DREAM BUILD GROW

A Female's Step-by-Step Guide for How to Start a Business

Francie Hinrichsen, MBA

For information contact:
https://www.herbusinessguide.com/

Cover and Interior Design by Nelly Murariu at PixBee Design
Edits by Rebekah Benham and Market Refined Media

Print ISBN: 978-0-578-36617-3

First Edition: February 2022

Founding Females™
PO Box 5061
Morton IL 61550
https://www.herbusinessguide.com/

10 9 8 7 6 5 4 3 2 1

DEDICATION

For Hans, my other half and A-Team. Thank you for making this possible.

For my first customers and best cheerleaders, my parents.

For Myla, can I be your mommy forever?

And for you, hopeful entrepreneur. Girl, you already have what it takes to build the dream in your heart. You can do this!

CONTENTS

FOREWORD

I started our business when I was 25 years old with just $2,000. In 2018, I retired with 75 employees, offices in six states, and a strong brand known throughout the world. I have traveled to 78 countries so far, with my next adventure right around the corner. Creating a small business was the right thing to do for me and you're reading this because you feel the same fire within you.

Three things helped me create our business: 1) unbridled ambition, 2) a focused plan, and 3) never saying someone works *for* me, because we all worked together.

Think about starting or improving your business like going on a hiking trip. You need a few essential items in your backpack: insect repellent, an understanding of the weather, food, a compass, and a good map or plan.

Dream, Build, Grow: A Female's Step-By-Step Guide for How to Start a Business is the exact plan you need as you start or improve your existing business. It is not intended to be read and placed on a shelf, but rather to be a working business manual for you to take your time and read and reread several times. It will explain things you need to think hard about to create a thriving business.

After you read a chapter, stop and think about what you just read and do the action items in each chapter. Some of them will be hard and take intensive thinking. Others will come easily. Your business plan is one of the most important maps you will ever create. So, spend time writing and rewriting it. After a few months or years, go back and re-read the action items from each chapter within this book. Your business will be fluid but the culture, core values, and ethics in your business will stay constant. One piece of advice I would like to offer you is that quitting is not an option. Stick it out, even when the going gets tough.

I know Francie Hinrichsen personally; I'm one of her biggest cheerleaders. I have watched her entrepreneurial spirit since she was teaching our neighbors sign language as her first business at a young age. She has the drive, communication skills, and experience to help you create or improve your business.

Whether you are an existing business trying to get better or a start-up in the beginning stages, read *Dream, Build, Grow: A Female's Step-by-Step Guide for How to Start a Business* carefully to think about your path so you arrive without getting lost or back tracking on your journey. Pausing and second-guessing yourself is normal when so much is a stake. Not following your plan could mean a loss of money, time, and energy that could delay moving forward in your business.

Some day you will look back and see entrepreneurship as a great opportunity in your life. Success, creativity, and wealth create freedom. Freedom allows so many options to a fulfilled life.

Follow your dreams, unleash your ambition, and make a plan.

Good Luck,

David K. Mueller

Founder of Insects Limited, Inc. and Fumigation Service and Supply, Inc.

INTRODUCTION

When your imagination takes hold, what do you envision your dream life to be? There, in your delightfully joyous state, serving your purpose and living your ideal destiny, can you hear the ring of successful transactions? Can you taste the unlimited supply of your favorite mocha latte as you type away at your computer managing YOUR business? Can you feel the warmth from satisfied customers?

Look closely at the vision of your future. Do you see yourself peace-ing out early from the workday to cruise over to your daughter's soccer game or sashay into happy hour with your best girlfriends at the new wine bar in town—without your boss giving you the disapproving side eye?

Or do you wince at the realization that you'll be dragging yourself out of bed in the morning to clock into a job that fuels the fire of someone else's dream business?

I don't know about you, but I like working. I thrill at the feeling of accomplishment. I enjoy an ongoing project. I love building a business that I *created!* Actually, it's work that *feels* like work that I avoid like a bandit on the run. Is it too much to ask for work that fuels my soul *on my terms*? The Merriam-Webster dictionary sites "freedom" as the power to do what you want to do. My definition of freedom is living life on my terms, using my time however I please. Entrepreneurship affords abundant freedom, which might be one reason you're considering starting a business.

Girl, dream on. Take a deep breath while you're entranced in the vision of your dream life. Soak up the reality that the freedom you crave is obtainable with business ownership. You have the exact guidance within this book to lead you into a life of freedom you'll love waking up to.

I've been where you are: frustrated, tired, overwhelmed, and fed up with the negative energy that comes with pouring into someone else's vision of success. I'm not there anymore. Today I own and operate two successful businesses and love going to work. I make my own schedule, choose clients I want to work with, and create value that positively impacts others.

Through the experience of starting and running my own marketing business, Simply Integrated, for seven years, I now have hard-earned insight and guidance to uplift women looking to become entrepreneurs. I run my second business, Founding Females™, with one goal in mind: *to inspire women to create businesses of impact.* I've guided clients as they've achieved incredible feats—accomplishments they used to only dream of. I knew documenting the processes would help motivated females like you through entrepreneurship when the female dreamers who read advanced copies of this book shared, "*This* is exactly what I've been looking for!"

Corporate executive or stay-at-home mom, business degree or school of hard knocks, none of it matters. You'll soon see all you need to start your successful business is the willingness to take action. This book walks through the step-by-step framework I have used to guide clients through starting their own successful businesses and transform the dream in their hearts into a reality. Now, I want to give you the guidance you need to satisfy the rumbling in your soul.

Dream, Build, Grow: A Female's Step-by-Step Guide for How to Start a Business is your blueprint to confidently plan, research, build, launch, profit, and scale your business. This book will take you from status quo to CEO. Think of it as your business bible. Its pages provide space to capture your thoughts and dreams. Its thought-provoking questions, action steps, practical guidance, pep rally-style support, checklists, diagrams, real life examples, and "oops, don't make the same mistake I did" insights help you write the start-up story of your dream company. You will build layer upon layer until you manifest a living, breathing business. With blueprint in hand, this guide is something you can refer to again and again as your company grows and thrives.

Some call it fate that you're reading this book. I call it God's grace and plan for your life. You are meant to read these words at this exact moment. He sewed the dream in your heart. It's your purpose—your responsibility—to unravel the extraordinary dream and assemble it step-by-step into a thriving business. *Dream, Build, Grow: A Female's Step-by-Step Guide for How to Start a Business* will teach you how.

Grab your gusto, dig in your heels, and leave behind the fear of the unknown, because we're unlocking the potential and drive buried deep inside you, and together we'll create the incredible reality of your dream business.

DREAM, BUILD, GROW YOUR WAY TO BECOMING AN ENTREPRENEUR

At least ten "how to start a business" books line the shelves of my home office from my early days of entrepreneurship. With each one, I was convinced the secrets within would be the answer to the clarity and progress I yearned for. Instead, I still felt empty after finishing each one because I knew *what* to do, but not *why* or *how* to do it.

Knowing what to do and actually doing it separates the dreamers from the doers. I finally realized if new entrepreneurs understood what to do, along with why and how to take each step as they started their business, we could overcome one of the biggest obstacles in female entrepreneurship: uncertainty.

First, there must be space in the midst of the learning process for ideas to flourish. Cue: The purpose of this guided journal. It's for taking action, for scribbling thoughts, for scratching out ideas when you find better ones, for putting dreams into words that drive results. Through each phase and every step in this process, there's an underlying call to action to *do, to step forward, to create a functioning piece of your business*.

Put pen to paper and then execute. Use these pages to pour out what's in your mind and on your heart. It's not enough to ponder each question without taking action. Ink up the pages. Articulate your thoughts into words so your brain creates a roadmap to bring results to life.

This journal is divided into six sections, or phases, which include direct steps to take, where to find the resources you need, practical business tips, and the confidence that *you can do this*.

Your ideas will become the foundation of a business that will transform your life. Let's take a sneak peek at what you'll accomplish in each phase:

Phase One: Clarify. Articulate your dream and connect it to who you are as a human being.

Phase Two: Research. Dive into purposeful research to better understand how your business will fit into the bigger business ecosystem of its niche industry, meet the needs of your potential customers, and impact your own life as a business owner.

Phase Three: Build. Create the core framework of your business—what it is, what it isn't, and how it will function.

Phase Four: Launch. Introduce your vision to the world and create the runway for your business's success.

Phase Five: Profit. Learn and implement the strategies successful businesses leverage to create the maximum profit margin possible.

Phase Six: Scale. Make the strategic shift from incremental growth to an influx of growth using fewer resources.

GIRL, YOU ALREADY HAVE WHAT IT *takes*

ACCESS A SUITE OF BUSINESS RESOURCES

There's much more to this book than what you're holding. You gained access to the exclusive Founding Females™ Resource Suite to support your journey when you purchased this book! Find downloadable templates and workbooks to support your start-up journey at www.HerBusinessGuide.com.

The customizable templates are resources you'll build once and reference time and again through the life of your business. You'll also find a vetted list of small business resources and a link to the Founding Females™ Start-Up Community full of peers you can grow with and learn from. It's a community of founders whose hearts speak the same language as yours—a language of grit, a "rise together" attitude, a personal growth mindset, and unstoppable ambition.

Once you launch your business, please get in touch with me at YesSheCan@FoundingFemalesCo.com to share your good news so we can happy dance together.

"IF YOU DON'T
LIKE THE ROAD
YOU'RE WALKING,
START PAVING
ANOTHER ONE."

Dolly Parton

PHASE ONE
CLARIFY

You did it! You made a thrilling decision to start the business on your heart, and you took action. Here you are ready to create a living, breathing, thriving business. You're a smart woman with an appetite for challenge!

It's time to cut through the confusion that often piggybacks on something brand new, like starting your first business. It's time to make a conscious shift into who you were made to become. There's nothing about starting a business we can't figure out together. Sis, it's time to define what your business will look like as the vehicle into the life you dream of.

Why would your Maker sew into your heart this beautiful, wonderful dream and remind you of it incessantly if you weren't supposed to chase after it with the fervency of 1,000 mustangs? You were *created* to bring your dream into the world. In fact, it's your responsibility. Your dream is yours alone, and there's a purpose, a reason, a future for what you're about to create. This is your moment to bring it to life.

Reading this book means you are equipped with everything you need to succeed. How do I know? It's not because this book has the answer to every question you'll ask during your business journey. It's because you choosing to open this book means you have the grit and initiative to flip back its cover and pour into its pages, to dare to dream, to venture into the unknown, to trade in the life you've always known for a life you can only imagine.

This book overflows with support and encouragement to let your imagination run wild. In this first section, **Phase One: Clarify**, we'll clarify your purpose, your why, and your motivation for the journey ahead. Taking time to cultivate the meaning behind starting a business—*your* business—is what will build the foundation to your success.

The steps included in **Phase One: Clarify** are:

- ▸ **Step 1:** Outline Your Business Idea

- ▸ **Step 2:** Pinpoint Your Purpose

- ▸ **Step 3:** Talk About Timing

- ▸ **Step 4:** Define *Your* Vision of Success

Your "someday" is finally here. You have the roadmap in your hands to begin your journey from dreaming about what could be to making it a reality. Most people think they must have the perfect business idea or the right amount of business knowledge to become a success. They only need the willingness to take action. If you're unwilling to quit, you cannot lose. Let's move forward creating your very own business.

DREAM ON, GIRL!

Your business building process is as unique as you. Your remarkable story, your special attributes, your detailed business dream can only be written by YOU. Life's triumphs and hardships have sketched a story the world needs to experience because your business will become an extension of you. That's right, sis. **The world needs more of you.** As you prepare to dive into the sections that follow, consider the most defining points in your life.

Recall your most impactful moments of meaning. Pull out important memories. Rummage through boxes of old keepsakes, yearbooks, reference letters about you written by people you admire, journals, resumes, vision boards, devotionals, gifts, old test results, social media posts, birthday cards, vacation souvenirs, photos, and mementos whose reminders will anchor you in what makes you, you. Think to when you were happiest, saddest, and proudest. Sketch out memories you want to keep and ones you're ready to pitch as you begin this new endeavor.

Phase One: Clarify offers a refreshing starting point, an intentional moment to salute the past and shake loose the chains keeping you captive to it. Cling to the remarkable woman you've fought to become and transform into the person you've always wanted to be.

More than ever, your future is yours for the taking and **Phase One: Clarify** is your starting block. Its purposeful guidance will help organize your thoughts so you can begin connecting each piece of your business's puzzle. Think of it like flipping on your windshield wipers and pushing aside the muck to provide clear vision into the future of your beautiful business journey. The time is now. Let's dive in!

STEP 1

OUTLINE YOUR BUSINESS IDEA

Exciting news! It's time to sculpt the vision of your brand-new business. This is the step where you lay everything on the table. Even the ideas you're not completely in love with get a seat at this table.

You never know where an articulated thought might take you once it's out of your mind and on paper. It's better to see the vision than to keep it locked away in your heart. Lay it all out! Give those ambitions hope! Delight in the chance to pour your heart out!

You may be tempted to skip this step but that would be like heading out for a road trip without first deciding your destination. In fact, this is the most important step you could take in becoming an entrepreneur because in business, clarity always wins. The only rule about brainstorming your business is you actually have to take action to do it.

Otherwise, throw all other rules to the wind. There is no "right" way to investigate your business idea except how your beautiful brain makes meaning naturally. Make a mess! Get loud! Or don't, and instead pause to meditate on your vision if that feels more your style. Whip out your thesaurus. Scribble, scratch, smile. Girl, it's impossible to mess up this step!

Start with a word, thought, feeling, memory, outfit, color, vision, object, song, poem, goal, situation, person, hope, dream, or fear. Hold that thought for a moment. Allow your mind to wander. Draw pictures, write a letter, make bulleted lists, scribble a series of words, ramble in a paragraph, create a diagram, riddle off rap lyrics, speak it aloud and then document it. Anything goes here. This is your space to dream in whatever "language" comes naturally to your brain.

As your thoughts begin to flow, journal what you see, hear, or feel. Then journal the next thought and the next until you could articulate the concepts into a paragraph if you had to.

The uninhibited flow of thoughts and feelings honors crucial space for your creativity. Right now, in this moment, you are a product of every situation leading to this one—the good, the unfortunate, and the magical. This is your opportunity to take what has shaped you (input) and create something incredible (output). You have a significant, powerful, necessary perspective the world needs. Let's get to it!

If you picked up this book without a business idea, you're in luck! The appendix has a resource you're going to love! Start brainstorming your business idea:

Now that you've downloaded your thoughts onto the page, let's add a tad more structure. Imagine you're headed out to grab coffee with your bestie who has encouraged you for months to start a business. Your bestie believes in you big time as the captain of your cheerleading squad, and you're ready to share the biggest secret of your life: your business idea. Prepare for the conversation by thinking through the following questions.

What people will you have involved in your business? Check all that apply.

☐ Business partner

☐ Employees/Contractors, like an admin assistant or web designer

☐ Supply vendor

☐ Team of advisors

☐ Community of peers

☐ Retailers who sell your product wholesale

☐ Networking contacts

☐ Customers (definitely check this one!)

What product or service (or both) will you offer? Describe it in detail.

....

....

....

....

....

....

What need does your offering meet for customers?

....

....

....

Where is your business's presence? Do you work from home, a coworking space, or a physical shop?

....

....

Where are your customers located? Locally or all over the country/world?

....

....

When is your business open? When will you be working your business? Is it seasonal or busy year-round? What do you expect its hours to be?

....

....

....

....

....

....

How does your business deliver its offering to customers?

....

....

....

....

....

....

Do your customers order online or in person or both?

Do you conduct meetings in person or via video conferencing?

How is the experience for customers buying from you and using your product?

Why does your business matter? Are there any special aspects that contribute to its purpose, like a "purchase with a purpose" social good aspect?

Now let's see if your business idea makes sense for you, the person ultimately responsible for its success. Use the following considerations to evaluate your business idea.

Do I enjoy the responsibilities required of me? When I finished school, I pursued the spa industry because I enjoyed the spa environment. Seems logical, right? It wasn't long before I realized running a spa isn't so relaxing. Direct experience taught me the role requires managing people, running numbers, and sitting in meetings. When I figured this out, my interest in running a day spa plummeted. Turns out I was interested in the industry, not in the responsibilities that would be required of me as a successful spa owner. Play forward what your entrepreneur role will be and the activities and responsibilities you'll assume in your business as its owner. How will you create a business that involves work you enjoy?

Do I believe in the idea? Gut check. To convince others to buy your offering, you'll need to fall madly in love with it. Can you talk passionately about the value you provide? For example, if you're a life coach who won't spend money on coaching, authentically convincing others of its value will be tough.

What are the risks and obstacles? Consider your risk tolerance. If your business idea involves risks that you're not willing to take, it may not be a good fit. If the obstacles you must overcome feel bigger than you're willing to bite off, you might want to reconsider the idea.

After thinking through these considerations, how are you feeling about your business idea? Does it still feel like a good fit for you? If not, don't be discouraged! Use the Guide in Appendix A to brainstorm more business ideas.

If your idea does feel like a great fit, keep exploring it and visualizing what it would look like for you. Develop a deeper sense of your business idea's fit for you with these action steps:

- **Journal** – Reflect over what it would be like to fulfill the role as the owner of the business. Journal about your lifestyle, job satisfaction, challenges, and opportunities. The goal is to imagine the business as if it were your own to gain a sense of whether it might be a good fit.

- **Talk with trusted friends and family about the idea** – Ask what opportunities and challenges they see.

- ▶ **Research and interview a business owner of that type** – Ask what the most rewarding and challenging aspects are, how they got started, and what you should know as someone considering leaping into the role.

- ▶ **Stand in the mirror and explain what you do and who you do it for** – See what feelings creep into your heart. Are they feelings of excitement or dread? Joyful anticipation or anxiety?

- ▶ **Dive into research** – If it's a brand-new concept to you, plug it into the search engine and see where it takes you. Click through websites and explore blog posts to see if you gain a sense of life as the owner of that business.

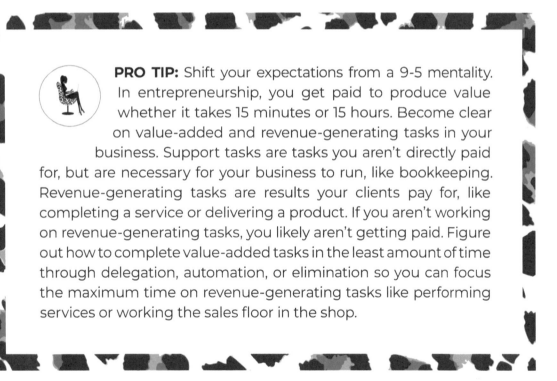

PRO TIP: Shift your expectations from a 9-5 mentality. In entrepreneurship, you get paid to produce value whether it takes 15 minutes or 15 hours. Become clear on value-added and revenue-generating tasks in your business. Support tasks are tasks you aren't directly paid for, but are necessary for your business to run, like bookkeeping. Revenue-generating tasks are results your clients pay for, like completing a service or delivering a product. If you aren't working on revenue-generating tasks, you likely aren't getting paid. Figure out how to complete value-added tasks in the least amount of time through delegation, automation, or elimination so you can focus the maximum time on revenue-generating tasks like performing services or working the sales floor in the shop.

Many people fall in love with a business idea and dive into developing its presence before ever analyzing the idea from a 360-degree perspective. Then, as time goes on, problems arise because they never stopped to view the business from all angles. Because of this, their decision-making is limited only to what they see. It would be like deciding to buy a house after only looking at the front side. One perspective means limited information.

Thoroughly defining your business idea is akin to walking around and through the entire house before buying. You're exploring every detail and looking at it from all perspectives. Just like fences create understanding about where one person's property starts and ends, clear understanding hinges on knowing what your business is and also what it is not.

STEP

PINPOINT YOUR PURPOSE

What is inspiring you to start your business? For me, it was the ability to make a big impact on many small businesses as an entrepreneur rather than a small impact on one large corporation as an employee. I felt deep in my core I could help shift the trajectory of women's lives through entrepreneurship. I believed my skills and knowledge could help propel entrepreneurial women to great heights. Pinpointing the difference you want to make organizes your countless thoughts about your business and streamlines them into your intended outcome. The difference you want to make equals your purpose. That's where your Why statement comes in.

Your personal Why statement is your deep-rooted purpose and motivation for starting your business. Your Why statement comes from having a vision of what you want. It's a concise statement about your intention for impact and reflects the difference you want to make in the world. Throughout the ebbs and flows and seasons of life, your Why statement engages your thoughts and behavior toward your goal.

This important ingredient creates cohesion for your own actions, but also for others—employees, advisors, customers, and collaborators—to create meaning behind your business's existence.

According to author and speaker, Simon Sinek[1], a compelling Why is crucial for people to believe in your offering. A strong purpose creates the drive that perpetuates successful businesses.

A Why statement looks like:

To .... so that ....

For example, my Why statement is: "To connect, educate, and empower women so that they can create businesses of impact."

Take Airbnb for another example. Its Why statement is: "To connect millions of people in real life all over the world, through a community marketplace—so that you can belong anywhere."

Your Why is important for building a long-lasting, sustainable business. It attaches meaning bigger than earning a paycheck. Working for money alone won't encourage customers to buy from you, and it certainly won't keep you feeling fulfilled, which is why having a deep sense of your Why is crucial when facing especially difficult challenges in your business. It will anchor you and help you keep sight of your long-term goals.

There will be hard days, barriers, times when you question what you're doing, days when you feel like running back to the safety of the 9-5. You wouldn't be doing it right if none of these things nagged at your ambition.

Remember to focus on the beauty of the entrepreneurial journey. You can do hard things and you will come out of them with growth. Knowing your Why is your ticket to pushing through challenges.

Let's explore important considerations for clarifying your purpose.

What is your primary motivation for starting a business? What difference do you want to make in the lives of the people your business impacts, like customers, employees, and the community at large? List all the factors that fuel your Why. For example, will you deliver resources to people who otherwise wouldn't have them to live? Will you empower clients to reach their full potential? Will you help busy moms unwind? Will you ignite important social change?

....

....

....

....

Write your Why statement. Your Why statement should be concise and actionable, and should pair the value of what you offer with your business's purpose for existing.

Example: If Dolly owned a coworking space that allowed business owners to enjoy their environment while they worked, her Why statement might sound something like this: "To provide a calm, resourceful, and collaborative work environment for entrepreneurs to thrive while accomplishing the work they feel called to."

Write your Why statement:

....

....

🔧 **TAKE ACTION! Write down your goals. Science says both writing down your goals and telling others where you are with your goals increases the likelihood that you'll accomplish them. It's not magic. It's accountability. In fact, research shows you become 42% more likely to achieve your goals and dreams by writing them down on a regular basis.[2]**

What are your personal life goals? Consider the moment you near your last breath. What will you look back on and rest peacefully knowing you accomplished?

....

....

....

....

....

What would you regret most if you didn't spend your life doing it?

What are your goals for this month, this year, and for the next five years?

Describe how your personal goals relate to the difference you hope your business will achieve?

Girl, your business will be a physical representation of how your brain works. Why? Because YOU are creating it. If your thoughts are disorderly, so too will be your business. If you're an action-taker in your personal life, so you'll also be in your business. If you tend not to finish what you start, that will likely also happen in your business.

Chasing what you want out of life and business are intimately related. Your business becomes a byproduct of you as a person. Your blood runs through your business's veins. That's why it's critical in the start-up phase to become crystal clear on what you want, why you want it, and what you'll do to accomplish it. It's yours for the taking! Beautiful, huh?

Your business can be the vehicle that chauffeurs you into the life you've always imagined. Whatever big goals you catch yourself daydreaming of, chase them. When you find yourself thinking, "Somebody should...", realize life often speaks to us in tiny, feather-like nudges. Rise up and choose to be the somebody who makes the difference.

Your purpose doesn't have to be curing cancer or ending world hunger. Something as seemingly small as spreading hope to one person each day is far more profound than failing to take action at all. Pinpoint your purpose and you'll have created a roadmap for a life of meaning.

"NEVER DOUBT THAT A GROUP OF THOUGHTFUL, COMMITTED CITIZENS CAN CHANGE THE WORLD; INDEED, IT'S THE ONLY THING THAT EVER HAS." – MARGARET MEAD

STEP

TALK ABOUT TIMING

I had the vision all mapped out. I'd gracefully walk across the stage to accept my diploma, probably with a job offer already waiting. That job offer would usher me into a management position in the luxury spa industry I had fallen so madly in love with.

Five or six years would fly by teaching me everything I could ever know about running a successful day spa. By then, I could easily manage that place with my eyes closed. I'd have a full staff performing their roles impeccably with candidates in the queue chomping at the bit for an open position.

My spa location's numbers would be pristine, out-performing all other managers' locations—duh. Naturally, the owners would basically beg me to take on their newest locations. Woe is me. By then I'd have grown ready for a fresh challenge. Primed with a business plan in hand, I'd resign from my role to start my own high-end day spa in a geographical location rich with opportunity no one had discovered yet.

Cringy, huh?

You don't need me to tell you my dream didn't play out that way. Not even close. After graduating, I pursued management in the spa industry, but my experience was nothing like what I'd envisioned. Turns out managing people isn't my strong suit and showing up to work at someone else's beck and call isn't exactly my ideal career.

My life crumbled when I was hit by a Mack truck. Okay—that was a bit dramatic—but suffice my misery to say, everyone on my favorites list would tell you my life was in serious disarray. I'm an Enneagram 3 and our egos don't fare well in the midst of failure. After saying to myself too many times, "There has to be more to life than *this*," I submitted a 90-day notice to my employer, fulfilled it, and thereafter became an entrepreneur making my own rules.

I became self-employed years earlier than I anticipated in my plan of life, more out of survival than careful planning. Life throws us curve balls, and we can't always perfectly time the start of our entrepreneurial journey, but it sure helps to try.

For me, the stars aligned. When my girl-power-loving, smart-as-a-whip Aunt Susie Mueller passed away, she left me a few thousand dollars. It's with that life-changing gift that my cat, Boo, and I lived on peanut butter and jelly and bought business cards to bootstrap my virtual assistance business.

I get it. Not everyone has a generous Aunt Susie to help them get a start and certainly not everyone is 25 and with enough moxie to leave behind a salaried position with health insurance and a 401K to start their own gig.

So what does "not everyone" do? While it may never feel completely safe, planning ahead can hedge major risk otherwise inherent in transitioning to self-employment. Even a healthy emergency fund can become the safety net for someone who stumbles upon entrepreneurship like I did.

Diving into self-employment is rarely "all or nothing." Many people run their own businesses for years, working at night and on the weekends while also working a W2 job. Keeping a close eye on your household budget, having a mentor to light the way, saving up, and creating systems to automate as many business tasks as possible to save you precious time are all steps you can take in advance to set yourself up for success when the time comes to officially become your own boss.

Take this opportunity to assess whether now is the right time to move forward in starting your business by answering the following questions.

What will it look like to start your business while still taking care of your life responsibilities (e.g. rent or mortgage, insurance, food, and bills)?

Are you at a place in life where you can afford to take on the risk of starting a business? If not, what needs to change to make it happen? Do you need to take a second job? Pull back on unnecessary spending? Find a business partner? Delay your timing? Launch your business part-time?

If you must first launch your business part-time while you work for someone else, what will your life look like during this season? Less social time? Less sleep? Using vacation time to grow your business?

How will this career change impact other priorities in your life, like how you spend time with your family or outside obligations like volunteer roles? Should you involve your family in your business venture so you can spend time together? Will you need to create healthy boundaries around spending, relationships, and time-management?

Starting a business often presents new financial risk. How will that risk impact your financial health and how will you take precautions to hedge that risk? Begin or increase your emergency fund? Tighten up your budget? Reroute your vacation fund into your business? Plan for a lean Christmas?

After consideration, is now the right time to start your business? Why or why not?

PRO TIP: Allow the process of becoming an entrepreneur to change you. Lean into it the unfamiliar. Create new habits. Redefine who you know yourself to be. Give yourself space to grow. Wake up in the morning and tell yourself you're capable of your wildest dreams, because, sis, you are. Challenge the status quo. Embrace mindset shifts. Don't feel guilty about your desire to make money or that your human makeup includes an extraordinary dream sewn into your heart. Don't feel guilty because your passions and personal satisfaction may look differently than your peers'.

Running a business can be a monumental challenge—maybe one of the greatest adventures you'll ever undertake. Throw poor timing into the mix and an otherwise homerun could turn it into a strikeout. Give yourself the timing advantage by first analyzing whether your ducks are aligned *enough* to dive in headfirst now. Don't confuse *feeling* ready with actually having access to the right resources, like capital, connections, and time, ready to deploy.

Excitement can create impulse. But spontaneously starting a business because you *just can't wait* could nullify your greatest strength: intentional forethought and planning. If you have determined now isn't the right time, it's not a "no" but rather "not yet." It's a pause. A moment to strategize. A wise decision for forethought. A huddle, a regroup. And it certainly doesn't mean you can't finish this book. It only means a longer timeline before you open your doors.

When we know better, we do better. Consider it a sign pointing you in the right direction about what you need to do first—save up capital, create time in your schedule, or coach yourself through self-limiting beliefs—before leaping off the starting block.

STEP 4

DEFINE *YOUR* VISION OF SUCCESS

"DEFINE SUCCESS ON YOUR OWN TERMS,
ACHIEVE IT BY YOUR OWN RULES,
AND BUILD A LIFE YOU'RE PROUD TO LIVE."
– ANNE SWEENEY, FORMER PRESIDENT OF DISNEY CHANNEL

Ever found yourself wondering when people will find you out? Or felt the weight of intimidation when you tried explaining one of your big dreams? I've wrestled with my dream of retiring my husband so we can off-road our Jeep (which we don't own yet) underneath rays of sunshine in the middle of a "workday" (gaspppp!). I've struggled to call myself a business owner at networking events and felt timid sharing that I run not one, but two, businesses. Once when I was asked to speak at a conference for entrepreneurs, my mind went blank. *Why would they ask me? I really don't know anything the audience couldn't figure out themselves*, I thought.

It doesn't stop there. I struggle to charge appropriately. Much of my knowledge is self-taught, so I often question how valuable it could *really* be since it's accessible for anyone willing to get gritty.

All of this is imposter syndrome, and it has a real effect on what we believe is possible. Imposter syndrome affects the standards we set for ourselves, and what we charge for the value we deliver.

Imposter syndrome is common among entrepreneurs. According to the American Psychological Association, imposter syndrome is "a form of intellectual self-doubt where high achievers often attribute their accomplishments to luck rather than to ability, and fear that others will eventually unmask them as a fraud."[3] In other words, you tend to feel on the verge of being found out. Too often, I hear clients say they "feel like they're faking it." They feel uncomfortably bold for breaking away from the norm, for believing they can create a successful business, as if others were silently judging or waiting for them to fail.

You may even grapple with imposter syndrome as you dream of your future successes, financial stability, and official job title. If you use terms to rationalize your endeavor like "small little side gig," or "What will they think if I…," it's a sure sign we need to chat about why you fear taking up your rightful space as a powerful, passionate, and capable business owner. I speak from experience, sis.

One way to counter imposter syndrome in business ownership is to create YOUR definition of success because it keeps you focused on what you want and helps you avoid measuring your results by someone else's ruler. I mentioned in the introduction of this book that my definition of success includes choosing how I spend my time. Money doesn't motivate me. Freedom of choice does. When you define your own success, you'll experience satisfaction from results that may or may not be tied to money. What does success look like for you? Use the following questions to help define what business success looks like on your terms.

What does your definition of success look like aside from a paycheck? Spending more time with your kids and family? Freedom to create a career you love? Giving to charities that matter to you? Putting your money behind causes that create social change?

In what ways does your definition of success differ from society's definition of success?

....

....

....

....

....

....

....

What are your business goals?

....

....

....

....

....

....

....

....

....

....

Now, take your ideas and create a vision board—a visual representation of your definition of success. Initiate your creativity. Glue pictures, magazine photos, or newspaper clippings onto the following space. Or use Canva (my fave!) to create your own like the one below. Write words. Draw images. Add whatever it is that cultivates an image you can later return to as a reminder for what success means to you. Here's an example.

It's true what they say about needing to know what your destination looks like in order to reach it. For some women, their dream business provides extra cash for traveling. Nothin' wrong with that. Other women won't be satisfied until they change the trajectory of their family tree. And still others set their sights on changing the entire world.

Create a vision in your mind of what YOU want. Detail every nitty gritty detail, smell, meal, wardrobe item, life you impact, even down to how you speak, think, and behave. If you fail to do this, your brain, wired for survival, will default to "Meh, good enough."

The reality is, "meh, good enough" doesn't justify the risk inherent in entrepreneurship. Be all in, babe, because you were not created to be "meh, good enough." You were created to thrive and to bring your dream business to life.

'PHASE ONE: CLARIFY' CONCLUSION

You have accomplished the hardest part of the process: starting. Way to go, sis! Your momentum will serve you well! You've officially taken action—the impetus for creating a successful business. Too many people never commit because they don't know where to start, but not you. You took action, and that's a major accomplishment!

You. Are. Doing. It. Sis!! You completed the crucial work of creating clarity on what's important to YOU, and clarity is your new business's golden propeller. Next up in **Phase Two: Research**, we'll dive into information-gathering so you're best equipped to make decisions as we continue to walk through building the framework for your business.

NOTES

"KNOWING WHAT
MUST BE DONE
DOES AWAY
WITH FEAR."

Rosa Parks

PHASE TWO
RESEARCH

When I started my first business in 2015, I faced major overwhelm. The learning curve felt like it swallowed me whole. And the frustrating part? I didn't know what I didn't know. Girl, do you feel me? I was lost. Uncertain. Unconfident. Gone were the days of studying the notes to get the right answers.

"If I could only figure out *what* I'm supposed to research, I'd be golden!" I'd rehash. For someone who was unemployed and pulling from savings, time was of the essence. I longed to feel purposeful, but instead felt like a magician who forgot to learn the tricks.

Alas, I dedicate this chapter to 25-year-old, messy, confused, ruffled Francie. It details what she wishes she'd known—the clarity to lead her along a purposeful path. It details the categories of information like a checklist she could have used to customize to her business model and strut into business meetings feeling like a rockstar. Since she couldn't have this insight, let it empower you.

You have clarity around your business idea. Now it's time to discover how to make it successful through purposeful research. Thoughtful exploration *first,* before diving into creating business assets (think, your website, social profiles, and brand), provides a more accurate context for making wise decisions later. Due diligence in researching your business is akin to mapping the most efficient route before traveling to your favorite vacay spot. You get to the right destination in the quickest way possible.

In **Phase Two: Research**, you'll uncover important considerations as you make all the many tiny and ginormous decisions to set yourself up for success in your new business. Who doesn't love knowing which activities drive the best results? Skip this critical step and you'll wander aimlessly, wasting time, resources, and energy.

Borrow my 20/20 vision: if you become overwhelmed, the best approach is to peek through the customer's eyes. If you don't know an answer, that's okay! My best ideas never come on the fly. Typically, I make a hard decision after a good journaling sesh or posing the question to my mastermind peers. You have permission to do the same.

The Law of Diminishing Returns says there comes a point where one more unit of investment (say, one additional hour of your time) begins to yield less and less return. Once you can explain the basics to, say, your mom, then move on. There may never be a point where you *feel* like you know it all. (You can't sit with us, imposter syndrome!) The reality is you'll likely have to commit to the next step forward *before* you feel ready.

Perfectionism will consume time and resources you can't afford to waste as a new entrepreneur. Learn the basics, then take action. This section reveals what to research as you prepare to build the foundation of your business.

Phase Two: Research guides you through how to do the following:

- ▶ **Step 1:** Trial Your Offering
- ▶ **Step 2:** Find Your Flock

- ▸ **Step 3:** Toast to Your Competition

- ▸ **Step 4:** Finance Your Future

- ▸ **Step 5:** Name Your Business

- ▸ **Step 6:** Get Legal Like Elle Woods

WISE RESEARCH STRATEGY

The best freedom you can give yourself is the permission to evolve. Research helps you do that. Of course, you don't know everything yet, but, sis, if you can self-teach, you can literally accomplish anything.

The best way to approach this phase is purposefully. Aside from that, you can't do it wrong. *You don't need to become an expert at everything to start and run a successful business*. You need a basic understanding that will inform your ability to _take action_.

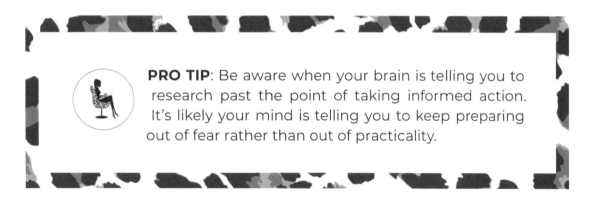

PRO TIP: Be aware when your brain is telling you to research past the point of taking informed action. It's likely your mind is telling you to keep preparing out of fear rather than out of practicality.

This is the stage of building a business that taunts us into believing there's a "magic bullet," a "secret," a "mystery waiting to be uncovered," revealed at the end of the next blog post, the next thousand-dollar course, or the next how-to book. Sis, developing an insatiable thirst for knowledge is one of your most powerful attributes, but it can also keep you paralyzed if you allow it to prevent forward progress. No amount of research can create a successful business. Only action and follow-through can.

Move forward intentionally to gather purposeful facts, weigh others' opinions against your experience, and surround yourself with people who have done what you're aiming to do. Find a community of people who carry an unselfish willingness to guide you in the right direction. If you can, your strategy is airtight.

Remember to trust your judgment and give yourself the freedom to change your mind later.

REPUTABLE INFORMATION SOURCES

So where do you look for reliable information about your business? Government websites, conversations with professionals with a proven track record for success, local organizations like the Chamber of Commerce or Rotary Club, vetted research articles, beta testing, and surveys are some of the most reputable sources for research.

Here are examples of resources you can generally trust.

Reputable Websites

▶ SBA.gov for small business information and resources

▶ SCORE.com for start-up and small business guidance

▶ ONetOnline.org for information on industries and occupations

▶ IRS.gov for tax information related to business

▶ Census.gov for information about people and the economy

Reputable Organizations

▶ The Kauffman Foundation for small business resources, including local chapters of '1 Million Cups'

▶ Local Chamber of Commerce organizations

▶ Local Economic Development Council organizations

Research Methods

- ▸ Check out your local college or university library for access to paid research subscriptions, like IBIS World, that provide detailed economic and demographic information about a variety of industries.

- ▸ Beta testing is the use of a nearly completed product or service by a group of target testers who can provide feedback and suggestions about what it was like to use the offering in an attempt to improve it

- ▸ Focus groups are groups of people intended to provide feelings and opinions about a business concept

PRO TIP: It's tempting to subscribe to every free checklist on the internet. Instead of breadth, focus on depth. Subscribe only to a handful of sources based on criteria that matters most to you, like an authority in the field, someone with a particularly interesting approach, or someone who offers cutting edge tips and tricks in your industry. That way, you'll resist "chasing shiny objects" and develop a keen focus on topics most likely to create forward movement.

Note: Surveys and polls are traditional ways of gathering data for decision-making, but be careful about how you approach them. The information they yield is not always accurate. People don't mean to lie, but they often report.

STEP

TRIAL YOUR OFFERING

"THE MIDDLE IS MESSY, BUT IT'S ALSO WHERE THE MAGIC HAPPENS." – BRENÉ BROWN

I love to see women use their smarts. All the time in online communities and in my own network of entrepreneurs, I see women creating prototypes, testing them out, and, after they receive feedback for improvement, finalizing the details of their offering. They know time is their most precious resource and ideal client feedback is the most efficient way to create a product that will sell.

Even the original iteration of this book went through the hands of three carefully-selected beta testers (Leann, Molly, and Amy, I could kiss your faces!). For each, I printed a spiral bound copy of the manuscript and asked them to mark it up so I could understand how to improve the delivery of the concepts. Their feedback became invaluable for deciding what information to keep, further explain, and omit altogether.

A successful business idea hinges on an offering people want to buy. Period. No perfectly executed business plan, no beautifully crafted brand, no darling brick and mortar shop positioned on the busiest corner in town could overcome the gaping hole created by an offering nobody wants. You need an offering people value, an offering that addresses a problem customers feel so deeply about that they're willing to fork over their moolah in exchange for the value they find in your offering.

It's critical to verify that there are customers willing to buy your offering. It's time to test your product. This section leads you through exactly how to do that.

YOU CAN'T COURSE CORRECT IF YOU'RE STANDING *still*.

If you test and find people are *not* willing to buy, gosh, that would suck. But undoubtedly more suck-y is wasting time, money, and resources on an offering nobody wants. Don't be afraid of bad news. Testing your offering in advance lets you make tweaks that better serve your customer and allows you to create an amazing business. Let's normalize failure starting now because there's a lot we can learn from daring to try.

Here are ideas for how to test your offering before you build your business:

Describe your offering and ask, "Would you buy this if I created it?" The audience you ask should be representative of people you expect to use the offering in real life. For instance, if your offering involves dogs, be sure to pose your offer to a group of people who love and own dogs to receive accurate feedback. Find these groups among your social media followers, social group communities, your network of friends and family, a college class, or anywhere groups of people congregate and who resemble your target audience. If they say they would buy it, you might have a viable offering. But don't stop there! Invite them to your waitlist. Cue sweet, precious, wonderful, lovely warm leads to sell to once your offering does exist. More on that in our marketing chat in **Phase Three: Build** (can't wait!!).

Build a waitlist: Create a form (Google Forms works great for this) where interested parties join the waitlist for your offering. There's magic about a waitlist—anticipation gets the best of us, and we become so darn excited about the unknown! Grab the link to the form and paste it anywhere you mention your upcoming launch (like, everywhere—your email signature, social media posts and profile, business cards, a QR code handy at the perfectly opportune networking moment). As your waitlist builds, you'll have interested people you can ask questions to and poll to develop your offering.

Leverage beta testers: Offer an early version of your product or service, potentially at a discounted rate or with an added bonus, in exchange for constructive feedback for improvement. Find beta testers in your network or in concentrated groups of customers who are likely to use your offering. For instance, if your offering is baby swaddles, post to a breastfeeding social media group full of mamas. If you're a new graphic designer creating logos for small businesses, contact the local Chamber of Commerce to see if they have any connections to new businesses. Make sure to clearly communicate up front what you'd like in exchange so you and the customer get the most out of the opportunity. Deliver the offering and follow up with an interview or survey asking questions where respondents' answers can be used to craft your marketing message in the future. Finally, don't forget to ask for a review or testimonial. (Highlighting past customers' experiences with an offering to encourage new customers to buy it is social proof that speaks for itself as future customers decide to buy from you.)

Let's talk about questions you might ask beta testers in your follow-up interview or survey after they have experienced the early version of your offering:

- [ ] Have you purchased a service like this in the past? If so, how did it compare? What did you pay previously?

- [ ] What range would you be willing to pay for this service?

- [ ] How would you describe the problem you face that this offering addresses?

- [ ] How does this problem make you feel?

☐ How would you describe the relief you feel from having your problem solved?

☐ What could make the experience better for you?

☐ Do you know of anyone currently offering this product or service? If so, what do you like about their brand, business, and offering? What don't you like?

As you can probably guess, the invaluable answers you'll receive will not only help you develop a valuable offering, but you'll also be able to leverage the insight in marketing messages in the future. Keep this information safe for future use.

Plan how you will beta test your offering.

What groups can you connect with whose members would be ideal to test it out?

What questions will help you gain clarity about how to develop your offering?

What information will help you determine whether a demand for your offering exists?

....

....

In your successful entrepreneur journey, you will face moments of necessary pivots. Change is where growth happens best. Your business won't survive without changing lanes or an occasional sharp turn into Plan B. I used to believe I needed to uncover the "right" way to success. Now I know countless roads lead there. Things don't need to be perfect to create success. Trust the process.

STEP FIND YOUR FLOCK

I've always gravitated toward communities of women for the camaraderie. In youth and college, I learned teamwork and cohesion through sports teams, Girl Scouts, and membership in a sorority. In adulthood, good-hearted, drama-free women have become my best friends through personal interests like business-related communities and church small groups.

I've experienced both toxic and uplifting communities of women. The toxic crowd was usually marked by individuals who aimed to shine solo. They were competitive, ingenuine, unpredictable, and catty. There always seemed to be a staleness in the room and eye contact was sparse. You can't grow with people who don't like how growth looks on you.

The uplifting communities were just the opposite: inclusive, generous with their time, talent, and treasures, warm, and dependable. It wasn't unusual for them to check in on life updates, somehow know to show up when they were needed most, and rally around me in my toughest moments.

There is power in women gathering for the good of the community. Girl, you were created for community. It's in your chemical makeup. If you channel it, community in business can become your greatest superpower. Much of your success will come from finding the right people to "row" alongside because, just like in life, prioritizing people and relationships is where many of the richest business opportunities take root.

Thoughtful relationship building opened doors in my business I never would have walked through otherwise. Paid speaking engagements, new clients, an invitation onto a nonprofit board of directors, and podcast interviews are examples of business opportunities I secured *because* of relationships. They knew my work was good, but more importantly, they personally knew me to be a dependable person who would provide an excellent result. In the same way many jobs are never posted publicly, but rather filled when current employees refer their own connections internally, so too are many business opportunities referred internally among trusted peers.

Relationships foster familiarity and trust. It's true we rise together. Stepping forward in the safe space of community has the potential to transform what the rest of your entrepreneur journey looks and feels like. It's in the context of community where you'll fill in the gaps and evolve most as a business owner.

Surround yourself with people navigating similar challenges, as well as people who are one step ahead of the challenges you face currently. The invaluable insight, support, and camaraderie cannot be over-exaggerated. Now is the time to lean in and develop business connections in your journey to build the business on your heart. It's never too early or too late, and it's an investment that pays dividends. Relationships provide rich opportunity for leveling up through actionable conversation and sharing best practices that will positively impact your business now and in the future.

Business-focused community groups produce successful results because they're predicated on motivated individuals focusing energy and ideas together. Members lend insight to one another in their respective areas of expertise. They "speak the same language" of an entrepreneurial heart. They contribute to the synergistic results of the group. They understand highs and lows and ins and outs of building a business day after day.

Have you ever felt alone in your dream to run a business? Ever poured your heart out to someone about your excitement only for the conversation to fall flat? My fellow entrepreneurs and I joke that our friends and families have no idea what we do. "So, tell me for the *fourth* time…Like, how does your business work?" #ButSeriously

For those who aren't entrepreneurs, it's challenging to grasp the possibility to create a business that never before existed, while also earning a viable income. These are the people you feel like smacking when they ask, "How's your *little* business doing?" as if starting a business were something cute you do in your spare time.

Engaging in community is the self-care of business ownership. Say goodbye to doing entrepreneurship alone and say hello to finding your new girl gang to level up with. Here are types of groups where you can do exactly that:

Mastermind Groups are organized peer-to-peer mentoring. Members discuss focused topics, provide support during difficult challenges, and brainstorm organic, new opportunities together.

Some of the brightest minds in history, like Andrew Carnegie, Napoleon Hill, Thomas Edison, Henry Ford, Harvey Firestone, Theodore Roosevelt, C.S. Lewis, Tony Robbins, and Grant Cardone trace much of their success back to the ideas and feedback they gained in mastermind membership.

To find a well-fitting mastermind group, search an organized meet up platform, check with colleagues, mentors, and community leaders, and reach out to local professional organizations. Of course, the Founding Females™ Mastermind is a lovely option for established entrepreneurs who are past the "proof of concept" phase of business. If you're still in the beginning stages of starting and growing a business, the Founding Females™ Start-Up Community could be an excellent fit. Find links to the Founding Females™ Mastermind and the Founding Females™ Start-Up Community at www. HerBusinessGuide.com.

Can't find a mastermind group that fits your needs? Consider starting one of your own!

Local Networking Opportunities – Organizations like the local Chamber of Commerce, Rotary Club, Women in Leadership, SCORE, or National Association of Women Business Owners (NAWBO) provide resources particularly focused on benefitting members of the local community and local businesses.

Local networking groups typically meet in person since members are in the same locale. In my experience, meeting in person creates stronger ties and better experiences.

Don't be fearful if you're an introvert or apprehensive about social situations. We all are from time to time. Networking colleagues turn into friends, so the more you show up, the easier it will become. Plus, it's a great excuse to reward yourself with some alone time and a glass of rosé while you send follow up emails after the event.

To find local networking opportunities, search local social media events, review the local Chamber of Commerce events page, or explore a platform designated for meet ups (think Meetup.com). Ask your connections which local organizations they're involved with or contact a business owner you know to ask for insight. National organizations with local chapters like Rising Tide Society and 1 Million Cups (organized by the Kauffman Foundation for entrepreneurship) with local chapters across the U.S. are two other great options.

Online Groups – Online groups come with plenty of flexibility. Many are hosted inside a social media setting or private online community, like Mighty Networks. The groups I love most are the ones organized intentionally to discuss relevant topics on a consistent schedule, and whose group rules support a positive experience for members. Social media sites and a detailed search in your browser can turn up options that fit you perfectly.

Look for groups with qualities that matter most to you, like members in a similar season of business or life and a similar schedule, or general guidelines like staying on topic during meetings.

Local Business Incubator – An incubator is a space designed to provide relevant business resources like meeting space, presentations rich in applicable content, and business and start-up counseling. Small businesses are beneficial for a local economy, so you'll often find free or low-cost training in business incubators as the local government's investment into the next wave of small business owners.

Ask about available resources like counseling, grant application assistance, and templates. Incubators are staffed by experts with guidance on the start-up process from proof of concept all the way up to scaling and eventually selling a business.

To find out if a local business incubator exists near you, locate the global network of incubators, accelerators, and entrepreneurship centers called the International Business Innovation Association at www.INBIA.org.

Coworking Spaces – Coworking spaces primarily focus on providing a physical space for people to work. Secondary benefits like access to a community and events that could support your entrepreneur journey are a fabulous perk. A quick online search or recommendations from gal pals in your area will help point you in the right direction. Research membership benefits and whether they offer a trial period so you can test out the fit.

One similarity exists among most coworking spaces: they're filled with a concentrated community rallying around small business ideas and goals. Organizations like these often team up to capitalize on resources, like sharing the cost of internet, subscriptions, printing equipment, and office supplies. Lowering costs? This is what entrepreneur dreams are made of!

🔧 **TAKE ACTION! Reflect below on which communities fit you best. Jump on the interwebs and do your research. Make it a goal to join at least one community in the next month.**

QUALITIES TO LOOK FOR
IN A BUSINESS COMMUNITY

▶ **Members are made up of peers within reach**. This means members of the community are in the same relative "season of business" – perhaps one step behind and one step ahead of where you are in your journey. It can be tempting to seek a community of business owners well beyond your phase of business. Someone who found success 10 or 20 years ago likely did it with different resources than what will shape your approach. Save this dynamic for a mentor-mentee relationship (More on this in **Phase Three: Build**.)

▶ **An expectation for initiative-taking**. It's not important all members are leaders, but it is important members know how to take responsibility for their own success. Entrepreneurship is an offensive game, and people who wait around for success to happen to them don't make lemon martinis from the lemons life hands them the same way you do.

▶ **"Enough success to go around" values**. The group(s) you join should encourage an underlying belief that there's plenty of success for all of us. As the saying goes, "a rising tide lifts all boats." Group interaction should pave the path for members to regularly contribute their "secrets to success" so each member can learn from another's experience.

What values and characteristics are important to you as you commit time to finding your tribe?

Consider developing relationships in 2-3 core groups. This number will allow a variety of expertise among members. Plus, you'll be able to stay up on and commit to engaging in conversation, but also won't likely inundate you with obligations or spread your time too thin. What kind of community will you draw from for support and guidance?

....

....

....

....

....

Find your tribe. Through the process of entrepreneurship, you'll cross paths with people on a mission to change the world. You'll surround yourself with dreamers whose passions fuel them to wake up at 5am, also. You'll catch the contagious thrill of self-improvement. These are the people willing to pack in long days because they love what they do. They wisely invest hard earned profits back into their business because they believe in themselves. They're the kind of people who give up watching TV so they can binge consume books, podcasts, and blog posts that will ignite mindset shifts and advance them closer to their goals. These people exist. They'll help you see the world differently. You are one of them and the tribe needs you, too. When you find them, hold on tightly.

STEP

TOAST TO YOUR COMPETITION

Intentionally researching the competition in your industry isn't about "beating" anyone. You can be in direct competition with another company and still root for their success. Rather, researching the competition is beneficial for becoming aware of the value available to your customers to create the best business you can. Building a successful business is creating work you love and fulfilling your purpose, and if you get to support other female-owned businesses in the process, what could be better?

In fact, two friends of mine, Reagan and Camie, both local interior designers, teamed up for a collaborative event. They weren't intimidated by the other's incredible talent, and they clearly know there's enough success to go around.

In the same breath, I often I see online boutiques support other online boutiques through social posts and events. Female businesses organize events with vendors who sell similar products to theirs. As a community, we're stronger together than we are alone. Isn't that wonderful?

As you move into this chapter about researching your competition, keep in mind when one of us does well, it's a benefit to all of us. The goal isn't to bash or wish ill will against a fellow entrepreneur. Find out what they're doing well and allow it to inspire you to greater heights. When one of us sets the bar just a little higher, let's all celebrate the example of what's possible.

If you're ever tempted into a scarcity mindset, remember how many gas stations are available in your community and how many coffee creamer types line the shelf at Target.

The following will help you gain a thorough sense of the value available to your customers. You'll then be able to craft the positioning and brand of your business to uniquely serve customers for whom you're the right fit.

Use this space to record information about your top three competitors. For each competitor, record:

- ▶ What is their digital presence like?

- ▶ What vibe does their brand (logo, color scheme, communication tone, etc.) offer?

- ▶ How do they connect with the audience?

- ▶ What is the customer experience like?

- ▶ What is their value proposition (which is the reason their customers choose to spend money with them)?

- ▶ What is their competitive advantage (which is how they compete in the industry)?

- ▶ What insights can you pull from customer reviews?

Not finding many competitors to your business? Hold up! A gap in the market could suggest rich opportunity, but it could equally suggest a red flag. Make no assumptions. If there is no competition in the niche or geographic location you're looking at, first find out why. The Chamber of Commerce or surrounding businesses might have insight.

If your business operates solely online, finding the source of a gap in the industry can be more difficult, but certainly not impossible. Talk to vendors and other similar businesses. Complementary businesses who target a similar audience to yours are great place to start.

Competitor #1: ....

For each category, check all that apply:

Digital Presence:

☐ Content is kept regularly up to date

☐ Competitor keeps a consistent brand (i.e. logo, color scheme, communication tone, type of imagery) across online platforms

☐ Website, social media platforms, and brand mentions are easy to find in a search engine

☐ The vibe appears to appeal to the intended audience

☐ The company positions itself as an authority in the industry

☐ The online presence feels relatable and authentic

Brand Personality:

☐ Brand has been clearly planned and executed

☐ The company's core values are apparent

☐ It's clear to a new customer what the company does and who it serves

☐ Fonts are consistent across platforms

☐ Images are consistent and professional

☐ The feelings and emotions expressed are appropriate to the brand and offering

How they connect with their audience:

☐ The company seems to have established several well-planned marketing channels (e.g. email marketing, website, social media, Google Business presence)

☐ Engagement appears to be up to date on social channels

- ☐ Company appears to be on all social media channels where its target audience spends time
- ☐ Contact information is easily accessible

What the customer experience might be like:

- ☐ The customer appears to be guided through an intentional process from lead to paying customer
- ☐ The customer is encouraged to engage with the company through social channels, emails, and on its website
- ☐ Content is a healthy mix of entertainment and sales messages
- ☐ Content is created in such a way that customers' questions/concerns are anticipated

Why customers buy:

- ☐ The company clearly articulates its purpose
- ☐ The company's value proposition is apparent (in other words, it's easy for customers to establish an affinity for the company's unique personality)
- ☐ Engaging with the company evokes positive emotions

How they compete:

- ☐ The company's competitive advantage is obvious (e.g. low-cost provider, high quality, convenience, ridiculously good customer service)

Insights from customer reviews:

- ☐ Customer reviews are available (e.g. Facebook, Yelp, Google, website)
- ☐ Customer reviews appear to be positive (4+ stars)

Competitor #2: ....

For each category, check all that apply:

Digital Presence:

☐ Content is kept regularly up to date

☐ Competitor keeps a consistent brand (i.e. logo, color scheme, communication tone, type of imagery) across online platforms

☐ Website, social media platforms, and brand mentions are easy to find in a search engine

☐ The vibe appears to appeal to the intended audience

☐ The company positions itself as an authority in the industry

☐ The online presence feels relatable and authentic

Brand Personality:

☐ Brand has been clearly planned and executed

☐ The company's core values are apparent

☐ It's clear to a new customer what the company does and who it serves

☐ Fonts are consistent across platforms

☐ Images are consistent and professional

☐ The feelings and emotions expressed are appropriate to the brand and offering

How they connect with their audience:

☐ The company seems to have established several well-planned marketing channels (e.g. email marketing, website, social media, Google Business presence).

☐ Engagement appears to be up to date on social channels

☐ Company appears to be on all social media channels where its target audience spends time

☐ Contact information is easily accessible

What the customer experience might be like:

☐ The customer appears to be guided through an intentional process from lead to paying customer

☐ The customer is encouraged to engage with the company through social channels, emails, and on its website

☐ Content is a healthy mix of entertainment and sales messages

☐ Content is created in such a way that customers' questions/concerns are anticipated

Why customers buy:

☐ The company clearly articulates its purpose

☐ The company's value proposition is apparent (in other words, it's easy for customers to establish an affinity for the company's unique personality)

☐ Engaging with the company evokes positive emotions

How they compete:

☐ The company's competitive advantage is obvious (e.g. low-cost provider, high quality, convenience, ridiculously good customer service)

Insights from customer reviews:

☐ Customer reviews are available (e.g. Facebook, Yelp, Google, website)

☐ Customer reviews appear to be positive (4+ stars)

Competitor #3:

For each category, check all that apply:

Digital Presence:

☐ Content is kept regularly up to date

☐ Competitor keeps a consistent brand (i.e. logo, color scheme, communication tone, type of imagery) across online platforms

☐ Website, social media platforms, and brand mentions are easy to find in a search engine

☐ The vibe appears to appeal to the intended audience

☐ The company positions itself as an authority in the industry

☐ The online presence feels relatable and authentic

Brand Personality:

☐ Brand has been clearly planned and executed

☐ The company's core values are apparent

☐ It's clear to a new customer what the company does and who it serves

☐ Fonts are consistent across platforms

☐ Images are consistent and professional

☐ The feelings and emotions expressed are appropriate to the brand and offering

How they connect with their audience:

☐ The company seems to have established several well-planned marketing channels (e.g. email marketing, website, social media, Google Business presence).

☐ Engagement appears to be up to date on social channels

- ☐ Company appears to be on all social media channels where its target audience spends time
- ☐ Contact information is easily accessible

What the customer experience might be like:

- ☐ The customer appears to be guided through an intentional process from lead to paying customer
- ☐ The customer is encouraged to engage with the company through social channels, emails, and on its website
- ☐ Content is a healthy mix of entertainment and sales messages
- ☐ Content is created in such a way that customers' questions/concerns are anticipated

Why customers buy:

- ☐ The company clearly articulates its purpose
- ☐ The company's value proposition is apparent (in other words, it's easy for customers to establish an affinity for the company's unique personality)
- ☐ Engaging with the company evokes positive emotions

How they compete:

- ☐ The company's competitive advantage is obvious (e.g. low-cost provider, high quality, convenience, ridiculously good customer service)

Insights from customer reviews:

- ☐ Customer reviews are available (e.g. Facebook, Yelp, Google, website)
- ☐ Customer reviews appear to be positive (4+ stars)

Summarize your findings. What are your top competitors doing well and what does that signal about what your customers might be expecting? In what areas do you see your competitors lacking?

Competitor Strengths	Competitor Weaknesses
....	....
....	....
....	....
....	....
....	....

Competing in the market is a very real consideration in business, yet the landscape is changing. More and more, women are banding together to rise together. Knowing your competition is about understanding alternative options and experiences available to your customers so you can elevate your own standards to remain a top consideration in their minds. It's not about rivaling another company so you look good and they look bad. It's about enhancing yourself and your business to be the best you can be so it positively impacts all stakeholders involved.

STEP 4

FINANCE YOUR FUTURE

"YOUR WORST WEAKNESS CAN BECOME YOUR GREATEST SINGLE STRENGTH." – BARBARA CORCORAN

You're a smart cookie. I see you exercising self-discipline and diving into the topic of managing money despite feeling tempted to skip this section altogether.

One of the most important steps to building a successful business is managing money well. How you manage money in your personal life is how you'll manage money in your business. Otherwise smart, capable people who can't manage money well are at a much higher risk of hitting choppy waters in business. It's okay if you don't have the best track record for money management. Good habits can start now.

Funds are stretched thin when you first start a business, which can add extra stress when you're already fenagling funds to pay yourself and cover start-up costs and invest money back into the business so it can grow. This part of starting a business is not glamourous, sis, but the good news is PB&J is sustainable and you have what it takes to get scrappy. As a kid with entrepreneurs for parents, we used to drink "Uncle Dave's Lemonade." That's what my dad called the concoction of tap water, lemon slices, and sweetener he'd make for us at restaurants so we didn't have to pay for real drinks with our meals. Channel your creativity to save on discretionary spending, especially in a culture where luxury is the norm, but not a necessity, for many people.

Knowing the money side of your business is the single greatest thing you can do to empower yourself to succeed. This section will help you pinpoint your money management strengths, discover areas for improvement, estimate how much you need to budget for start-up costs, explore start-up financing options, and plan ahead for taxes and retirement savings to best prime yourself for the financial side of running your very own business.

First, let's take inventory on where you are with money management. Things are about to get real. You owe total honesty to your future self.

Take the money management quiz below. Give yourself one point for each habit you practice. Do you...

- ☐ Live within your means?
- ☐ Keep a healthy emergency fund of 3-6 months of expenses?
- ☐ Practice delayed gratification by saying "no" to excessive spending?
- ☐ Use money to furnish the future you want with savings and investments, rather than furnishing your current lifestyle?
- ☐ Act consciously to avoid lifestyle creep, which is the tendency to spend more as you make more?
- ☐ Consider, "Do I need it, and can I afford it?" before buying?
- ☐ Set strict parameters for taking out a loan and stay accountable to paying it off?
- ☐ Limit debt to necessities?
- ☐ Pay bills ahead of time or on time?
- ☐ Study financial literacy?
- ☐ Set a budget and visit it monthly?
- ☐ Track your spending and evaluate your bank/credit card statements on a monthly basis?
- ☐ Limit credit card usage by paying the balance in full on or ahead of time always?
- ☐ Buy luxury items only when you can afford them?

☐ Set boundaries with people who don't have good financial habits themselves?

☐ Put money into savings monthly?

☐ Pay for luxury items and experiences with cash on hand, including travel and vacations?

☐ Regularly practice generosity with money?

☐ Value and appreciate what you have?

☐ Use a surplus of income to invest into income-producing assets, like real estate or the stock market?

Your Money Management Score: ....

17 – 20 – Way to go! You have likely developed strong money management habits. Keep at it and apply that transferable skill within your business.

11 – 17 – Girlfriend, you're on the right track. You've developed a good foundation for financial habits with room for improvement. Focus on your money management habits and the value of delayed gratification. Consider taking a course on money management to strengthen your good habits and learn to adopt new ones.

0 – 10 – Hang in there, friend. Strong financial habits are lacking, and you could be at risk when it comes to running a business. The good news is you're finding out about it now rather than after stumbling through avoidable future money struggles. Before going farther, develop an action plan for how you'll learn and adopt sound financial habits so that cash flow challenges in business don't hinder your success. It's imperative for you to take a course or find a money mentor who can help get you on the right track now so you can learn and implement strong financial habits in your business.

BUDGET

A budget outlines the amount of money you have allotted for start-up costs (one-time costs to open your doors) and monthly expenses (recurring costs). It details how much money is necessary and available to make each purchase. You may hear the word "budget" and think "Womp-womp – there goes my freedom."

Actually, a budget creates freedom. It's the sifter through which you send all spending decisions. If it fits in the budget, go for it! If it doesn't, your decision is easy. Want something not in the budget? Your next immediate thought should be, "*How* can I afford this?" and ta-da! Your mind gets to work solving the challenge. You'll either increase your income or reduce your expenses to make it work.

The Bureau of Labor Statistics cites that 50% of businesses don't make it past the 5-year mark.[4] According to SCORE, the nation's largest network of volunteer business mentors, 82% of businesses fail because they run out of cash.[5] When businesses run out of cash, they're unable to finance activities like paying bills, maintaining inventory, or paying employees—activities critical to keeping the doors open.

How do you prevent that? A wise place to start is by tracking spending carefully with a budget, keeping tabs on how much it costs to produce your offering, and carefully planning revenue generating activities.

Let's dive into this concept by first talking about start-up and on-going costs.

START-UP AND RECURRING COSTS

Learn to love doing things that scare you. When you do, fear can't control your destiny. Empower yourself with the financial side of business, beginning with determining costs you'll incur to run your business.

Start-up costs are the cost requirements to open your doors. After that you'll keep track of how much it will cost to *stay in operation*.

Given most entrepreneurs overestimate how soon their business will turn a profit and sustain itself (meaning that revenues are enough to cover the costs to operate), it's easy to see how they underestimate capital requirements to keep the doors open. This is one reason why an emergency fund is a necessity and should be calculated to cover the business's costs for three to six months.

The following list will help you assess your business from several angles.

COSTS SPREADSHEET

The Costs Spreadsheet below lists common costs businesses incur to become an established business and then remain operational. The purpose of the spreadsheet is to record how you'll allocate funds as you start your business.

Not all costs listed must apply to your business and you'll find space within each category to add costs not already listed. If a cost applies, but you can make do with a free option, go for it! For example, a free spreadsheet or Google Drive will be more than sufficient to get your business up and running rather than paying for accounting software.

Researching each cost is where you channel your spending savvy. Sleuth the best prices by comparing several retailers' listed prices online and consider online marketplaces for a gently used option (printer, for instance) at a discount price.

Then, use the spreadsheet to fill in your budgeted amount for items that apply to you. If the cost is recurring, check the box in the far-right column.

Want a downloadable version of the spreadsheet below? Find it at www.HerBusinessGuide.com.

THE FOUNDING FEMALES™ COSTS SPREADSHEET

OFFICE EQUIPMENT		
Desk and office chair	$	☐ Recurring
Computer	$	☐ Recurring
Printer	$	☐ Recurring
Office supplies	$	☐ Recurring
Other:	$	☐ Recurring
Other:	$	☐ Recurring
SUBSCRIPTIONS		
Email marketing platform (try to go with the free version as long as you can)	$	☐ Recurring
Customized/branded email address such as Hello@YourBusinessName.com	$	☐ Recurring
Customer Relationship Management software (CRM)	$	☐ Recurring
Project management software	$	☐ Recurring
Video conference software	$	☐ Recurring
Invoicing/Accounting software	$	☐ Recurring
Website	$	☐ Recurring
Word processor software	$	☐ Recurring
Social media scheduler	$	☐ Recurring
Graphic design software	$	☐ Recurring
Other:	$	☐ Recurring
Other:	$	☐ Recurring
Other:	$	☐ Recurring
MARKETING		
Business cards	$	☐ Recurring
Ads	$	☐ Recurring
Stock photography and video or licensed music	$	☐ Recurring
Branded photo shoot by a professional photographer	$	☐ Recurring
Logo/brand designer	$	☐ Recurring

Other:	$	☐ Recurring
Other:	$	☐ Recurring
Other:	$	☐ Recurring
Other:	$	☐ Recurring
UTILITIES		
Rent	$	☐ Recurring
Cell phone	$	☐ Recurring
Internet	$	☐ Recurring
Office space rental / coworking rent	$	☐ Recurring
Water/Sewer	$	☐ Recurring
Electricity	$	☐ Recurring
Gas	$	☐ Recurring
Other:	$	☐ Recurring
Other:	$	☐ Recurring
Other:	$	☐ Recurring
WEBSITE COSTS (NOT ALREADY LISTED UNDER SUBSCRIPTION)		
Domain	$	☐ Recurring
Hosting	$	☐ Recurring
Apps or plugins	$	☐ Recurring
Designer	$	☐ Recurring
Other website costs not listed under subscription	$	☐ Recurring
PROFESSIONAL FEES		
Membership fees, such as the Chamber of Commerce, Business Networking International (BNI) groups, or Rotary Club	$	☐ Recurring
Legal fees	$	☐ Recurring
Accounting fees	$	☐ Recurring
Insurance and permits	$	☐ Recurring
OPERATING EXPENSES		
Courses for becoming educated or certified	$	☐ Recurring

Professional clothing (this could be a suit or scrubs – whatever is appropriate to your business profession)	$	Recurring
Operations equipment	$	Recurring
Inventory	$	Recurring
Paying yourself	$	Recurring
Employees or contractors	$	Recurring
Travel expenses	$	Recurring
Other:	$	Recurring
Other:	$	Recurring
Other:	$	Recurring
Other:	$	Recurring
Total Start-up Costs:	**$**	

Total all costs required to start your business and write it in the last column. This is your total start-up cost.

Total all recurring costs required keep your business running on a monthly basis. This is your operational cost.

Ongoing monthly operational costs $ ....

This number is your starting point. If it seems overwhelming, that's normal! Break it down into manageable goals. Right now without customers, it's likely you have more time than money, so consider investing in time-saving resources *after* you start generating revenue. For now, keep in mind that there are many ways and options to raise cash or finance your business, which we'll talk about in the following sections.

PRO TIP: Stretch your money as far as it will go. Here are some additional tips to help you do that.

▶ Ask, "Does the item you need for your start-up have to be brand new or could you purchase it second hand?" For example, a moving company might consider purchasing a fleet of used vans.

▶ If it's not customer-facing, you may not need to splurge. For instance, I initially purchased colored printer ink, but after that, I realized grayscale was more than sufficient for my needs since my customers weren't seeing printed documents.

▶ Get in the habit of asking yourself, "Do I need it, and can I afford it?" Robert Kiyosaki mentions in his book *Rich Dad Poor Dad* that he and his wife buy luxury items only from the profit of their real estate investments. Aim to fund "nice to haves" by first becoming profitable in your business.

▶ It's enticing to think paying for the annual subscription is the smart choice, because annual subscriptions often offer a discount over monthly subscriptions. I recommend paying monthly for at least the first two months to find out if the cost is a necessity. If it is, pay for the annual subscription thereafter.

Maintaining a budget is one of the best ways to keep yourself accountable. Whether you use accounting software or document financial activity in a traditional spreadsheet, use the list provided above as a starting point for creating a monthly budget. Then, put a recurring date on your calendar to address finance and accounting activity for the month.

We've covered what you should know about planning and tracking start-up and operational costs with a budget. Then, once you dive into building your business, **Phase Three: Build, Step 2: Find Your Financial Finesse** addresses the remaining financial statements you'll use to keep the financial side of your business healthy: the profit and loss statement, balance sheet, and cash flow statement.

START-UP FINANCING OPTIONS

Knowing how to acquire financing can feel overwhelming. Traditionally, bank loans, peer loans, and investors were the primary sources of start-up capital. However, the landscape is changing. As more players enter business ownership, they introduce diverse ideas into the mix for leveraging capital.

Three things to keep in mind when you seek start-up financing:

- ▶ No one-size-fits-all approach exists.

- ▶ Each business idea comes with its own costs and needs.

- ▶ Each business owner has a unique financial situation.

There is no completely risk-free financing option. Every financing option comes with benefits and drawbacks. Take using personal savings ("bootstrapping"), for instance. This is the financing option I chose. The enticing part of bootstrapping is less financial risk, but it leaves many people wondering how to make water out of wine because no funds = no forward movement.

This section will guide you through choosing the financing option best suited for your situation, which might mean combining two or more of the following options. Think carefully about the start-up costs you listed in the Costs Spreadsheet on the previous pages. Remember that many businesses fail because they run out of cash. Whatever financing option(s) you choose should be enough to help you stay operational *until you can earn consistent revenue*. In my experience, new entrepreneurs tend to underestimate how long it takes to generate consistent revenue, so research carefully and adjust your goals as you go.

In the following pages, we'll explore a variety of financing options including personal savings, small business loans, investors, crowdfunding, and small business grants. Consider whether each option might fit your needs and write your personal advantages and disadvantages along with how you might go about securing each particular option.

Personal savings. Costs of starting a small business have generally decreased as technology and start-up resources have become more attainable. By staying "lean" and managing expenses carefully, it's possible to begin a lucrative business with just the cash you have sitting in the bank rather than taking out a loan. However, if you don't have savings or if using the savings you have is too constricting, you might need to explore other financing options. Do you have personal savings you could use to fund all or part of the start-up phase of your business? If so, outline the details below.

Personal Savings Pros	Personal Savings Cons

A plan for acquiring the funding:

Amount available: $

Small business loans – The two main types of business loans are secured loans and unsecured loans. A secured loan is one where a business with assets uses them as security. (Assets are items of value the bank could turn into cash if you default on your loan, such as equipment, inventory, and property). This means the bank can repossess the assets if the owner is unable to repay the loan. Unsecured loans, on the other hand, don't use assets as collateral, but often require qualification based on a credit rating and might come with higher interest rates. Note that in **Phase Three: Build, Step 1: Assemble Your A-Team**, we'll walk through finding a banker who's a good fit for you. Is acquiring a bank loan on your radar? If so, outline the details below.

Small Business Loan Pros	Small Business Loan Cons

A plan for acquiring the funding:

Amount available: $

Investors – Venture capital firms, angel investors, and corporate investors are individuals or organizations who provide financial support, often in the form of an exchange of equity (taking a portion of ownership) in the company. The landscape for securing outside investment is competitive and often focused on start-ups with the ability to grow extensively and quickly. In exchange for the equity the business owner gives up, the investors often provide capital, valuable ideas and connections, and business expertise which can overcome the challenges of bringing an offering to market. Is acquiring capital from an investor a viable option for your business? If so, outline the details below.

Investors Pros	Investors Cons

A plan for acquiring the funding:

Amount available: $

Crowdfunding – Crowdfunding is a collective effort of gathering small amounts of capital from many individuals. Usually the investors, or "backers," receive some kind of incentive for supporting varying levels of the crowd-funding campaign. Other times the financial commitment is "in kind" as a way for backers to simply show support for the business or individual. Types of crowdfunding include peer-to-peer lending, peer-to-business lending, reward-based crowdfunding, and equity crowdfunding.

As the business landscape changes to include more women in financing conversations, crowdfunding and women-led businesses are emerging and touting "by women, for women" by putting their money where their mouth is. Girl power! Is crowdfunding an option for your business? If so, research crowdfunding platforms and then dive into the advantages, disadvantages, and method(s) for acquiring it below.

Crowdfunding Pros	Crowdfunding Cons

A plan for acquiring the funding:

Amount available: $

Small business grants – Grants are sums of money that do not have to be paid back and are available for businesses looking to start or grow. Generally, the receiving company doesn't give up any company ownership or pay the funds back, but in turn, grants are highly competitive. Since it's essentially free money, grants often come with high stipulations or requirements for approval, like how the money can be spent.Therefore, only apply to grants for which you qualify and can meet the conditions of the grantor.

Types of grants include private grants through corporations and large businesses through a philanthropic initiative and government grants available at the federal, state, and local levels. Grant funders typically secure funds in an effort to support specific industries or demographics. For instance, if you're a minority business owner or a business that promotes social good in your operations, there may be grants available specifically for you.

The following are some places to begin looking for small business grants:

▶ The Small Business Administration (www.sba.gov)

▶ Initiative by the Office of Management and Budget (www.grants.gov)

▶ Economic Development Administration, a U.S. Department of Commerce agency (www.eda.gov)

▶ Local small business development center (SBDC) (www.americassbdc.org)

▶ The National Association for the Self Employed (www.nase.org)

Are grants an option for starting your small business? If so, outline the details below.

Small Business Grants Pros	Small Business Grants Cons

A plan for acquiring the funding:

....

....

....

....

....

....

....

Amount available: $ ....

DECIDING WHAT TO PAY YOURSELF

What you pay yourself depends on several factors, including your region's average cost of living, the legal entity you have chosen for your business, and whether you're profitable. Working with your accountant or a bookkeeper could provide strong guidance into this question. Here is what you should take into consideration:

- ▶ Are taxes, fixed costs, and payroll covered?

- ▶ When your business drives consistent revenue, can you pay yourself a certain amount consistently at the same interval – perhaps monthly, bimonthly, or weekly?

- ▶ What is your legal structure? "Reasonable compensation" is the amount of money the government would expect you to take from your business, which is an especially important consideration in businesses legally considered "corporations." Sole proprietors have more freedom in terms of what to pay themselves whereas incorporated businesses (including S-corps) have stricter guidelines where the business owners must be on the payroll just like any other employee.

PRO TIP: Avoid lifestyle creep. Lifestyle creep is when you spend more money just because you make more money rather than out of necessity, and this can happen in business ownership, too. Once you determine a viable wage for yourself, pay yourself regularly and then allow the profits in your business to grow. The freedom a cash flow offers can positively impact your business. You'll be thankful when you can afford to hire help, invest back into your business, attend conferences or other skillset-related education, or upgrade the quality of your equipment.

Once your business earns a recurring, predictable revenue and you as the business owner maintain a handle on its costs, you can consider giving yourself a reasonable raise. Some years I've taken a 3%-5% raise, and some years I've opted to take no raise at all and instead invest that profit back into the business. If you're anything like me coming out of a 9-5, I felt entitled to an annual raise, but, friend, then I learned that's not how entrepreneurship works.

In fact, in 2019, I made the decision to forego giving myself a typical raise so I could buy a plane ticket to California and a conference registration for The Impact Summit—a conference for entrepreneurs and online course creators.

During those three days, I earned more than a raise could have ever given me. I learned about creating passive income and running my business more intentionally. I soaked up inspiration from trailblazers like Amy Porterfield, Chalene Johnson, Brendon Burchard, Rachel Hollis, and my self-appointed SEO mentor, Neil Patel. It was blissful and so worth it.

After that conference, I glowed for weeks and took with me precious benefits that would later transform my business. Sure, a 3% raise would have been nice, but experiencing the conference was a far greater perk.

TAXES AND RETIREMENT SAVINGS

When it comes to paying taxes, you have a choice: you can either plan ahead or scrounge up the money you need later. Either way, paying Uncle Sam what he's owed isn't optional. Since you won't have an employer paying your taxes or providing the benefit of a 401(k), you'll need to make a habit of setting money aside.

Thirty percent of what I make immediately upon payment from a client is transferred to cover quarterly tax estimates and contribute to a retirement savings account. The rest goes into a business checking account I use to pay myself once monthly and cover the business's expenses. Reach out to your accountant (finding an accountant is covered in depth in **Phase Three: Build, Step 1: Assemble Your A-Team**) and financial advisor to talk through best-suited options.

And while we're on the topic of saving for retirement, I'll be the friend urging you to take control of your personal finances. Managing your personal finances is more than dispersing your income. It means paying off debt, investing, building an emergency fund, and creating additional income streams, **on. your. own.** Start an investment account. Balance your checkbook. Interview and choose a financial advisor. If you're waiting for Prince Charming to knock on your door, ready to manage these things for you, either you're kidding yourself or you have a massive trust fund, which you need to be in control of anyway.

If you haven't yet started saving for retirement or have no idea why you'd need a Roth IRA, girl, it's time to wake up. Decide today to take ownership for your financial health and future. That's not the topic of this book, so I'll only plant the seed for this new goal of yours, because I'm in your corner with your best interest in mind.

I'd love nothing more than to slow clap for more savvy, well-off boss women changing the world through generosity while running insanely profitable businesses and enjoying financial freedom. You cannot do that if your finances aren't in order or if you aren't diligently planning for YOUR future. Barbara Stanny has you covered with two of her financial literacy books titled *Prince Charming Isn't Coming* and *Secrets of Six Figure Women*. Both are excellent.

Financials can feel foreign because it's a subject that adults are typically expected to wake up one day and suddenly know how to do well. Sis, I'm right there with you, but don't forget that us movers and shakers lean into difficult challenges, and we know it's never too late to start taking control of our own results. Even though many people never become formally educated on how to create a budget, manage money, and plan for retirement, it's still a vital part of running your business well and you can do this! Regardless of your background in managing money, you'll need to choose to be in the driver's seat, lean into the challenge, and take control of the money aspect of your business.

STEP  5

NAME YOUR BUSINESS

Naming your business is a big deal. I stewed over the name of my first business, Simply Integrated, LLC, for weeks. Looking back, I agonized over it so deeply that I paid a designer to help name my second business, Founding Females™, where I guide female entrepreneurs into and through entrepreneurship. I speak from experience when I compassionately say, girl, I feel your pain!

If you're one of the lucky ones who stumbled upon a name naturally or always knew what you wanted the name to be, props. For everyone else, this section will help you walk through the process of naming your business.

If you have a name picked out for your business, list it here:

Even if you have a name picked out, I encourage you to walk through the exercises within this section to make sure it passes the checklist.

If you don't have a name picked out yet, the following exercise will help you generate a brainstormed list of possible names with questions below to help analyze each.

Spend time thinking and writing all words that come to mind based on the following:

- Different viewpoints of your business by stakeholders, like customers, collaborators, and employees.

- The transformation you aim to take your customers through.

- Feelings you'd like customers to experience.

- Different scenarios where you'll introduce your business: competitors, local business professionals, your girl gang, family, and customers.

With a list of 15-20 words, consider which ones resonate the deepest with the impact you aim to make.

Next, experiment with different combinations of words. Consider whether each option is something easy for the customer to remember and repeat. The following will help you consider your options from all angles.

- What do you do and who do you do it for?

- Is the name easy to pronounce and introduce? Is it something you'll feel proud sharing with a wide variety of audiences?

- Is the name memorable?

- Stand in the mirror and pretend you're introducing yourself as the founder of your business. How does it feel?

- What would your name look like in a website address?

- Is your desired website address already taken? Typing your desired website address into an option like NameCheap or GoDaddy will help you find out.

- Consider the length of the name and think ahead about all the places your business name will be written, like email addresses, social media accounts, and on business cards.

- Plug each name on your brainstorm list into a search engine. What results do you find? Has a business in the industry already become synonymous with the name you're considering? If the name has been taken by someone else, you may not legally be able to use it, and/or your audience could get confused.

- Has the name been trademarked? Visit www.uspto.gov to find out.

HOW FAR CAN YOU PUSH YOUR *dream* IN THE NEXT 24 HOURS?

For inspiration on selecting a business name, check out the book *Hello, My Name is Awesome: How to Create Brand Names that Stick* by Alexandra Watkins.

After reviewing the important considerations for choosing a name for your business, list your top options in the space below. If you're still stuck, keep in mind that some graphic designers offer the service of helping develop a name for your business and finding a graphic designer is something we'll cover in Phase Three: Build.

....

....

....

....

....

....

Aside from a few legal parameters, which we'll talk about next in **Phase Two: Research, Step 6: Get Legal Like Elle Woods,** the sky is the limit in taking the dream on your heart and narrowly defining it into a single word or two. Meaning is created from the name you chose to call your business. Of course, there's a heavy load of pressure in getting it right! Don't rush the process, but also don't let a speed bump turn into an insurmountable mountain.

Ride the process of brainstorming names and themes to who, what, when, where, and why. If you're still struggling to find a name you love, hire a designer! Some of the best money I ever spent was investing in the help of a dahhhling designer who helped me choose Founding Females™.

STEP  GET LEGAL LIKE ELLE WOODS

"LIVE EVERY DAY LIKE YOU ARE ELLE WOODS AFTER WARNER TOLD HER SHE WASN'T SMART ENOUGH FOR LAW SCHOOL." – REESE WITHERSPOON

All I knew was I wanted to be on the right side of the law, and I needed an expert to help keep me there. When I started my business, meeting with an attorney was one of my first to-dos. My attorney walked me through definitions of legal structures and what kind of risk I'd be looking at with my business model. Later, he pointed me in the right direction in starting a second company and connected me with other excellent professionals in his network throughout the process…all because I sat down in his office one day as a blank slate ready to be led.

Even though rookie business me Googled the definition of "pro bono" walking into my first attorney meeting, I learned as I went. The goal wasn't *just* to have someone to help me get started. No, it was more far-sighted than that. The goal was to establish a relationship with someone I could turn to with every seemingly stupid "pro bono"-type question that followed in my business journey.

There is no substitute for wising up over the legal impact of your business. It's vital to protect yourself and your future. The legal space can feel confusing and intimidating, yet it's one of the most important aspects to secure the longevity of your business as an asset. Good news: you're in good hands.

Phase Three: Build shares details for adding an attorney to your advisor team of support. For now, we'll walk through the "need to know" you can use to prepare for meetings with your attorney or, if you feel equipped, tackling the legal tasks on your own. In this section, we'll cover common legal structures, registering your business with the IRS, trademarking, protecting your intellectual property, securing permits and licenses, and the legal differences between hiring employees and contractors.

CHOOSE A LEGAL STRUCTURE

Choosing the right legal structure isn't one-size-fits-all. Your legal structure sets the standard for key factors in your business, like taxes, liability, and day-to-day operations. Ya know, the stuff you *really* want to get right. I recommend working with an attorney, and/or an accountant to determine the best legal and tax structure for you. This section will prepare you with the fundamentals so you can walk into your meeting much more confidently. Let's talk about legal structures.

SOLE PROPRIETORSHIP

A sole proprietorship is one of the most basic forms of legal structure. Should you operate a business and not register your business as a legal entity, it will be considered a sole proprietorship as a default. With this legal structure, there is no separation between which assets and liabilities are the business's and which are yours personally. While this structure can work well for low-risk businesses, the owner is personally responsible for debts and obligations of the business, along with any legal suits brought against the business.

In essence, a sole proprietorship can provide little protection in the case of litigation, meaning that anything you own personally, like your home or car, can be taken if you get into legal trouble. An advantage of the sole proprietorship is that it's simple and a disadvantage is that it can be riskier legally than other forms of legal structures.

LIMITED LIABILITY COMPANY (LLC)

An LLC allows business owners to benefit from some of the advantages provided to corporations and partnership structures, including tax rates and protection from personal liability. This is the legal structure I chose. With LLCs, profits and losses are passed through as personal income. LLCs are the most common business structure as they are relatively flexible, inexpensive to set up and maintain (in most cases), and offer a clear boundary between business assets and personal assets.

PARTNERSHIP (LP OR LLP)

A partnership is appropriate when there are two or more people who own a business together. The two kinds of partnerships are limited partnerships (LPs) and limited liability partnerships (LLPs), with the difference being how much liability (and generally also control) each partner has. There are important tax implications with partnerships regarding how profits are reported on tax returns. Multi-member LLCs are usually taxed as partnerships unless you make other arrangements.

CORPORATION

While there are several forms of corporations, the important thing to note is corporations are legal entities separate from owners and can be held legally liable. The differing forms of corporations include C-corporations, B-corporations, close corporations, and nonprofit corporations.

S-corporations are a tax designation you can select by filling out an IRS form allowing you to stay organized as an LLC, but be taxed as a corporation. There are some increased expenses with S-corps, so check with your accountant about when it makes sense to switch to this tax election and put yourself on a reasonable salary. Each structure is characterized differently in how profits are taxed, what kind of recordkeeping is required, the cost of forming the entity, the risk that's appropriate, and ownership.

🔧 **TAKE ACTION! Still have questions? The Small Business Administration (www.SBA.gov) offers expansive information on legal structures.**

Reflect on which legal structure(s) might be a good fit for your business vision and why: ....

....

....

....

REGISTER YOUR BUSINESS
(AND SECURE THE DOMAIN)

Hallelujah! This is officially happening! You determined which legal structure fits your business best. Now it's time to register or incorporate the business in the state where you live. To some, this may seem like a small thing, and it can be a fairly simple process, but don't kid yourself. This accomplishment earns you a dazzling happy dance. You're really doing it!

If you choose a sole proprietorship, your tax ID will be your social security number. Registering your business under any other legal entity will establish a new tax ID also known as an EIN (employer identification number), which you'll need for some business activities like hiring employees, securing licenses and permits, opening a business checking account, and filing taxes. It's time to make your business official! You can get your EIN for free at the IRS website with the following steps[1]:

1. Visit www.irs.gov.

2. Click "File."

3. Click "Business and Self-Employed."

4. Click "Small Business and Self-Employed."

5. Click "Employer ID Numbers."

6. Click "Apply for an Employer ID Number."

There are a few ways to make your business name official, including registering it with the state, trademarking the name at the federal level, or perhaps registering under a DBA (stands for "Doing Business As"). Your specific requirements depend on the laws in your state and your business's legal structure. The section below briefly explains each.

REGISTER YOUR BUSINESS NAME

Registering your entity name within your state is how your state identifies your business. Generally speaking, your state will require your business name to be unique (meaning no other businesses in the state could use the exact same name) and be reflective of your organization. With a few exceptions, registering your name with the state provides protection that no one else in the state can operate a business under the same name.

The Small Business Administration (www.SBA.gov) is an excellent resource for finding your state's specific requirements. Registering your business is also a task a business attorney can help with if you decide to hire one (more on this in **Phase Three: Build**).

Since developing a strong brand image is important across platforms, registering your desired domain name, even if you don't plan to immediately build your website, can ensure brand consistency in the online space. There are many registrars available, like Network Solutions, NameCheap, and GoDaddy, where domain names can be registered. Find the Founding Females™ recommended list of registrars in the resource suite at www.HerBusinessGuide.com.

TRADEMARK YOUR NAME

Your business is as unique as you are! Trademarking your business's name at the federal level prevents other businesses in the same or a similar industry from using the same business name for the same type of goods or services as you. Once you've selected the name you're considering, double check it against the United States Patent and Trademark Office's official trademark database at www.uspto.gov/trademark and follow the process for submitting your business name for trademark registration.

Trademark searches can be a nuanced process where you will need to look for your intended name plus alternate spellings, pronunciations, hyphenations, transliterations, plurality, and even foreign language equivalents. In addition, trademarking can require quite an investment and tends to be a long process. (Mine took over six months.) If you love your name and plan to investing in it as a true "brand," consult with a trademark attorney early to clear your naming runway and set yourself up for success.We'll cover getting a lawyer business bestie on your advisory team in **Phase Three: Build**.

PROTECT INTELLECTUAL PROPERTY

Have you created something like an invention, book, e-book, online course, handouts, blog posts, audio, video, music, photograph, illustrations, artwork, choreography, or sculpture? That's your intellectual property (IP)—ideas YOU have dreamed up and brought to life—and you'll want to protect your ownership of it.

Here are three examples of how to protect your ideas.

- **Copyright** – Copyrights protect original artistic and literary work. Each author automatically has the exclusive copyright to his or her creation once it leaves her brain and is fixed in a tangible form. However, registering a copyright at www.copyright.gov provides additional benefits to enforce those rights.

- **Patent** – Patents protect inventions for a set period, especially the sole right to exclude others from making, using, or selling an invention. File for a patent at www.USPTO.gov.

- **Trademark** - Trademarks protect brand names and identifiers, like words, phrases, symbols, and/or designs that identify and distinguish the source of the goods of one party from those of others. File a trademark at www.USPTO.gov.

Reflect on which, if any, of your ideas will need intellectual property protection via copyright, patent, or trademark:

....

....

....

....

....

....

Others' Work

It is also important to note that other intellectual property has protection as well. Be a good steward of content creation as you grow your business. Do not use the work of anyone else without permission (even if you credit or @ tag someone). Not all sharing is caring, and getting written permission is the best practice to use the original work of any third party. Use reputable stock sites for stock photography, stock music or stock video, use written contracts with any creative freelancers (designers, virtual assistants, web developers, branding designers, videographers, and photographers), and make sure you always have the commercial rights to use any work as part of your business.

PERMITS AND LICENSES

What permits or licenses, if any, will you need to operate your business? The list below reflects examples of licenses some types of businesses need to operate legally:

- ▶ Fire department permit
- ▶ Liquor license
- ▶ Sign permit
- ▶ Parking permits
- ▶ County permit
- ▶ State licenses
- ▶ Sales tax license or reseller's permit
- ▶ Health department permit or food handling permit

For specific instructions regarding which licenses and permits your organization will need, contact your city's business license department. Find their contact information through an internet search. Most cities do not require any kind of license or permit for a virtual or home-based business, but always check with your local jurisdiction and their rules. Use this space to jot down notes and thoughts:

HIRING HELP

There is an important difference between an "employee" and a "contractor." They are treated differently by the law and should be leveraged differently in your business. Let's say you own a small boutique. You might hire an employee to help run the store, wait on customers, stock the shelves, etc. As their employer, you set their hours, pay, and even determine the dress code. But you might hire an independent contractor to handle your company's marketing needs. This person isn't considered an employee, but rather someone you would establish a mutual agreement with regarding what they will do for you at what price. We'll dig into this deeper in a minute.

There is an extensive legal test that differentiates employees from contractors. You need to be sure you're clear on the characteristics and requirements of both for your business because state and federal labor laws could enforce costly legal ramifications for misclassification.

Let's review the criteria for both options. Refer to the Equal Employment Opportunity Commission's website at www.eeoc.gov and the IRS's website at www.IRS.gov for additional information. You may also want to enlist the help of your accountant or a human resources or employment law specialist to check on helpers in your business, especially as their roles may evolve over time, to see if a classification switch needs to be made.

An **independent contractor** operates under a separate business from your business and invoices for work completed. They must have certain freedoms, including choosing their work hours and how the work will meet the desired result.

You are not required to withhold income tax, social security tax, unemployment tax, or Medicare tax for independent contractors who perform work for your business. The income earned by an independent contractor is subject to self-employment tax, which they pay. An independent contractor is also not owed benefits or employee incentives.

Typically, an independent contractor and a business agree on expectations in the form of a contract on an ongoing or project-contingent basis. The contractor usually uses her own equipment and has the freedom to offer services to other clients and customers. You cannot use any non-compete language with an independent contractor and typically have little to no control over their dress code, their schedule, or the manner in which they perform their job. They are supposed to be trained and ready for whatever skill they are providing for you.

An **employee**, on the other hand, is subject to stricter guidelines regarding behavior on the job, such as what hours are worked and how the work should be completed. Employees can wear many hats within the organization—a role that doesn't typically fall on an independent contractor. Employers are also required to pay certain benefits for each employee, including social security taxes, workers' compensation insurance, disability insurance (in certain states), leave benefits, and unemployment insurance (in certain states). It is common, though not required by the government, for employers to offer benefits like health insurance, a retirement plan, and employee incentive programs. Employers must withhold payroll taxes for their employees and should consult with their accountant or an online employment provider like ADP or Gusto to help with employee compliance.

From a business decision-making standpoint, it's important to run the numbers about whether your business can afford the cost before you commit to hiring. Contractors often cost more per hour, but they can be a much more flexible way to leverage a competent skill set until you're ready, and before it makes financial sense, to hire an employee.

Tease out your hiring needs with the following questions:

Will you need help in your business from either a hired employee or a contractor? If so, which one and why?

If you cannot afford to hire an employee right away, what business milestone will signal the need for an employee? A certain revenue threshold? A certain number of clients? A certain growth percentage? Create an idea of what your target might be so you can track progress along the way.

Don't hire just for the sake of growing your team. Girl, there's a better way. Determine first how each employee will contribute to the profitability of the company. Set expectations before you hire regarding what kind of skillset and output each employee or contractor will need to produce to justify the cost of bringing them onboard. Do this by comparing how much output they can produce for the company to how much you'll need to pay them. Four X is the standard, meaning an employee should drive four times the amount of revenue than what they are paid to justify their role.

In your business, describe how the employee's or contractor's output will justify their costs?

You can't manage what you don't measure, so think about this. The average revenue per employee is calculated by dividing a company's annual revenue by the number of its FTE's (full time equivalent employees).

For example: $650,000 in revenue / 6.5 employees = $100,000 revenue per employee

This equation also measures how efficient a company is with its labor resources. Bigger companies like Fortune 500s are typically the most efficient with labor resources, but for small businesses like ours, the standard revenue per full-time equivalent is about $100,000.

What might your revenue numbers need to look like in order to bring an additional employee on board?

....

....

....

....

Skilled labor is more expensive than general labor. In addition, many business owners find that even employees with past experience don't perform to expectations in their own company because the employee was trained under a different company's procedures and standards. Consider Patrick Lencioni's thoughts in his book, *The Ideal Team Player*[2]: could you hire a "hungry, humble, and smart" personality type *without* experience and train them according to your company's values, processes, and expectations?

What skill set or role within your company will be your first hire, and how do you plan to find the right employee?

....

....

....

....

PHASE TWO: RESEARCH CONCLUSION

Bring it in for double high-fives! You made it through **Phase Two: Research** and your future self will thank you for your due diligence. It's not easy to bear down and address the nuts and bolts, but you did it!

Sis, you are now armed with the research and knowledge to design the blueprints for your business and build a successful company!

Hold on tight. Life is about to become magical because in the next phase of *Dream, Build, Grow*, you will add viability to this business in your heart.

NOTES

"DONE IS BETTER THAN PERFECT."

Sheryl Sandberg

PHASE THREE

BUILD

To this point, *Dream, Build, Grow: A Female's Step-by-Step Guide for How to Start a Business* has helped organize your dreams and feelings into intentional words. Are you ready to breathe life into your researched thoughts and ideas? Girl, let's go!

Phase Three: Build is full of everything your business needs to become legit. These official steps will escort your business out of your mind and into the world.Creating official plans and documents outlining your business ignites the shift from having an intangible idea to creating a tangible, real business. It's happening! As you work through the development of each important piece, think deliberately, reflect, and don't rush this step.

The truth is, this is likely the most time you'll ever have to carefully build each brick, layer upon layer. It's critical you address the steps in **Phase Three: Build** now because decisions you'll make within this phase will allow you to work fluidly once your business operations increase momentum.

In **Phase Three: Build**, you will be guided through how to do the following:

- ▶ **Step 1:** Assemble Your A-Team

- ▶ **Step 2:** Find Your Financial Finesse

- ▶ **Step 3:** Develop Your Own 'Dolly'

- ▶ **Step 4:** Craft Your Brand Identity

- ▶ **Step 5:** Draw Up Your Marketing Plan

- ▶ **Step 6:** Dream Up Your Digital Space

- ▶ **Step 7:** Figure Out Your Physical Space

- ▶ **Step 8:** Breathe Life into Your Business Plan

Call this the "everything you'll wish you would have known" chapter about becoming an official business. Work you complete in this phase will allow you to *feel* confident that you have the cornerstones in place as you chart new territory. Doing the work by laying the systems and creating your business's "personality" will allow you to spend precious time on revenue-generating tasks. You'll be one step ahead with your ducks in a row, leaving you maximally prepared for whatever opportunities present themselves. Revenue-producing opportunities equal profit, and a healthy profit in your first year of business is totally possible with the right forethought and planning.

By the end of **Phase Three: Build**, you'll have a complete business plan.

Take that to the bank (literally!).

STEP

ASSEMBLE YOUR A-TEAM

"YOU EDUCATE A MAN; YOU EDUCATE A MAN. YOU EDUCATE A WOMAN; YOU EDUCATE A GENERATION." – BRIGHAM YOUNG

One of the best decisions I made was to surround myself with a team of advisors to guide my entrepreneur journey. Your advisory team is your A-Team. It consists of professionals in their areas of expertise. They are not hired employees within your company, but a circle of experts you can turn to for guidance. They are professionals in their realm of expertise, and you typically become their customer so you can leverage their expertise without having to become the expert at everything yourself. Their aim is to help you succeed.

The best time to build relationships is before you need them. As you begin building your advisory team, consider people you already know who could fill the role well. Then ask trusted friends, family, and business colleagues for recommendations. Research thoroughly. Look up reviews, ask for examples of past projects, and don't hesitate to interview candidates for these support positions because you'll be paying them and investing in their guidance.

Your advisory team might consist of any or all of the following:

- ▶ Attorney
- ▶ Banker
- ▶ Insurance Agent
- ▶ Accountant

- ▶ Graphic Designer
- ▶ Web Developer
- ▶ Supplier
- ▶ Business Coach

- ▶ Marketer
- ▶ Mentor
- ▶ Human Resources Consultant

Let's review each advisor—why you need them and what to ask to be sure they're a good fit. Before we do, take a minute to review your values and your Why. Adding someone to your team who doesn't uplift your values will counter your efforts. Think critically about the qualities you want influencing your business so you can make an appropriate selection for each spot on your advisor team.

Remember that whomever you allow at your table is likely to open their network for your leverage. This alone can be worth the cost of working together.

ATTORNEY

First, let's talk about your business attorney. There can be lots of legal parameters to navigate in business, so it's important to have someone in your corner who can help interpret what you need to do to abide by the law and protect yourself. I don't recommend DIY'ing the legal side of your business. Could you? Possibly. Is it wise? Nah.

The beginning phase of launching your business is a fabulous time to establish a relationship with an attorney. Their guidance can help shape the trajectory of your business. Use their guidance to establish your business as a legal entity, write up contracts, and complete other foundational to-dos.

This groundwork allows you and your attorney to interact purposefully. You'll find it valuable to have a connection established in case you ever face a future challenge where it's vital to be on the right side of the law. At that point, your attorney already knows the important details about your business matters leading up to your legal challenge and can offer insight about how to proceed and/or connect you with their network of contacts. Look for an attorney with experience with business entity selection (corporation, LLC, not-for-profit, etc.), entrepreneurial law, and employment.

Note some attorneys will work pro bono on a small project in the beginning of your working relationship, such as filing your legal entity, with the understanding that a trusting relationship must be established for the relationship to grow. ("Pro bono" work means services that are free or are at a reduced fee.

Many professionals also offer a free initial consultation, but don't assume this is the case. It's best to ask for their fee structure.)

There are different types of attorneys who may be helpful as you start and grow your business. Typically, you'll look for someone who practices in:

- ▸ Small/Start-up business

- ▸ Intellectual property/Copyright/Trademark: you want to protect and grow intellectual property and its legacy value in your business

- ▸ Product safety/Compliance: if you are manufacturing a physical product, particularly in any children's goods industry

- ▸ Employment: help hiring, firing, drafting handbook policies, HR compliance

- ▸ Litigation: if you get sued, you need an attorney who practices civil defense litigation

Ask your network for recommendations or research attorneys who might be a good fit for your advisor team. Narrow your list to three options and contact each for an interview:

Name/Interview Date

....

....

....

Questions to consider as you research the right attorney for your business:

- ▸ What do they charge? Do they require a retainer?

- ▸ What type of clients do they usually work with?

- ▸ What are their specialties?

Use this space to document additional questions that come to mind:

....

....

....

....

....

....

....

....

....

BANKER

Having a relationship with a banker is often underrated by new entrepreneurs. Why would you want one? First, bankers often have a wide network of connections. Second, bankers tend to know about quality business opportunities. Third, if you need a loan, having an established relationship with a banker can make a profound impact on the process. After all, people do business with people they know, like, and trust.

As you research banking options in your area, consider which hometown banks are available. Many entrepreneurs find a more tailored, personal relationship comes with choosing a hometown bank or credit union over a commercial institution.

According to the Independent Community Bankers of America[1], obtaining a loan can be easier through hometown banks because they often have more flexibility to whom they loan, less red tape, and are more apt to make character loans, which means the relationship holds some weight in the loan decision rather than solely financial indicators. Even if you don't need a loan immediately to start your business, your business might require one in the future if there comes an economic downturn or if you need a loan to scale your business. Established rapport could mean the difference between financial stability or lack thereof.

Ask your network for recommendations or research bankers who might be a good fit for your support team. Narrow your list to three options and contact each for an interview:

Name/Interview Date

....

....

....

Questions to consider as you research the right banker for your business:

1. What industries does the bank specialize in?

2. Is the bank familiar and comfortable enough with your industry to provide guidance?

3. What do the following look like for business checking accounts?

    a. Introductory offers

    b. Interest rates for savings and checking

    c. Interest rates for lines of credit

    d. Transaction fees

    e. Early termination fees

    f. Minimum account balance fees

7. Does the bank have the mix of products and services you're considering, like credit cards, online banking, a smartphone app, or SBA (Small Business Association) loans?

8. Are they able to establish a relationship with you over the long-term to provide insight and guidance as you take your business journey?

Use this space to document additional questions that come to mind:

....

....

....

....

....

....

....

....

....

....

....

....

....

....

....

....

INSURANCE AGENT

The type of insurance appropriate for your business model and whether insurance is a "nice to have" or "gotta have" for your business varies by the type of business you own, your legal designation, your aversion to risk, and whether your business has employees.

The three primary types of business insurance are general liability coverage, workers' compensation coverage, and commercial auto coverage. Consider contacting a local independent agency in your area who works with multiple carriers. They will be able to provide options and insurance recommendations uniquely tailored to the operations of your business.

Ask your network for recommendations or research insurance agents who might be a good fit for your support team. Narrow your list to three options and contact each for an interview:

Name/Interview Date

....

....

....

Questions to consider as you research the right insurance agent for your business:

1. Have they worked with businesses like yours before?

2. Which insurance companies do they represent?

3. Does the history of their agency align with your values?

Use this space to document additional questions that come to mind:

....

....

....

....

....

....

....

ACCOUNTANT

Many times, I've heard business owners say the best investment they made was hiring an accountant. Depending on the complexity of your business model, an accountant can play an important role in keeping the financial side of your business in order as frequently as weekly or monthly to as infrequently as filing annual taxes. In a relatively straightforward business model, such as a freelancer who provides services to a handful of clients each month, you may only need minimal help from an accountant.

The benefit of having an accountant on your business's advisor team is having eyes on changing tax laws and opportunities you're unlikely to be in the conversation to hear. Your accountant's role is more than getting the correct documents to the IRS—they can also lend insight from a strategy perspective as your business evolves and grows.

It's especially important to work with an accountant experienced and comfortable with businesses like yours. The impetus is on you, as the business owner, to have your accounting in order, and if you face auditing from the IRS in the future, you'll want someone in your corner already familiar with your business to guide you through the situation.

Ask your network for recommendations or research accountants who might be a good fit for your support team. Narrow your list to three options and contact each for an interview:

Name/Interview Date

....

....

....

Questions to consider as you research the right accountant for your business:

1. What industries or small business types does the accountant specialize in?

2. Is the accountant familiar and comfortable with your industry?

3. How can the accountant help guide the evolution of your business?

4. What does the tax filing process look like?

5. Do they provide any resources for you to manage the accounting processes within your business like a tax checklist, organization guidance, or a monthly newsletter on changing regulations?

6. What additional services do they provide outside of filing taxes?

7. What will the accountant handle and what will you be personally responsible to manage?

Use this space to document additional questions that come to mind:

....

....

....

....

···

···

···

···

GRAPHIC DESIGNER

A graphic designer is the support team member responsible for helping build the vision, personality, and feeling your audience will experience through visual and written elements of your business's brand. Outsourcing brand development typically allows for the thorough development of precise details—details often overlooked when brand development is only one to-do item on an entrepreneur's exhaustive list of tasks.

Ask your network for recommendations or research graphic designers who might be a good fit for your support team. Narrow your list to three options and contact each for an interview:

Name/Interview Date

···

···

···

Questions to consider as you research the right graphic designer for your business:

1. What are their design strengths and weaknesses? Then ask yourself if their strengths align with your priorities?

2. Do their past projects and style align with your vision for your business and brand?

3. What services do they offer aside from brand development?
    For instance, if you need help naming your business, is this a service
    they offer?

Use this space to document additional questions that come to mind:

....

....

....

....

....

....

....

....

WEB DEVELOPER

It's normal for small businesses to ask, "Do I really need a website if I'm just a small business?" Increasingly, the answer is "yes." A good looking and well-functioning website can make you money while you sleep because it serves as YOU any time someone is looking for your offering online. It speaks to your credibility for customers who are already searching for your product or service online, especially those who have never heard of you.

However, just because you need a website doesn't mean you have to outsource creating it. Designing and developing a website is one of the aspects of running a business that has become user-friendly with lots of few-tech-skills-needed options on the market.

Before you decide whether to outsource or DIY, ask yourself which functions of a website are priority to you and then research which platforms might work best for your unique situation. Especially if your start-up budget is small, consider building your own website.

Name/Interview Date

....

....

....

If you decide to DIY, take the following steps:

1. Research website platforms to decide which is the best fit for you. See a vetted list of suggestions in the Founding Females™ Resource Suite at www.HerBusinessGuide.com.

2. Secure your domain name (if you didn't take this step in **Phase Two: Research**) by heading to a domain name registrar, checking if the domain is available for purchase, and completing the transaction. A vetted list of suggested domain name registrars is available in the Founding Females™ Resource Suite atwww.HerBusinessGuide.com.

3. Map out beforehand which pages you'll need on your site (Home, About, Testimonials, Services or Products, Blog, and Contact, for instance), along with sections and features each page will contain.

4. Add plenty of calls to action with buttons and hyperlinks leading visitors from page to page. This can positively impact your website ranking and deliver visitors a curated, purposeful experience. Remember, if you don't tell visitors where to go or if they become confused on your site, they'll likely leave. Think intentionally about the site experience to purposefully build "know, like, and trust," eventually leading them into a sale. We'll cover more website strategy and best practices in **Phase Three: Build, Step 6: Dream Up Your Digital Space** when you create your online presence.

5. Consider how to use your website for repeat touch points. Repeat touch points are intentional "collisions" with your target audience that

build familiarity. Give visitors a reason to return to your site. Regularly scheduled blog posts, free resources or value-packed downloads, or an informative video series that delivers value could do the trick!

If you choose to hire a web designer, consider asking the following:

1. Do you have a portfolio I can view?

2. Do you offer services aside from web design, like ongoing support, maintenance, or search engine optimization?

3. Will I own and have full access to all aspects of the site after completion?

4. How much will it cost and what does the cost include?

Use this space to document additional questions that come to mind:

SUPPLIER

Suppliers are critical to product-based businesses because purchasing store items at retail prices cuts into a business's potential profit margin. While the price a supplier can offer is important, there's more to consider. The right supplier can become an important information source by alerting you of upcoming trends or identifying potentially promising opportunities. Don't hesitate to reach out by phone or email. Like most everything else in your business journey, all good things start with taking action.

Qualities to look for: a sense of urgency, lead time for getting products to you after submitting your order, quality of products, price, and a good reputation in the industry.

Ask your network for recommendations or research suppliers who might be a good fit for your advisor team. Narrow your list to three options and contact each for an interview:

Name/Interview Date

....

....

....

Questions to consider as you research the right supplier(s) for your business:

1. What is their track record for reliability? Can you find any information online about what other businesses have said it's like working with the supplier? If you're able to find a current or past customer of theirs, try reaching out to see if you can ask questions. Also consider asking the supplier directly for references you can contact.

2. Will you be a large customer of a small supplier or a small customer of a large supplier? The difference could mean being a priority.

3. How long has the supplier been in business? A business with at least 5 years is a positive signal of stability.

4. Does the supplier have access to the latest and most advanced products?

5. What are their payment terms?

Use this space to document additional questions that come to mind:

....

....

....

....

....

....

....

....

....

....

BUSINESS COACH

Consider a business consultant or coach on your advisor team either now or in the future. A coach can help you effectively work through immediate challenges and develop the "big picture" for where your business is headed. For instance, if you plan to scale your business in the future, it could be wise to access support and direction through a professional who has already carved that path and can lead you through the transition, avoiding speedbumps and pitfalls.

Ask your network for recommendations or research business coaches who might be a good fit for your support team. Narrow your list to three options and contact each for an interview:

Name/Interview Date

....

....

....

Questions to consider as you research the right business coach for your business:

1. Does their resume and/or LinkedIn profile demonstrate a track record for success?

2. Do they have a list of references you can contact?

3. Does their expertise fill the gap for your shortcomings? Look for someone whose skillset complements yours, not mirrors it.

4. What do their reviews/testimonials highlight about benefits or drawbacks to working with them?

5. What past client success stories demonstrate they could also help drive success in your business?

Use this space to document when additional questions come to mind:

....

....

....

....

....

....

....

....

MARKETER

You're bright, sis, so you might already know leveraging marketing channels, like anything else, comes with a learning curve. Using social channels to drive profit can require different know-how than managing your own personal social media accounts. Since many small businesses only market via social media and minimally through other marketing channels, they assume marketing a business will be a walk in the park. This often isn't the case.

You could manage your marketing yourself, and there are many advantages of doing so, but it may not be the best use of your time. Here's why. Social platforms have ever-changing algorithms, so keeping up with changes can feel like a full-time job. Pair that with managing multiple marketing avenues at once and the responsibility quickly becomes complex and time-consuming. Many business owners who opt to do their marketing on their own quickly find themselves too busy with other tasks of running their business.

Many small businesses make the following marketing mistakes:

1. Executing marketing strategy intermittently, if and when the business owner has time, creating an inconsistent presence

2. Marketing solely through social media

3. Prioritizing marketing efforts only when sales are low

4. Neglecting planning, leading to insufficient attention allocated to the effectiveness of the marketing message.

Don't leave your marketing to chance. Serving as the marketing manager in your business pulls your attention from growing your business, developing the internal structure, managing employees or contractors, and attending to revenue-generating tasks. If marketing is a responsibility you can manage well for your business, go for it!

However, if complexities of marketing seem too much to handle, consider delegating marketing responsibilities to someone who can devote focused, consistent attention. You'll feel a breath of relief knowing one of the most important aspects of your business is handled. Plus, you'll have time and energy to focus on revenue-generating tasks that more naturally fit within your wheelhouse.

Ask your network for recommendations or research marketers who might be a good fit for your support team. Narrow your list to three options and contact each for an interview:

Name/Interview Date

....

....

....

Questions to consider as you research the right marketer for your business:

1. What are their marketing strengths and weaknesses? Do their strengths align with your priorities?

2. Will they focus on earning your business an ROI (return on investment)? Request specific examples.

3. Do their past projects align with your vision for your business?

4. Could they develop a message that resonates with your audience and sounds like your brand? (You'll outline this in **Phase Three: Build, Step 4: Craft Your Brand Identity.**)

5. How do they stay up on emerging marketing trends?

Use this space to document additional questions that come to mind:

....

....

....

....

....

....

....

....

....

....

....

MENTOR

Myth: Successful people don't need a mentor. Reality: A mentor shines light on your path to success. You don't have to figure out business ownership alone. Be coachable enough to believe in the power of learning from others' wins and hardships.

Whereas your business coach helps develop the growth of your business, a good mentor will help refine you as a human being. Finding a mentor is a process you don't want to rush. It takes time, forethought, trust, and commitment from both parties to develop a mutually rewarding mentor-mentee relationship. Some mentors volunteer their time and others prefer to be paid.

Give ample airtime to events where leaders gather. It's hard to find a worthwhile mentor without intentionally immersing yourself into community affairs. Think of it like a soirée with an ever-growing social network. The people who can develop and sharpen you likely value and show up for community involvement because a good mentor knows how to build and sustain relationships.

This is how I found Doris. The first time we crossed paths, she sat across the table as my appointed SCORE counselor. What a Godsend! SCORE is a large network of seasoned business owners who offer free counseling, and I took advantage of it during my start-up phase.After that, it's no surprise I bumped into Doris any place where community leaders gathered. With almost celebrity status, the whole town adored her, and she was unbelievably well-connected. Asking new connections, "Do you know Doris?" became a rhetorical question. Plus, Doris was head over heels for supporting woman-owned businesses (YASS!!), and that alone was enough to earn my respect.

As time passed, we connected often at group events and during 1:1 lunch and coffee dates. Eventually, I asked her to be my mentor, and her response surprised me. Now I know it's because she took my question very seriously. She paused and stared back into my eyes long enough for me to feel sure I was getting rejected, and she said, "I'll only be your mentor if you promise to give your business five years." That seemed like a fair trade, and still today, I hear from Doris weekly. Our conversations involve business topics occasionally, but more often, Doris pours into my personal life, leading me in topics of friendship, motherhood, and marriage. There is no amount of money I could pay for the value I receive from this relationship.

As you evaluate connections you already know, or as you consider the type of person you'd like to develop a mentor-mentee relationship with, keep the following characteristics in mind:

- They possess high moral and ethical standards.

- They follow through by doing what they say they will do.

- They take action.

- They understand how to develop relationships and are generally liked among peers.

- They're well-rounded and good decision makers.

- They are emotionally intelligent.

- They're good listeners.

- They aren't afraid to provide critical feedback. Remember, the unwise only look for praise while the wise look for constructive criticism from people they trust and respect.

- They're giving of their time in an intentional way. You don't want a people pleaser who promises the world but can't follow through.

- They believe in your business idea and you as a person.

- They have found success in a way that you'd like to someday. Their success doesn't have to be in your exact field, though that's tremendously helpful, too.

Use wisely the time you invest into finding a mentor. Start with organizations whose members are several steps ahead of you. Recall **from Phase Two: Research, Step 2: Find Your Flock**, your community of peers should be "within reach," but your mentor should be seasoned enough to know the backroads, shining light on stumbling blocks they know about from a depth of experience.

Once you have an idea of who you'd like to ask to be your mentor, converse with the person to see if it's a good mutual fit. More than likely, the person will be honored to mentor you; however, set up a formal conversation to discuss expectations out of respect for the time and effort you'll receive.

Brainstorm who in your life could be a good fit as a mentor:

....

....

Don't know anyone who could mentor you? Many people choose a well-known thought leader as a mentor. Instead of meeting with the thought leader in person, they intentionally consume their content from afar and study their success path. Organic conversations with a mentor can be invaluable, but if that's not an option, studying someone with the qualities and career path you'd like can still have advantages. Don't forget to look up their "before it worked" phase of business for a realistic idea of how they developed over time. Often, we only see people in the spotlight *after* they've persevered through difficulties.

HUMAN RESOURCES CONSULTANT

More than likely, a human resources consultant is an advisor you'll add to your team in the future rather than now. Even small businesses with employees typically can't justify a full-time human resources manager. Abiding by laws governing employment is crucial for the viability of every small business. Thankfully, an HR consultant can lend insight on a contracted basis until your business grows enough to sustain a human resources manager on staff.

Human resources issues include everything from managing benefits to hiring and firing, and workplace disputes. Seek guidance from a human resources consultant on your advisor team who stays up on laws in your state.

Ask your network for recommendations or research human resources consultants who might be a good fit for your support team. Narrow your list to three options and contact each for an interview:

Name/Interview Date

....

....

....

Questions to consider as you research the right human resources consultant for your business:

1. Does the HR consultant specialize in the services your business needs, like writing an employee handbook, advising on the hiring and firing process, setting up and handling a 401K program, and recruiting?

2. How does the HR consultant stay up to date on laws, continuing education, and industry trends?

3. How does payment work? Retainer? Packages? Hourly rate?

Use this space to document additional questions that come to mind:

....

....

....

....

....

OTHER SUPPORT TEAM MEMBERS

What other roles deserve a seat at your advisor table? Get as creative as your business's personality. Perhaps it's the role of cheerleader, rest mandator, or accountability partner. We've just discussed the typical roles business owners need as they build their dream, but your business comes with unique needs as you carve out its place in the world.

🔧 **TAKE ACTION! Make connections. Set up interviews. Send those emails. It's time to officially create your team of support for your new business!**

Not every advisory member listed above will make your 'A-Team' right now. Some may never make your team. You're the architect in defining what roles your business needs and who is best fit to fill them.

The caliber of people you choose to surround yourself with will have a tremendous impact on the slope of your learning curve. Entrepreneurs are often also natural born leaders. However, coachability is imperative, and someone who yields to the guidance of experts shows wisdom. You don't have time to make every mistake yourself.If you want to fulfill your dream more quickly, choose a team who will help you avoid stumbling blocks and notice opportunities.

STEP  2

FIND YOUR FINANCIAL FINESSE

Early on, my business wasn't growing as quickly as I wanted, and here's the reason: I hadn't nailed down the habit of investing time into income-producing activities. Why? I had no clue what income-producing activities were. Now I know they're activities that impact your bottom line. The direct result of an income-producing activity is making more money. Examples: networking, consult calls, upselling existing clients, and following up with potential leads.

I'm a figure-outter, so after a few months of 'meh' income, I pushed myself to create a solution. That solution was accountability. I began documenting each day's billable work in a spreadsheet. If my client book wasn't full, I made a rule for myself that I would attend four networking events per month until it filled up... and guess what! It worked. My client load filled, and I started surpassing monthly revenue goals.

Nothing about it was magic. Documenting my billable work into a spread-sheet helped me clearly see where I was in relation to my daily, monthly, and annual goals. If I wasn't meeting goals, there was no denying it. If I was meeting goals, we (my husband, our bulldog, and I) would celebrate. What was left to do besides invest time in activities I knew created the result I wanted?

The same goes for tracking your financials. There are four main accounting state-ments that reflect a business's health: a budget, profit and loss statement, balance sheet, and cash flow statement. Just like my accountability spreadsheet, these statements paint a clear picture of what's going right and what isn't.

Even if you choose to work with an accountant or bookkeeper, you'll need to keep the financial side of your business dealings orderly. Ultimately, you're responsible.

Tracking your expenses, invoicing properly and on time, and withholding the appropriate amount of taxes and retirement savings are all tasks you're responsible for in your business. Whether you opt for a simple accounting software (see our recommendations at www.HerBusinessGuide.com) or keep track of your finances in a spreadsheet, it's important to be deliberate and consistent in managing the financial side of your business.

Most importantly, maintain strict separation between your business finances and your personal finances! Have separate business bank accounts for business and for personal, and do not commingle funds. Mixing your personal and business assets is one of the only ways to ruin your LLC protection and to make yourself vulnerable in the event of a business lawsuit. Resist the temptation to use a business credit card for personal items or vice versa, or to use a common account, such as PayPal, for mixed personal and business spending.

Knowing where to start with finances can feel like a tall feat because it's not exactly like distributing your childhood allowance into neat little envelopes. If embracing the responsibility of finances makes you want to throw in the towel, forget the world, or book a flight to Tahiti, I've got you! Remember to manage your mind to empower yourself. Money is still a taboo topic so unfortunately most people don't grow up talking about it, especially women. Don't let that stop you.

Many of us were raised to believe women are incapable of understanding finance concepts. One day we'll look at this like the absurdity it is, but for now it's many people's reality. We have been fed covert messages conveying investing and general money matters are a man's responsibility. Until recently, it was common for people to believe learning about money was unnecessary for a woman since her husband would manage it for her. The tales of "Prince Charming" and the "knight in shining armor" assume a man will swoop in, manage the household's money, and leave the woman not to worry about a darn little thing.

Since personal finance is rarely taught in the public setting, many women feel confused and intimidated during money discussions. Even though women are taking more responsibility for household finances, including investing (holla!!), many women feel like the topic is a foreign language. If the financial aspect of running a business feels scary to you, lean in and empower yourself by embracing the challenge. You've absolutely got this! We'll get through it together.

Running out of cash is one of the main reasons businesses fail, so it's important to develop an informed projection about what revenue and expenses will look like in your business. Doing this will afford you a better chance of acquiring enough financing, the opportunity to hire appropriately, and generally set you up well to plan how your business will use cash strategically. A deficit of cash is a recipe for disaster. It can force an otherwise strong business into bankruptcy or foreclosure.

Hope is not a strategy. Become financially literate so you can make the decisions that accompany difficult challenges in your business that would otherwise flatten it like a wrecking ball. For instance, once in our mastermind, I encouraged members to begin thinking *now* about how to build cash reserves if an economic downswing were to come in the next 12-18 months.

When it comes to sharp turns, businesses are cruise ships, not speed boats. Challenging circumstances require forethought."Putting out fires" rarely leads to an ideal outcome. On the flip side, there aren't many problems that cash on hand can't solve. In this section, we'll cover financial documents that will help you read the financial health of your business, manage its cash, plan for the future, and become a good decision-maker in running your business.

In addition to the budget we laid out in **Phase Two: Research, Step 4: Finance Your Future**, three additional financial documents will equip you with a sound strategy moving forward: 1) Profit and Loss Statement (sometimes called an "Income Statement"), 2) Balance Sheet, and 3) Cash Flow Statement.

Downloadable templates have been provided in the Founding Females™ Resource Suite at www.HerBusinessGuide.com. Let's talk through the purpose of each now.

PROFIT AND LOSS STATEMENT

A Profit and Loss Statement (sometimes called an Income Statement) outlines projected profit or loss after revenues, costs, and expenses over a period of time. This document is especially important if you plan to acquire financing from a lender. They'll want your detailed plan for becoming profitable to determine if you're a safe bet.

If you'd rather print it out, download the Founding Females™ Balance Sheet provided in the resources suite at www.HerBusinessGuide.com. Then plug your information in to see your projected profit or loss over three years and include a copy in the financial projects section of your business plan when you create it in **Phase Three: Build, Step 8: Breathe Life Into Your Business Plan.**

The Profit and Loss Statement looks like the financial document below.

BALANCE SHEET

A balance sheet compares assets (what you have), liabilities (what you owe) and shareholder's equity (what investors own). Together the three views show a business's net worth in a single snapshot rather than over a period of time.

If you'd rather print it out, download the Founding Females™ Balance Sheet provided in the resources suite at www.HerBusinessGuide.com. Then plug the information into the fillable Founding Females™ Balance Sheet and be sure to include a copy in the financial projections section of your business plan when you create it in **Phase Three: Build, Step 8: Breathe Life Into Your Business Plan.**

The Balance Sheet looks like the financial document below.

BALANCE SHEET

TIME PERIOD

ASSETS
CURRENT ASSETS
    CASH $
    INVENTORY $
    OTHER ASSETS $

    TOTAL CURRENT ASSETS $

LONG-TERM ASSETS
    PROPERTY $
    FURNITURE AND FIXTURES $
    GENERAL EQUIPMENT $
    TOTAL FIXED ASSETS $
    ACCUMULATED DEPRECIATION ($)

  TOTAL ASSETS $

LIABILITIES
CURRENT LIABILITIES
    LOAN PAYABLE IN 12 MONTHS OR LESS $
    CREDIT CARDS PAYABLE $
    TOTAL CURRENT LIABILITIES $

LONG-TERM LIABILITIES
    LOAN PAYABLE IN 12 MONTHS OR MORE $
    TOTAL LONG-TERM LIABILITIES $

OWNER'S EQUITY
    NET INCOME $
    PAID IN CAPITAL $
    RETAINED EARNINGS $
    DISTRIBUTIONS / DRAWS ($)
    TOTAL OWNER'S EQUITY $

TOTAL LIABILITIES AND OWNER'S EQUITY $

CASH FLOW STATEMENT

Think of the Cash Flow Statement similar to a bank statement. It projects the cash coming into and going out of your business. Adequate cash to cover expenses to stay in operation is critical to the success of your business. Just like paying rent on an apartment, it's hard to pay your landlord (cash going out) if your employer is late paying you (cash coming in). If your employer is late paying you, it's still your responsibility to pay your landlord. Having enough cash built up to cover costs if something doesn't go as planned lessens your risk. A general rule of thumb is to have enough cash on hand to pay your expenses for three to six months if something out of your control happens.

The Cash Flow Statement identifies expected cash in and cash out. If you'd rather print it out, download the Founding Females™ Balance Sheet provided in the resources suite at www.HerBusinessGuide.com. Then plug the information into and include a copy in the financial projections section of your business plan when you create it in **Phase Three: Build, Step 8: Breathe Life Into Your Business Plan.**

Some of the hardest tasks in your business will be the ones most integral to its success. If it were easy, everyone would do it. Girl, if you feel in the dark, let nothing stopping you from building the financial literacy to totally crush the management of your business's financial health. Getting friendly with your financial documents will empower you as the decision-maker of your business. With confidence in your decision-making, you'll find it much simpler to control the operations of the business and guide it in a direction well-aligned with your vision so you can leverage it to lead a life you love and create a profound impact in the world.

The Cash Flow Statement looks like the image below.

CASH FLOW STATEMENT

FINANCIAL YEAR END:

CASH FLOW FROM OPERATING ACTIVITIES

NET EARNINGS	$
DEPRECIATION	$
INCREASE IN INVENTORY	($ _____)
NET CASH FROM OPERATIONS	$

CASH FLOW FROM INVESTING

EQUIPMENT	$
NET CASH FROM INVESTING	$

CASH FLOW FROM FINANCING

NOTES PAYABLE	$
PERSONAL DRAW ASIDE FROM SALARY	($ _____)
NET CASH FROM INVESTING	$
CASH FLOW FOR FINANCIAL YEAR _____	$

STEP

DEVELOP YOUR OWN 'DOLLY'

Forget about *your* caffeine addiction. What kind of coffee does your customer drink?

Forget about where *you* like to shop. (It's Target, isn't it?) Where does your customer spend her money?

Forget about what life pains hassle *you*. What challenges keep your client awake at night?

Knowing your customer's lifestyle, behavior, thought patterns, preferences, and tendencies will solve many of your business challenges because the question always comes back to, "How does my customer see the world?". An ideal client persona is a prototype of the characteristics you believe your customers to have. It's a detailed description of who they are as a person, what matters to them, and what it's like to live their life. The persona outlines their unique life situation, including spending habits and factors influencing their spending decisions.

Having an intimate understanding of who buys your offering helps you develop a message that "speaks their language." Your word choice, tone, and even punctuation will be affected when you nail down your ideal client. The more targeted you can craft a message to the type of audience who needs your offering most, the more you can position yourself as the exact solution the customer can trust.

People buy from a place of emotion, rarely from a place of logic. When people feel understood, their emotions take hold. They're most likely to buy from companies whose brand honors their unique life circumstances. The level of clarity provided by ideal client personas allows you to see through the customer's lens of the world and craft tiny details that affect how a person feels about your brand and company.

The important details that comprise your business's ideal client personas help you craft a message that resonates intentionally and leads *potential* customers to become *paying* customers. It's vital you narrow down who your marketing message is intended for, and you do that with an ideal client persona. Why? Because marketing to *everyone* makes the product feel valuable to no one. An ideal client persona provides direction for marketing an offering that could technically be well-suited for a variety of customer types. However, the insight a well-curated ideal client persona lends helps you craft a message that speaks to a specific person, making the offering feel like it was created when their unique needs in mind.

Let's tease out the benefits of developing an ideal client persona. Lots of different people drink coffee, but if you try to market to *everyone,* you'll dilute your message and marketing resources ($$). Instead, you might choose to focus your marketing message toward busy mamas who need a special blend of awesome sauce to handle tiny tantrums and Talkative Tammy in the carpool line.

Of course, your coffee isn't made only for busy moms—Average Joe could enjoy it just as well—but the vision you create with your marketing message helps busy mamas feel notable moments of hallelujah, like the coffee was specially blended precisely as fuel to get through their toddler's feisty meltdowns. See? The message conveys how the product meets her exact needs and is therefore more likely to resonate and lead to a sale.

Do you have to choose only one ideal client persona? It's possible and likely you'll have more than one ideal client persona. For example, Founding Females™ serves three types of female business owners: DIY Dolly, Passionate Pearl, and Full-Scale Fiona. Let's meet these fabulous females!

'DIY Dolly' dreams of owning her own business. She's a woman living in a digital world. At this point, she's collecting information about how to start her business, and perhaps she's taken a few steps to get started. She's eager to learn about running a business and knows she can make her vision success-ful with the right guidance. Do you recognize DIY Dolly? I've got your back, babe!

'DIY Dolly' becomes 'Passionate Pearl' once her business generates consis-tent revenue. 'Passionate Pearl' is the second ideal client persona our company cares for. She has proof of concept in her offering and her brain has become wired to look for ways to improve her business. Her workload is a mix of some revenue generating tasks and some business management tasks. She'll outsource or hire when she can afford it. She continues working hard to develop her understanding of business and she's an initiative taker.

'Passionate Pearl' becomes 'Full-Scale Fiona'—our third ideal client persona—when she's ready to scale or expand her business. She runs her business full-time and focuses on its growth by spending more time working "on" her business with tasks that help it grow and scale rather than "in" her business with tasks that produce the revenue directly. She's ready to take her business from operational to lucrative. Fiona is a total boss. She's capable of large-scale success and leading a team to get there.

The difference between DIY Dolly, Passionate Pearl, and Full-Scale Fiona is where they are in business. As such, each ideal client persona faces different challenges. The world each persona lives in looks and feels differently. It's no wonder the message must be crafted differently for each woman.

As you can imagine, it's imperative our business recognizes how to serve our three types of customers differently based on their unique challenges. If we simply sent marketing messages saying we help women entrepreneurs, that wouldn't be nearly as impactful as a message telling *how* we help solve a problem she previously thought only she could articulate. Crafting a message that speaks directly to your persona's deeply rooted, agonizing pain is how you can cut through a space rampant with marketing messages. How could you understand what it's like to deal with that pain unless you develop an idea of the person who grapples with it in real life?

As business owners, we must insert ourselves into the client's world. We work hard to craft messages according to the unique challenges each faces so we can convey value in the form of guidance and help them understand how our offerings meet those unique challenges in words that sound like their own thoughts.

This topic can become pretty detailed. Use this section to guide your thoughts and research about your ideal client persona, but don't feel pressured to answer every question.

LIFESTYLE

What 3-4 words/phrases describe your ideal client's life? Ambitious? Laid back? Well-regarded in the community?

....

....

....

....

What is your ideal client's family life like? Young kids, older kids, or no kids? Is she the cook, Uber driver, cleaning lady, and sports cheerleader?

....

....

....

....

What is your ideal client's age range? From this, what can you infer about his/her "season of life"?

....

....

....

....

Does your ideal client have a career? If so, what is it like? If not, how does she spend her time?

....

....

....

....

What are your ideal client's life responsibilities? Is she a mom? A wife? A caretaker for her parents? A community volunteer? An elected official in the community?

....

....

....

....

PROBLEM

Grocery delivery meets the pain busy families feel when they don't have time to grocery shop. A brand designer's business naming service helps new business owners with the agonizing struggle of finding a name they feel confident in. An appliance repair technician helps families save time by getting their broken dish washer up and running again.

What pain is your ideal client experiencing that will be met by your offer?

....

....

....

How does your ideal client describe their problem? What feelings and emotions do they experience as a result of the problem? Identifying the attached emotion/feeling will be integral in crafting your marketing message later. Is it frustration? Fear? Confusion? Shame? Stress? Dissatisfaction? Anxiety?

....

....

....

How is your ideal client currently meeting their problem? For example, is it via a competitor's product? An alternative method? Perhaps they're not meeting it at all.

....

....

....

HANGOUTS

Does geographic location of your ideal client matter? If so, where does your ideal client live?

....

....

What does your ideal client's daily routine look like? Early bird or night owl? Daily meditation? Commuting to work? Caring for kids? Cooking meals and grocery shopping?

....

....

Where does your ideal client spend time online? You'll want to know this when you create your online presence. Social media sites? Pinterest? YouTube? Reddit? Online newspapers? The local university earning a degree?

ASK YOURSELF, "*Who* IS BUYING MY OFFERING"? YOUR ANSWER MAY BE DIFFERENT FROM THE PERSON USING YOUR OFFERING.

Where does your ideal client spend time in person? Kids' ball games? The gym? Target or Walmart? The local coffee shop?

....

....

What hobbies and leisure activities does your ideal client enjoy? Dirt biking? Kayaking? Garage sale-ing? Yoga? Reading?

....

....

....

....

....

....

What does your ideal client's social life look like? Tot Time at the local library? Happy hour after work? Knitting club? Golf league?

....

....

....

....

....

BRAND AFFINITIES

Where does your ideal client like to shop? Saks or Goodwill? Cute local boutiques or Lululemon? TJ Maxx or Amazon?

Describe your ideal client's style. Edgy or classic? Preppy or casual?

What brand(s) does your ideal client typically buy? Apple or Samsung? Beats or Bose? Nike or Under Armor? Coach or Louis?

What might this insight convey about the experience your ideal client will expect in doing business with you?

....
....
....
....
....
....

BUYING POWER

What are your ideal client's spending habits? Spendy? Frugal? Somewhere in between?

....
....
....
....

What is your ideal client's household income range?

....
....

Who in your ideal client's family makes most of the spending decisions? Research says the majority of women make the spending decisions for their households. Is that true in your case?

....
....

MOTIVATIONS

What are the core values your ideal client lives and dies by? Their faith? A "we rise together" attitude? Their own individuality? Equality? Supporting small businesses?

....

....

....

What are your ideal client's political views? What might this tell you about how they see the world?

....

....

....

....

What does your ideal client find rewarding in life? Hobbies? Art? Hard work? Being a mentor? Volunteering at church?

....

....

....

....

What are your ideal client's life goals? Have a family? Travel? Create a non-profit?

....

....

....

....

What does your ideal client see when they picture their ideal self?

....

....

....

IDEAL CLIENT PERSONA, MADLIB-STYLE

Now gather what you know about your ideal client to create a description using the provided mad lib-style outline. Then memorize it. Be able to pick your ideal client out in public. If you have more than one ideal client persona, head to www.HerBusinessGuide.com to download additional templates.

.... (ideal client persona's name) is .... (descriptive characteristics to illustrate him/her generally like age, gender, profession). He/She dreams of .... and feels .... (emotion) about .... (his/her pain, want, need, or challenge)..'s (name) life is characterized by .... (important information like time allocation, family life, career, etc.). His/Her responsibilities include ...., ..., and .... In his/her free time, he/she likes to .... and ....'s (Name) favorite places to shop are ...., ..., and ....

Factors shaping how he/she views the world are ...., ..., and .... (values). .... (Name) cares deeply about .... (life goals) and is continually trying to become .... (ideal self /

self-improvement). When .... (Name) has an extra $50 at the end of the month, it's spent on .... (what he/she spends discretionary income on). When he/she has an extra hour in the day, it's spent thinking about .... (passion). A typical weekend for .... (Name) would look like .... (how he/she spends leisure time).

.... (Name) regularly spends time .... (online hangouts) and .... (in person hangouts). When .... (Name) consumes information, it's usually via .... (preferred information outlets).

.... (Name) deals with .... (problem your offering solves). It affects his/her day in the following ways: .... When he/she is with friends, the conversation sounds like ....

....

Solving a real problem is everything in entrepreneurship. Become well-versed on the problem you're solving with your offering and how the person who buys your offering experiences the problem. Then, you can articulate the problem and the corresponding solution in a "language" your ideal client speaks. You'll earn trust when you convey understanding and compassion. A carefully crafted message is your bestie for cutting through the noisy ecosystem your customer navigates daily.

STEP

CRAFT YOUR BRAND IDENTITY

One of my favorite pastimes is browsing pop-up boutiques in my hometown in Central Illinois, supporting fellow female small business owners. I load up the stroller, strap my daughter in, and together, we twist and curve around the pop-up tents, finding treasures along the way. I've noticed that trends come and go. Often, several booths will sell items that look and feel similar in nature with little or no differentiation—bows, cups with vinyl designs, and boutique clothing, for instance.

The booths that stand out the most—the ones I gravitate to and the ones I remember after the event—are the ones with a carefully crafted and visible brand. Why? Because brands help our brains create associations and meaning. They set the tone for the quality and consistency customers can expect.

Creating a memorable brand for your business is a non-negotiable. More than anything, a brand legitimizes your business as viable and trustworthy. In this section of *Dream, Build, Grow: A Female's Step-by-Step Guide for How to Start a Business*, we'll discuss exactly what elements go into creating a recognizable brand you can feel proud of. What you create in this section will be included in a marketing document called your Brand Standards, which defines and details the nuanced look, feel, and message of your brand.

What is a brand? It's a representation of a company's identity and extends beyond a logo and color scheme. A brand becomes an all-encompassing personality of a company and a critical means of differentiating one company from another to build familiarity and trust. A carefully designed brand can incite a mood, feeling, and psychological connection. Even the small, subtle details like a color shade (Tiffany blue), word choice ("My pleasure" at Chick-fil-a), or distinct font ('The New York Times' English Towne font style) set the tone for customer expectations from engaging with a company at any point along the buyer's journey (We'll talk through what different stages of the buyer's journey look like in the next section, Step 5).

Many small businesses only go so far as to assemble a logo and color scheme, but as we will see, a brand encompasses much more than visual elements. Tiny details, like where a product is placed inside a store and ideals a business's brand associates with, like unprecedented customer service at Zappos, set a perception for what kind of experience customers can expect with each interaction. Left undetermined, a company leaves the definition of its brand open to interpretation.

Does a small business – a solopreneur, even – need a brand? Yes. Brands = quality. Brands which are inconsistent or the absence of a brand incite confusion and mistrust in customers. A brand defines what the company is, what it is not, and helps a company aim for its target. Small, subtle details are how brands sew themselves into customers' hearts. They reach beyond the obvious details of their brand and define the almost unconscious elements which form a customer's perception - the smell of the shop, the margin around the logo, the always-fresh flowers in the window, or the signature manner in which employees greet customers.

The elements below outline the look, feel, and messaging your brand should convey and are components of your Brand Standards document:

▶ Color scheme

▶ Logo & Logo specifications

▶ Font

▶ Attributes

▶ Visual elements

▶ Word choice and communication tone

▶ Description of your company history

▶ Statement of purpose

▶ Mission

▶ Core Values

▶ Big vision goals

▶ Ideal experience

- ▸ Target audience
- ▸ Elevator speech
- ▸ Positioning

- ▸ Feelings and emotions
- ▸ Social media guide + policy
- ▸ Web guidelines

A well-defined brand is critical for creating a positive perception in the minds of your customers. Authenticity is vital. Sis, your audience wants *your* business. They don't want an imposter of someone else's business. Build the brand your audience craves. While it's important your brand looks and feels authentic to you, it's ultimately your audience who your brand should resonate with most.

Before you solidify your brand in the coming pages, revisit the last section: **Phase Three: Build, Step 3: Develop Your Own 'Dolly'** as a refresher of who your ideal client is and what matters most in her world. Then, use the following space to develop your brand.

Let's first dive into big picture elements of your business's identity before narrowing in on the details.

Sometimes it's easier to begin by identifying what your brand is not. Take a moment to describe elements (colors, words, fonts, shapes, graphic types, tone) that are not a good fit for your brand:

....

....

....

....

Are there any non-negotiable elements you feel must be included in your brand? For example, a word, color scheme, or value?

....

....

....

....

Close your eyes and imagine customers interacting with your brand—first on your website, then feeling happy using your offering, then telling their friends about your business. Use this space to identify any details that come to mind.

Who should your brand appeal to? Kids? Young adults? Men or women? An older generation?

Consider the almost intangible feeling your business embodies and think intentionally about the tiny details which bring the feeling to life in a repeatable way. Detail your thoughts below.

REFLECT ON ELEMENTS OF
YOUR BRAND STANDARDS

Color Scheme

From a psychological perspective, think about what feelings colors naturally evoke and whether you want to align your brand with any of those often preconceived assumptions. (For instance, the color green is often used with Earth-friendly products, food, and freshness. The color red is known to invoke strong emotions.)

What colors represent your brand?

....

....

Note: you'll want to narrow your choices down to the exact color code to create consistency across all platforms.

Logo & Logo Specifications

What does your primary logo look like and what variations are acceptable? For instance, some people have their business's name written in a logo but also use a smaller, more condensed logo with just the acronym. Other logo specification questions include: How much of a border should be left on all sides? What backgrounds are acceptable to place the logo over? If your logo is yellow, perhaps one of your logo specifications is for the logo to never be placed over a red background. If you're DIY'ing your logo, be sure you create one that looks clear on all marketing material, including digitally and on print. Having access to a logo file with a transparent background is important for professionalism and versatility!

Record your ideas below.

....

....

....

....

....

Fonts

Typically, companies select two to three fonts to represent their brand. These fonts are used on ad copy, on the website, business cards, and any other marketing material where copy is included.

Which fonts are best for your brand?

....

....

....

....

....

Attributes

Attributes are descriptive adjectives that help shape a well-rounded picture of what your company is and what it is not. Is your business silly or serious? Trendy or timeless? Innovative or traditional? It's wise not to try to be all things to all people. Pinpoint attributes to define the true personality of your business.

Record your ideas below.

....

....

....

....

....

Visual elements

What kind of photos or illustrations are appropriate to associate with your company? For instance, are stock photos acceptable or should all photos include actual employees of your business? Are bright, minimalist photos appropriate or does your brand align more closely with a dark and moody photo editing style?

Record your ideas below.

....

....

....

....

....

Word Choice and Communication Tone

Communication style, including word choice, is the personality of the company in written form. It defines in writing how prim and proper or how casual a company is. Tone can break down relational barriers as your ideal client reads your copy and formulates what the conversation might sound like between themselves and you. For instance, do you call your audience "girl," "friend," or some other word choice to convey closeness, or do you maintain a more formal tone such as "Dear Valued Customer..."?

Record your ideas below.

....

....

....

....

....

Description of Your Company History

The best brands tell stories. What stories tell how your brand came into existence and how it has benefitted customers? What feelings can you convey through words to give your business meaning?

....

....

....

....

....

Statement of Purpose

What's your business's reason for existing? This will be come your official statement of purpose. Fill in the blanks: "We exist to .... so they can ...."

....

....

....

....

....

Mission

What difference will your business make in the world?

....

....

....

....

Core Values

What ideals are important to you? Now, more than ever, customers vote with their dollars. They consciously decide to spend money with companies whose values align with their own.

How do you intertwine your moral compass and ethics into your business practices?

....

....

....

....

....

....

Target Audience

As we've discussed in **Phase Two: Clarify** and previously in **Phase Three: Build**, narrowing your target audience allows you to present a concentrated message where your audience already spends time. Craft your message according to the unique language your audience speaks. You already defined your ideal client in detail in **Phase Three: Build, Step 3: Develop Your Own 'Dolly.'** Plan to use a copy of your ideal client persona in your Brand Standards. For this section, provide a brief description of your ideal client persona.

Describe your target audience below.

....

....

....

....

Elevator Speech / Company Synopsis

It sounds silly, but many people struggle to define what their business does and who they do it for. "Elevator speech" is one of the most worn-out phrases in business, but the purpose behind the concise description is powerful. It forces you to convey only the most important components of your business in a short, concise way.

New introductions provide little time to share what you do and who you do it for. Craft a short paragraph sharing about your business in all its glory clearly in the least amount of time. Include who you help, how you help them, benefits they can expect, and how to purchase your offering in 30 seconds or less, i.e. the amount of time you would have to tell someone about your business during a ride on the elevator.

Example: "Have you ever struggled to meal plan for the week? Isn't it a pain? At Mealtime Happy, we help busy moms create meal plans their families love with a personalized meal plan subscription starting at just $9.99/month on our smartphone app."

Jot down your elevator speech.

Positioning

Positioning sets the tone for the perception you'd like your customers to have when they think of your business. For instance, Canada Goose® is a high-end luxury cold weather wear company whose coat product offerings start at around $500. At the time of this publication, the company's marketing strategy is simple. Canada Goose® situates its products where their target audience spends time—film festivals. It positions its products alongside brands and pastimes targeting the social elite. You won't find their products inside of department stores like Target or Walmart because those stores don't align well with their high-end positioning.

Reflect on the positioning of your own offering:

....

....

....

....

....

Feelings and Emotions

Feelings and emotions are primary motivators for buying. That's why crafting a brand to evoke feelings and emotions you intend customers to experience is integral for setting the stage. When customers feel something, they can come to know, like, and trust your brand.

What feelings and emotions would you like customers to experience?

....

....

....

....

....

Social Media Guide and Policy

Limitless opportunity exists for one-on-one contact with customers through social media platforms. This also allows ample opportunity for a brand image to become skewed through direct messages, commenting, and posting. Every company using social media for promotion should outline what is and isn't permissible in a social media guide and policy. Determining the tone and vibe of the overall message creates consistency.

What's your goal for social media activities? Informative? Entertaining? Personable? You'll train your audience on what to expect starting with the first post, so determine your strategy in advance.

Web Guidelines

Crafting your web presence according to your style is just as important as welcoming someone into your home. Avoid trying to be all things to all people by determining in advance goals for your web presence. Specifically, determine:

1. how to lead your audience into a presence you have control over from different marketing channels

2. standards for consistency

3. a system for ensuring your web presence remains up to date to create a positive impression for anyone who enters into your online "ecosystem."

What web guidelines should your company abide by?

Who will need a copy of your Brand Standards to ensure all parties crafting your business's foundation follow precise guidelines? Circle the following that apply to your business:

Graphic Designer

Web Developer

Social Media Manager

Virtual Assistant

Employees

Collaborative Organizations

Ad Managers

Other: ....

Other: ....

Other: ....

🔧 **TAKE ACTION! Now you've created notes for what your brand will look, feel, and function like. Solidify your brand by downloading the Founding Females™ Brand Standards template in the Founding Females™ Resource Suite at www.HerBusinessGuide.com.**

STEP 5

DRAW UP YOUR MARKETING PLAN

In my experience consulting with start-ups, a common theme reverberates through new entrepreneurs' thinking: "If you build it, they will come." Let's address this misconception head on. Even the best businesses go under if nobody knows about them. How do we avoid that? By crafting intentional messages to an audience primed to buy through carefully selected marketing channels. Don't worry. You'll be a pro at this by the end of Step 5!

Marketing is one of the most necessary parts of running a business because it helps create the flow of turning new customers into repeat customers, yet it's a responsibility many business owners neglect. Some of thetop reasons business owners avoid marketing include:

- ▸ They assume simply *having* a business means people know about the business.

- ▸ They assume they have to be pushy to make sales.

- ▸ They don't have clearly defined goals or processes to follow. Since they don't have repeatable processes, they can never refine what works and what doesn't.

- ▸ The marketing responsibility feels obscure, messy, and uncertain, so they avoid it all together.

You can build the greatest offering with the greatest mission, but if you fail to market your business, all its glory will be kept in the dark. Girl, it's not magic! Successful businesses get that way when they meet a need people are willing to pay for and are marketed well to an audience who's a good fit to buy. Let's look at some examples of strong marketing.

Airbnb: Airbnb is in the business of connecting property owners with renters. It's is a fine example of marketing because it leverages storytelling in a way people understand to capture hearts and encourage customers to invest time and money into experiences.

Amazon: Amazon redefined how people shop. In their online marketplace, they leverage social proof with reviews which allows customers to have a say in voting for products and influencing others to buy them.

Disney: Disney is a mass media and entertainment company whose mission is to entertain and inspire the world. Their marketing deserves a "dang girl!" because they know their product is aimed at kids, so their target audience is adults with spending power. They convey through stories exactly how the whole family can enjoy time together.

Airbnb, Amazon, and Disney provide well-known and widely-consumed examples of strong marketing. In fact, when was the last time you used one of these businesses? It very well could have been today. Raise your hand if you'd like Airbnb, Disney, or Amazon on your team!

You might be thinking, "Girl, I'm no Airbnb, Amazon, or Disney...I'm just a small business in my tiny corner of the world doin' my thing." I love you for saying that, but remember every business once had a small beginning and even if you don't plan to grow big, a strong foundation helps you grow strong. Strong marketing is what propels a clear understanding for leads to become first-time customers and first-time customers to become loyal, repeat customers.

Let's start with the basics and define what marketing is.Think of marketing as helping qualified leads become aware of and interested in your offering's promise. Good marketing has:

- ▶ **Clarity** – Simple and concise explanations.

- ▶ **Calls to Action** - Instructions for where to go or what to do next.

- **Repeat touch points** – People are more likely to buy with familiarity.

- **Social Proof** – Peer experience helps us understand the risk and reward involved.

- **Stories -** The human brain is wired for stories.

Good marketing means making offers to help. You can do this if you commit to being in places where your audience is already spending time. Speak a message that already matters to your unique target audience. Engage with them. Tweak your strategy over time.

The objective of **Phase Three: Build, Step 5: Draw Up Your Marketing Plan** is ultimately to walk you through crafting a simple marketing plan. Before we do that, let's cover some basic concepts that are important to understand before you fasten your marketing plan together.

THE BUYING CYCLE

The goal of marketing is to move your customers through the path to purchase, or the Buying Cycle. To provide customers with a well-designed experience as they journey from lead, to prospect, to paying customer, to repeat customer, you should tailor each message to a phase of the Buying Cycle:

Deliver well-curated messages to the customer depending on which phase they are at in the Buying Cycle. Each phase is marked by best practices for connecting with customers and intentional calls to action to move them to the next phase, which we'll talk about below. For example, strong calls to buy are typically effective in the third phase of the Buying Cycle *after* a customer has learned to trust your brand. Why? The awareness phase builds rapport, and the consideration phase educates on what it would be like to buy from you. Only when customers feel trust and clarity are they ready to buy.

Generally, a customer 1) realizes a need, 2) compares options, 3) makes a purchase, 4) repurchases if the experience was positive. The message you offer at each stage of the Buying Cycle should help the customer move to the next phase. How long a customer rests in each phase of the Buying Cycle depends on many things, like urgency of the need and the availability of the product.

Let's review important aspects of each phase of the Buying Cycle:

Awareness

In the awareness phase, a customer realizes a need (a dress for an upcoming girls' night out, a pain in her tooth, or a rumbling in her belly signaling hunger) and begins generally seeking out solutions to fit the need. Positioning yourself as an authority who informs on the topic and delivers value is a great way to establish yourself as a trusted source for customers to rely on.

Consideration

In the consideration phase, customers compare their available options. The conversation in their head sounds like a customer comparing two competitors' products or comparing a purchase to an alternative method of meeting the need (think, running on a treadmill or running outside). Here, highlighting a value proposition, like a social responsibility component or superior quality of your offering, helps companies stand out from the competition.

Note the customer may come in contact with your business several times after realizing a need and before moving to the purchase phase. In my work, I have heard authority figures estimate 7-21 touch points are necessary for a customer to feel ready to buy.

Purchase

Strong calls to action to buy tend to work well in the purchase phase because customers are equipped with the information they need to make a buying decision. Don't get in their way. Craft your product pages intentionally to deliver any information they might need to make a decision, such as product use videos, testimonials, and detailed information on how the offering works. Or, if you're selling on a consult call, ask the customer if they see any deterrents to purchasing so you can help them work through the issue.

After-Sale

An often-forgotten phase of the Buying Cycle is the after-sale phase. Customers who have already purchased from you are typically easiest and least expensive to sell to. What does this mean for you? Driving down marketing costs. Consider how you can customize automated components of repeated contact points. Give them a reason to come back by continuing to deliver value (not just selling). This is a great opportunity to develop a brand experience rather than a one-off buying opportunity.

Let's review an example of how a customer travels through the Buying Cycle.

Awareness: One night while scrolling her phone, Dottie stumbles upon a cute clothing boutique on Instagram. She clicks the link in bio and browses the website: first the 'home' page to feel out the brand's personality, then the 'about' page to learn more about who owns the company, and finally through a few collections in the online shop.

Consideration: Before exiting the site, she enters her email address into the pop-up tempting a 20% off coupon to use on her first purchase. Then she exits the site.

Purchase: Two weeks down the road, she receives a wedding invitation and decides she'll dig up the boutique's email containing the 20% off coupon and use it on a dazzling new dress.

After-sale: Dottie arrives home from work to find her package has been delivered. She opens it up, reads the 'thank you' card from the boutique's owner, and tries on the dress. Perfection! The look and feel of the dress were just what she was going for, and in fact, Dottie gets several compliments on the dress at the wedding. She vows that the boutique is her new go-to, so the next week when she receives an email asking her to provide a product review, of course she clicks the link and gives it 5- stars and a raving written explanation for why the boutique is the literal best.

AWARENESS

One night while scrolling her phone, Dottie stumbles upon a cute clothing boutique on Instagram.

She clicks the link in bio and browses the website: first the 'home' page to feel out the brand's personality, then the 'about' page to learn more about the company, and finally through a few collections in the online shop.

CONSIDERATION

Before exiting the site, she pops her email address into the pop-up tempting a 20% off her first purchase.

PURCHASE

Two weeks down the road, she receives a wedding invitation and decides she'll dig up the boutique's email with her 20% off coupon and use it on a dazzling new dress.

AFTER-SALE

Dottie arrives home from work to find her package has been delivered. She opens it up, reads the 'thank you' card from the boutique's owner, and tries on the dress. The look and feel of the dress were just what she was going for, and in fact, Dottie gets several compliments on the dress at the wedding.

She vows that the boutique is her new go-to, so the next week when she receives an email asking her to provide a product review, of course she clicks the link and gives it 5- stars and a raving review.

Reflect below on what the Buying Cycle might look in your business:

....

....

....

....

....

....

....

....

MARKETING MESSAGING

Let's tap into the hard work you invested in **Phase Three: Build, Step 3: Develop Your Own 'Dolly'** focused on developing your ideal client persona and **Phase Three Build, Step 4: Craft Your Brand Identity** focused on creating your business's identity. Knowing how your ideal client persona experiences life will guide you in crafting a crisp marketing message your potential buyer can't refuse.

The words you choose matter. We all have dreams and ambitions of living a better life, so offer a path to transformation. Talk about their perspective frequently until the dialogue comes naturally, as if you too experience their pain. (You probably do, if you came up with a solution for it!) Your audience wants to know how to make decisions in a way they can understand. Talk about moments of meaning. Carefully consider the feelings and promised experience your brand offers and nail down words that represent those feelings and promised experiences.

Apple takes the cake for clearly explaining its product to customers in language they can understand. In the notorious example, Steve Jobs debuted the iPod on stage in his signature black turtleneck on October 23, 2001. To the eager audience, he described the new technology as, "500 songs in your pocket." Simple, concise, I get it.

In your messaging, answer the questions your audience members are likely already asking themselves:

- ▸ Is it simple?

- ▸ Will it work for me?

- ▸ Can I do it?

- ▸ How will it benefit my life?

- ▸ Where do I buy it?

Reflect on what the messaging in your business sounds like and how it deeply resonates with your audience.

....

....

....

....

CALLS TO ACTION

A call to action is the part of a marketing message or advertisement telling the audience what to do next. Commit this to memory: If you don't tell the audience what to do next, they'll get distracted doing something else. The call to action should be clear and manageable, meaning they know what to do and how to do it, and they feel confident they can manage completing the action on their own.

Consider how you can remove the friction that might prevent the audience from completing your desired action.

For instance, in my marketing business, Simply Integrated, LLC, I find myself making one primary recommendation in ecommerce website audits for clients. Website audits are a service I offer where I review their website to analyze where they're leaving money on the table and deliver results in report style so they know what improvements to make on their website.

The recommendation I make most often is for clients to remove social media icons from conversion-oriented pages. For example, I tell them not to include their social media icon on a product page. Why? Because the intention is for website visitors to complete a transaction. The business's goal should be for visitors to move forward in the process of completing a transaction. Social media icons can distract visitors from completing a transaction and prevent the intended outcome. Yes, in any other circumstance where clinching a customer is not on the line, I'd love to gain a social media follower. But completing the transaction, and in turn, gaining their email address to deliver repeat touch points is a far bigger priority than gaining a follower on a platform I don't have full control over.

The same concept works for every marketing message you deliver. Think intentionally about what your intended result is with each message, no matter the marketing channel. Ask yourself what series of actions the customer needs to complete in order to achieve your main objective. Picture the customer moving through the Buying Cycle. With each phase, consider what the call to action will sound like. What will those calls to action feel like to the customer? What finite details must you cover to make the call to action obvious?

Calls to action within your marketing channels should drive traffic to a space you have control over—like your website or email list—where you have control to determine the tiny details to shape customers' perceptions.

If you don't tell customers what they should do next, you run a higher risk of losing the sale. How will you build your message in each of your selected marketing channels to lead customers through the buying process and into a sale?

What calls to action feel like a good fit for your brand, offering, and ideal customer persona? Check all that apply.

- ▸ Subscribe
- ▸ Order now
- ▸ Add to cart
- ▸ Book a consultation
- ▸ Donate
- ▸ Commit
- ▸ Adopt
- ▸ Give now
- ▸ Support

- ▸ Join us
- ▸ Sign up
- ▸ Refer
- ▸ Download
- ▸ Learn more
- ▸ Find out how to start
- ▸ Snag it before it's gone
- ▸ Click here
- ▸ Reserve your spot

COMPETITIVE ADVANTAGE AND VALUE PROPOSITION

Your business is the only one of its kind because it came from your heart. That means even if you're following a franchise or parent company's business model, only YOU can infuse your unique passion. Two important concepts explain how you'll compete in your industry and why customers will choose to buy from you over your competitors: competitive advantage and value proposition.

Both concepts describe your "secret sauce." Your competitive advantage and value proposition are often closely related, but not always. Whereas a competitive advantage is how you compete against other businesses (for instance, highly skilled labor, brand image recognition, and a unique product attribute), your value proposition is why your customers choose your value offered over the competitors' (for instance, the user interface experience, the brand's promise like Eco friendliness, and the handcrafted nature of high-end watches).

Your aim should be to develop your value proposition to the point where you become so known for delivering the qualities customers care about that it's embedded in the meaning of your brand. For example, Zappos is known for customer service. Walmart is known for low prices. Nordstrom is known for quality. Tesla is known for innovation.

What quality do you want your brand to become known for? Try to narrow your value proposition down to one to two words. More than one to two words and it becomes too complicated for customers to make the connection. Keep it simple.

Let's start by looking at competitive advantages. Remember, these are the strategies you use to complete against your competitors.

EXAMPLES OF COMPETITIVE ADVANTAGES

Economies of scale (price)	buying in bulk to create efficiencies and drive per-unit costs down
Variety	offering a wide selection of available options
Expertise	having the best knowledge or experience
Processes	focusing on efficiencies to drive down costs
Culture	how things get done internally
Access to capital	investing opportunities that come with having more money to leverage
Reputation	clout from earning a good name, character, or status
Intellectual property	delivering a unique offering and protecting research and design costs with copyrights, patents, and design rights
Relationships	being well-connected
Location	being physically well-positioned, such as a busy corner in town or in a new market rich with ideal customers
Advanced technology	providing a new, innovative way to serve customers with the latest and greatest technology

Heed warning, dear friend. Competing on price alone is a nearly impossible strategy to succeed with for small businesses. It's often referred to as "a race to the bottom" for good reason. The strategy works for businesses able to purchase enough quantity of an item from suppliers to drive down the cost of each item considerably.

These companies are often considered "low-cost providers" (think, Walmart) because of the volume they can afford to purchase. Since they're selling so many of an item, the small profit margin adds up and "economies of scale" creates a hard-to-obtain competitive advantage. When small businesses try this strategy, their cash becomes tied up in large amounts of inventory and they often go under. This is why I recommend developing a competitive advantage that doesn't rely on offering the lowest price. In other words, figure out what YOUR secret sauce is aside from low prices and your customers will love you for it.

Which competitive advantage(s) from the list above will your business embody?

How can you leverage your competitive advantage(s) to position your business well in its industry?

EXAMPLES OF VALUE PROPOSITIONS

(Remember, value propositions are the value the customer sees in your offering.)

Quality	customers' willingness to pay more for access to a better product or service
Ease of use	consuming an offering is easy to use because of its simplicity
Unique experience	promising to deliver a distinct or rare interaction with your product or service
Quality of life	enhancing customers' lives with improvement in the status quo
Convenience	removing barriers to use an offering, saving time, brain power, or effort
Values	using products or services aligned with customers' core values
Customer service	standing behind an offering to reassure customers that if something goes wrong, the customer will still be taken care of
Style	allowing customers to express their individuality

Which value proposition from the list above will your business embody?

How can you leverage your value proposition to gain and maintain customers?

SERVICE PACKAGES

If you're in the service industry, it's likely you'll need to create packages so customers can easily understand the value of your offering. Bundle your services together in an attractive (and possibly discounted) way. Packages help you charge for the value of an end result and help you avoid trading time for money as in the case of charging by the hour. Other benefits to charging by the package over hourly rates include the ability to serve more clients, selling more services to the same client, and earning more profit. Take the following tips to create your packages:

- ▶ People like options. Offer two to four packages so potential clients can compare their budget with their desired result and easily make sense of the value provided.

- ▶ Include premium results in a second or third tier to entice an upgrade for anyone sitting on the fence.

- ▶ Remember, many people assume price reflects quality, and there are some people who always opt for the premium choice.

- ▶ Consider how you can pack more value into the higher tiers without committing more time for results. For example, you could offer recorded webinar training access exclusive to those who choose your top tier package. Record it once and sell it over and over.

Now consider what your offering looks like and how you can organize it into packages to help customers select the best option for their needs:

MARKETING PLAN CONTENTS

Now that we've covered a few basic Marketing 101 concepts, let's dive into the exciting part—the sections of your official marketing plan! Sections will include: Market Research, Marketing Objectives, SWOT Analysis, Marketing Channels, Marketing Metrics, Marketing Budget, Sales Strategy, and Marketing Roles. The following information will help you make clear decisions before you fasten it all together with a simpleMarketing Plan Template at the end of the section.

MARKET RESEARCH

Reflect back to **Phase Two: Research, Step 1: Trial Your Offering** and **Phase Two: Research, Step 3: Toast to Your Competition** when you tested your offering and evaluated industry competition. Let's summarize your findings.

How has your marketing and industry research affected the evolution of your business idea?

....

....

....

....

What does the competitive landscape that you'll be stepping into look and feel like? For example, what trends are taking place? Is there lots of competition or very little? Is customer demand increasing at a fast pace, steady pace, or slow pace (this will signal new competitors entering the market)?

....

....

How will your business and offering fit into the competitive landscape? Do any competitors have the exact offering? Where do your prices fall in relation to other businesses' prices?

....

....

....

....

....

....

MARKETING OBJECTIVES

Marketing objectives are the smaller to-dos that make up your overarching goals. Objectives should be quantifiable with a specific amount of time attached. Leverage your resources wisely by pairing each marketing objective to the action you'll take to meet it. How do your objectives help meet your goals, like gaining market share and meeting sales goals? Plan to measure your progress on a regular basis, monthly for example. Examples of objectives include:

1. Land five major contracts in six months.

2. Accomplish 100 transactions in the first two months of business.

3. Be featured as a guest on five podcasts during your business launch.

4. Enroll 50 students in your online course within three months of your launch.

Brainstorm possible marketing objectives that fit you and your business well:

1. ....

2. ....

3. ....

Reflect on your marketing objectives. How will you turn your objectives into reality?

....

....

....

....

SWOT ANALYSIS

SWOT Analysis: SWOT stands for Strengths, Weaknesses, Opportunities, and Threats. A SWOT analysis helps you develop an idea of what's working to your advantage and what's not. Consider back to **Phase Two: Research, Step 3: Toast to Your Competition** where you identified your main three competitors. Take that information into consideration as you perform a SWOT analysis.

Strengths are your competitive advantage(s) over competitors, value proposition(s), and your personal skill set, experience, knowledge, and abilities. Don't overwork yourself girl! You can pull some of this information from the 'Competitive Advantage and Value Proposition' section above.

Weaknesses are areas where competitors have an advantage over your business, your "blind spots," and your areas for opportunity to improve as a business.You likely uncovered some of this in **Phase Two: Research, Step 3: Toast to Your Competition** when you evaluated three other players in your industry.

Opportunities are market opportunities, ways you can leverage your strengths to create value for the customer, and the ways you can take action to position your business in a positive light to your audience. They differ from strengths in that opportunities are intrinsically action-based.

Threats are ways your competitors take action to stay competitive, shortcomings within your business operations (such as shortage of cash flow), and trends that could negatively impact your business. You likely uncovered some of this throughout **Phase Two: Research** as you uncovered new findings and evaluated the viability of your business and differing.

Journal thoughts on your strengths, weaknesses, opportunities, and threats:

Strengths: ....
....
....
....

Weaknesses: ....
....
....
....

Opportunities: ....
....
....
....

Threats: ....
....
....
....

MARKETING CHANNELS

Girl, you want to work smarter not harder! As the new kid on the block in my business venture, I lacked direction because I never stopped to consider how best to share my message with potential customers. I dove in headfirst and tread water as I went. I wised up over time. For instance, a clear Pinterest strategy helped me build my email list to over 1,000 subscribers in less than one year. One page and a little intention is all it takes to sketch your marketing blueprint.

To make a marketing plan, you'll have to first select which marketing channels are a good fit for your business, your audience, and you as a person. Creating a presence *everywhere* is costly and unrealistic. Consider where your audience already spends time. Of those options, which channels feel most authentic to your business and brand personality?

Let's review a variety of marketing channels. Then choose which are a good fit for your business. Put a star in the box next to the channels that seem to fit best.

☐ **1-to-1 relationship development.** Intentional relationship development is more than networking; it's getting to know the other person on a personal level. For instance, as a thank you for using their services, an insurance provider takes a team of decision makers on an annual two-day golf trip. In another example, a web designer and graphic designer team up to co-host a girls' night out event for a group of local entrepreneurs.

☐ **Car decals.** Magnetic car decals work similarly to yard signs, only in mobile form. They're flexible enough to take off or change when you need to and boast the benefit of significant exposure while you're parked in a parking lot, driving on the highway, or in line at school pick up.

☐ **Cold calls or cold emails.** Cold calling or emailing means reaching out to an audience who isn't yet primed to buy from you. Your list of leads could come from referrals, a detailed internet search, or by accessing a list of attendees from a carefully selected event. The important consideration is that people on your list have a need your offering meets. Rather than leaning on the power of repeat touchpoints or long-standing relationships, cold calls and emails take the approach of first informing the lead about the offering and immediately making a pitch.

☐ **Content marketing.** Blogs (written articles) and vlogs (video content) are methods for sharing information with an audience. It's likely the most underestimated and misunderstood marketing tactic I've seen in my work helping small businesses market. Intentionally developing strong content to support consumers in their decision to make a purchase is powerful. The strategy involves researching topics the audience is already looking for, using optimized keywords, and referring traffic internally to other places on the site or online space.

☐ **Developing your own community.** By developing your own community—in-person or virtual—you're able to intentionally choose topics of conversation, decide how information will be presented, and deliver value to a warm audience.

☐ **Digital advertisements.** The advantage of digital advertisements on social media and search engines is that the data available helps serve your detailed and unique message to the exact audience it's suited for. A word of caution–while paid ads can produce a high return on investment (ROI), there can be an expensive learning curve to first figuring out what works and what doesn't. Before you throw money at them assuming they're a sure bet, make sure you have the monetary and time investment to work out the kinks.

☐ **Direct mail.** From a small business, the personal touch of a postcard or newsletter can feel endearing and unique. For instance, I send postcards out a few times each year with encouraging sayings and a handwritten note. Sure, it's a marketing expense, but it's a great way to reach a warm audience and strengthen the relationship with the customer from a different angle.

☐ **Email marketing.** Email marketing is the strategy of sending curated emails to customers, typically through a platform designed to deliver messages in a sequence to nurture the new lead and guide them along the path to purchase.

☐ **Giveaways.** Giveaways are one way to entice your audience to pay attention to your message. Here, you offer a reward to one lucky winner who participates in the rules of your contest. Giveaways often "cut through the noise" of the busy online space. Why? Because there's something in it for them!

☐ **Guerilla marketing.** Guerilla marketing is a strategy that focuses on low-cost, unconventional marketing tactics to make a big splash. You'll know it's guerrilla marketing when you see characteristics of a "surprise effect," simplicity, being easily understood, and likely to create buzz and word of mouth. For example, the brand Gold Toe dressed New York City statues in oversized shirts and underwear when it launched its newest line in 2010. Their brand was hard to miss, and it was hard for New Yorkers to resist laughing. Once while I was on a jog along Old 98 in Destin, Florida, I repeatedly passed tiny two-inch wooden crosses lying along the paved path and stopped to pick one up. When I turned the cross over, the Bible verse "John 3:16" was written on the other side. Maybe Jesus uses guerilla marketing, too.

☐ **Hosting events.** Hosting in-person or virtual social events is your chance to be a difference maker. Since marketing works best with repeat touchpoints, consistently hosting or organizing social events helps an audience become familiar with you. Social events might include a community clean-up day, a triathlon for a cause, or a local meet up.

☐ **Leaving business cards strategically around town.** As you attend meetings at local coffee shops and restaurants, see if they offer a corkboard or area to leave business cards.

☐ **Membership organizations**. Membership organizations, like the local Chamber of Commerce or National Association of Women Business Owners (NAWBO), can offer perks like free entry into events, inclusion in a member directory, free advertising opportunities, and referrals.

☐ **Networking.** Networking takes many forms, though the goal is to expand connections. People do business with other people they know, like, and trust, and networking helps build trust and connection.

☐ **Podcast interviews.** Podcasts are a method for distributing audio content, often discussions on specific topics. Being interviewed on a podcast comes with a host of benefits, including being positioned as an authority on a topic, having marketing collateral to share with your own audience, and reaching an audience of potential customers who already have an interest in your topic. How do you get featured on podcasts? Don't wait around to be invited. Reach out to the podcast host and ask.

☐ **Referral program.** A purpose of a referral program is to incentivize existing customers to recommend the business to their circle of influence. The recommendation is backed by social proof. Since we humans tend to hang out with other humans with similar interests, socioeconomic status, income level, and world views, referrals are a powerful way to expand your reach to a larger circle of ideal customers. For example, Dubsado, the business management software I use to send client contracts and onboarding in-take forms and to collect payments, offers a referral program. Each customer gets a unique code to share with others. When a new customer adds the service from the existing customer's code, both the new and existing customer receive a free month of the software service.

☐ **Search marketing strategy.** Build your brand visibility and drive traffic to your website with search marketing. Use keywords and content that your potential customers are already using in their internet searches (think of search engines like Google, Pinterest, and YouTube) to make YOUR website show up in their search results. You can do this through search engine optimization (SEO), where you include those keywords on your website to drive traffic to your site organically and for free. You can also run paid ads that are triggered to display in search results based on keywords.

☐ **Secure a booth at a local vendor pop-up or farmer's market.** By securing a booth, you have an opportunity to interact with attendees primed and ready to buy. Some businesses operate solely at these kinds of events and do well because they carefully select the events they'll attend based on the kind and size of audience who typically attends.

☐ **Social media marketing.** Social media marketing is the use of social platforms to connect with ideal customers, develop brand awareness, and drive sales. You can do this through posts, ads, groups, direct messages, and more.

☐ **Speaking engagements.** Speaking engagements include any opportunity where you're in a position to teach others on a topic. Paid or free, large audience or a small one, virtual or in-person—everything counts. The big takeaway is you're positioned as the expert. This opens you to an audience, gives you something to talk about in your marketing material, and helps you hone your speaking and presentation skills.

☐ **Sponsorship.** Sponsorship is paying an organization to feature your business before their audience. Examples include conferences, little league teams, athletic events, and even social media influencers. What I love about sponsorship is you can typically negotiate your terms, so get crafty! In my experience, sponsorship has included the opportunity to speak to an audience, prime real estate on event signage, t-shirt visibility, visibility on the registration site, welcome swag, and much more.

☐ **Traditional marketing.** Traditional marketing like radio ads, billboards, or TV advertisements isn't dead, but it can be expensive and more difficult to target a narrow audience. Still, integrating traditional marketing with internet marketing where appropriate and with the right audience can be effective.

☐ **Yard signs.** Yard signs, especially placed along well-trafficked areas, can be effective for reaching a large audience. Remember to keep signs simple and legible with a clear call to action so viewers understand the point quickly while passing. Consider asking friends and family if you can place a sign on their property, and always abide by the law when placing signs in public spaces.

MARKETING METRICS

You can't manage what you don't measure. Marketing metrics help you know what's not working and more importantly, what is working. This insight comes with time after developing a basic understanding of the factors affecting your goals.

For instance, to gain sales on your website, you must first drive enough traffic. The average ecommerce conversion rate is around 3%, so you'll need to drive at least 100 customers to your site to earn three sales. If your sales are under-performing, examining the data to ask "Why?" leads our brains to discover new opportunities.

Key performance indicators (KPIs) are indicators of forward movement toward an intended result. Knowing your KPIs helps you do more of what's already working. In the beginning, it's most important to become familiar with your baseline key performance indicators. These are the core metrics that help you "feel the temperature" of your marketing efforts.

If you're unfamiliar with your business's KPIs, like how many daily site visits your receives, what its average conversion rate is (how many people buy compared to how many people visit), or what its abandoned cart rate is (how many people reach checkout but don't buy), you won't be able to pinpoint how you can improve. This information is typically available in your website's dashboard. You can also link Google Analytics and other third-party apps, like Data Box, to your site to glean the data. Numbers can feel overwhelming, so take it slow if you need to.What can sound like a foreign language initially overtime becomes familiar dialogue. At this point in building your business, it's unlikely you know all the KPIs important that will help you manage your business well. No biggie! Tuck this insight in the back of your mind for the future. Familiarity will come with time. Be patient and open to the opportunity to learn.

The following is a list of example KPIs:

Conversion rate. Conversion rate is the number of successful results compared to the number of total visitors. A good average conversion rate varies by marketing medium and industry, so research will help you find your industry's average conversion rate.

Website visits. Site visits are the number of times your website has been visited in a defined period of time, usually one day or one month.

Time spent on a site (also called "dwell time"). Time spent on a site is how long a website visitor stays on a site before leaving. It's one metric search engines use to gauge whether visitors are having a positive experience on a site. Note this metric often correlates with other success indicators, like transactions made, number of pages viewed, and engagement.

Leads generated. A lead is an organization or individual who finds out about your offering and considers buying. Consequently, leads generated is defined as the number of leads created by a certain marketing effort. To understand which marketing channels are most effective for generating leads, create systems to help you connect the dots. For instance, to pinpoint how many leads are generated from a marketing campaign, you could segment your email list based on which form on your website a subscriber signed up through or ask leads via sales consultation how they heard about your business.

Monthly recurring revenue (MRR). Monthly recurring revenue is the income a business can depend on every month. This number often accompanies proof of concept when a business is generating revenue predictably. To find this number, multiply the average number of paying customers per month by the average revenue per customer.

Sales calls made. Sales calls made are just that—the number of sales calls to prospective buyers. "Sales calls" and "cold calls" are often interchanged. Data trends come with consistent action. This means you've consistently maintained a marketing effort long enough to see patterns in the results. Let's say your sales call rate of success is 4%. That means you'll have to make 100 calls in order to secure four sales. The average conversion rate for sales calls is around 2%.

Return on investment (ROI). Return on investment measures the gain or loss by a particular investment. ROI is calculated by subtracting the initial investment by the total amount yielded, then dividing by the initial investment and multiplying by 100%. For example, if you pay $100 in social media ads, and make $247 in sales, the ROI would be calculated as following:

ROI = (($247-$100) / $100) X 100% = 147% Return on Investment

Customer satisfaction score. Customer satisfaction score is a metric companies define and use to understand how overall satisfied a customer is with a particular experience or interaction. It's a way of putting subjective feelings into a measurable metric.

Social shares. Social shares is a social media metric that indicates how many times customers are mentioning a brand on social media. Seeing themes or patterns in content shared should indicate the type of content your audience wants to see more of because they found it interesting or entertaining enough to share with their own audiences.

Followers. In social media terms, a follower is someone who has subscribed to an account.

Click rate (sometimes known as a "click through rate"). Click rate is the percentage of people who click on a link, button, or image within an email compared to the total number of subscribers the email was sent to. Click rate can also be defined as the number of people who click an ad or organic search result compared to the number of people who were presented the ad or organic search result. A good click through rate varies by industry and marketing medium.

Email open rate. Email open rate is the percentage of subscribers who open an email compared to the total number of subscribers the email was sent to. It's one metric companies use to understand how effective their email marketing strategy is. A good email open rate varies by industry. In my experience, I've seen 3% to be considered good for one industry and 25% to be good for another.

Email sign ups. Email sign-ups are the number of people who opt into your email list. Measuring the number of people who subscribe to your emails given a certain marketing strategy (such as a pop up on your website or sign ups through a social media account) helps gauge interest in your offering.

Unsubscribe rate. Unsubscribe rate is the number of people who opt out of an email list compared to the total number of subscribers. A good unsubscribe rate is less than 1%.

Reflect on which KPIs might indicate success in your business.

....

....

....

....

....

....

....

MARKETING BUDGET

I've never met a new entrepreneur with a huge marketing budget and that's okay! Why? It's important to test out your product or service initially until you gain proof of concept. You want to gain proof of concept before you invest lots of money in marketing.

Proof of concept (PoC) is evidence that proves your offering is feasible because it shows people are willing to pay for it. It's one of the reasons you spent time testing your product in **Phase Two: Research, Step 1: Trial Your Offering**. Until you gain proof of concept, you'll garner valuable insight about what you thought would happen versus what actually happens. It's in the space of taking action where all the valuable lessons are revealed. Once you gain clarity through proof of concept by taking action, then you can wisely invest money in ads and marketing spend, because with proof of concept often comes a better return on investment (ROI). Keep in mind, 7% - 8% of revenue is the average company's spend on marketing, so plan to work up to that figure in the next five years.

Here's a sample marketing channel dispersion based on budget.

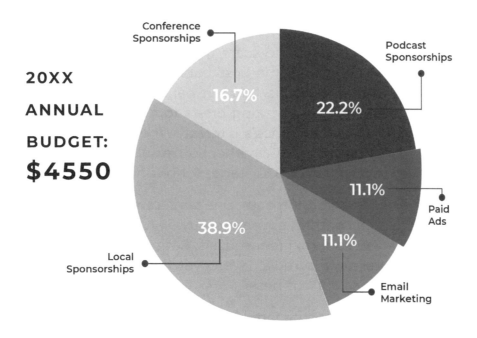

20XX ANNUAL BUDGET: $4550

- Conference Sponsorships — 16.7%
- Podcast Sponsorships — 22.2%
- Paid Ads — 11.1%
- Email Marketing — 11.1%
- Local Sponsorships — 38.9%

Reflect on what your marketing budget currently looks like and what you'd like it to look like as your business grows. This is the perfect place to add your "wish list" for how you'll spend your marketing budget. Then in the graph below, sketch out your ideal marketing channel dispersion.

YEAR:

ANNUAL BUDGET:

SALES STRATEGY

For whatever reason, sales seems to scare many people. Even hearing the word "sales" is enough to make some boss babes run scared. Let's change that today! Sales and marketing go hand in hand. Sales means fostering and managing relationships and making offers to help. Marketing is creating messages to spark your audience's interest. Whether or not you need a robust sales strategy depends on whether you're selling B2B or B2C (B2B stands for business to business or B2C stands for business to consumer).

Sales strategy can be incredibly intricate. One conference I went to even laid out a 12-step process for "getting anyone to buy anything from you." If that last sentence made you squirm, I feel you, sis. Rather than suggesting you memorize an overwhelming formula, let's cover the basics for developing sales relationships within your business.

- ☐ Do your research - Become familiar with your connection as a person. Who are they? How can you help them solve a nagging problem? What are their goals?

- ☐ At the end of the day, people want to do business with people they know, like, and trust. What are you doing to build trust?

- ☐ Be a good human being even when no one is watching. (Someone is always watching!)

- ☐ Listen more than you speak during business conversations. You cannot make an appropriate offer to help others when you haven't understood what life is like through the other person's eyes.

- ☐ The best business owners don't sell; they offer a solution to address a specific problem and offer to help.

- ☐ Set goals – Define your aim and work backward outlining actions you can take leading up to accomplishing your goals.

- ☐ Be personable – Develop a genuine interest in creating value for the other person rather than just trying to make money.

- ☐ Plan for objections (like your customer saying "no" on a consult call because they don't have the money) and play forward how you'll overcome those objections in a helpful way.

☐ Gatekeepers are the people who stand between you and the person you're trying to get your sale on with (like the CEO or a department head). Gatekeepers often have more influence on the sale than what their title might suggest. Treat them like the CEO.

☐ Assume the person you're selling to is standing next to you – in the elevator, in line to get coffee, or at the stoplight waiting to cross the street.

☐ Follow up as many times as it takes to get a response. The sale is in the follow up.

☐ Ask for the sale.

☐ Secure your work together with more than a handshake. Get a signed contract, prospective timeline, and payment deposit.

☐ Be respectful of hearing "no," but consider it a "not yet."

Knowing that sales is about developing relationships and making offers to help, what might the sales process look like in your business?

....

....

....

....

....

MARKETING ROLES

It's probable many of these marketing responsibilities will fall on your shoulders as the business owner—especially in the beginning. If you have help with marketing while getting your business off the ground, take time to consider and communicate with key players which marketing responsibilities fall under which role within your organization. Examples of roles include social media manager, content creator (graphics, written, blogs, video, and emails), and digital marketing specialist.

Role #1: ....

Marketing Responsibilities: ....

....

Role #2: ....

Marketing Responsibilities: ....

....

Role #3: ....

Marketing Responsibilities: ....

....

OFFICIAL MARKETING PLAN

Ready for the fun part? All that hard work you just walked through means you're ready to create your official marketing plan—and you already have all the pieces to put it together! In addition to your Brand Standards and ideal client persona, your Marketing Plan Template anchors all marketing activity in your business.

In a world where businesses tend to market haphazardly, creating and following a solid plan for marketing your business undoubtedly gives your business an advantage. Customers travel through a psychological process of buying. Knowing the questions they ask in their minds (often subconsciously) as they familiarize with a new brand provides a roadmap for tailoring your messaging to their needs.

Marketing is a long-sighted game. Messages sent early and often and tailored to your target audience are the recipe for marketing success. Your marketing plan equals accountability for how, why, when, where, and to whom you'll spread awareness about the value of your business.

Use this space to identify your marketing plan starting point.

MARKETING PLAN

1. MARKET RESEARCH SYNOPSIS

2. MARKETING OBJECTIVES

1.

2.

3.

3. SWOT ANALYSIS

STRENGTHS   **WEAKNESSES**

OPPORTUNITIES   **THREATS**

4. MARKETING CHANNELS

1.

2.

3.

4.

5.

5. MAIN MARKETING METRICS (KPIs)

1.

2.

3.

4.

5.

6. ANNUAL MARKETING BUDGET

$_____

7. SALES STRATEGY SYNOPSIS

8. MARKETING ROLES

ROLE #1 _____

RESPONSIBILITIES:

ROLE #2 _____

RESPONSIBILITIES:

ROLE #3 _____

RESPONSIBILITIES:

STEP 6

DREAM UP YOUR DIGITAL SPACE

"The only thing that ever stays the same is change." I learned this from our family friend, Myron. He was a wise man with a good heart, and it seems like every day, his wise advice becomes more and more accurate. The key to crushing the online space is willingness to evolve.

At a female business conference in 2019, I heard TikTok was about to blow up. Then it did."Everyone will be using it," they said. Then, for a short while, it was Clubhouse. Next year, some new social media platform will burst through the noise, and everyone will flock to it.

So how do you know which emerging trend is worth your time? Like everything else, you research whether your target audience is (or will be) using the space. Make it an obsession to find out what your customers feel, think, and want.

Your business's online visibility depends on many things, including where your target audience spends time, which media outlets your audience uses and also align with your brand, the cost in time and budget of maintaining your presence, and you, as the business owner—how many online responsibilities you can handle, your savvy with online systems, and whether spending extensive time on social media aligns with the needs of your mental health, to name a few. Because of the variables playing a role in your success, your blueprint is one only you can create.

Recall in **Phase Three: Build, Step 5: Draw Up Your Marketing Plan** that you carefully selected marketing channels based on which ones were a good fit for your business, ideal client, and you, personally. Here, we'll focus specifically on the digital marketing channels you chose.

As you craft your online presence, keep brand consistency at the forefront of your efforts. A customer jumping onto your site, social presence, and email newsletter, for example, should experience a consistent feeling and experience on all platforms. Let's first think through what your online presence will be like from a general perspective.

Circle options that align with what you'd like your online experience to be like:

Informative

Supportive

Engaging

Entertaining

Community-oriented

Trend-setting

Well-branded

Positions you as a thought leader

Visual with unique photos or graphics

Easy to navigate

Seamless

Safe

Edgy

Professional

Playful

Other: ....

Other: ....

ONLINE CONTENT CREATION

Content strategy includes the planning, creation, execution, and management, of online content. Content can include social media posts, blog posts, videos, website copy, and any other type of message delivery. Your content strategy has many benefits, including:

1. serving as a vehicle to convey value to your audience

2. giving your audience a reason to buy

3. providing the context for search engines to determine what you do and who you do it for.

PRO TIP: Lead customers where you want them to go in emails, on your website, in social media posts, and in conversations. Make it easy for them to give you money. I received an email recently from a small hometown company. They noticed I hadn't signed my daughter up for the next round of dance classes. Their email invited her into the next session but didn't include direction where I could view the class schedule or make the transaction online. In the context of our busy lives, this may as well have been a roadblock and as a result, I didn't sign her up. Go through the online experience as your customers would to uncover costly hiccups in the process. Simplify the process of creating a conversion in as few steps as possible.

Content is too often poorly executed by small business owners because a vast number of responsibilities fall on their shoulders. Often, content creation and execution is the task which:

▶ is executed intermittently if/when the business owner has time

▶ is completed by hurriedly throwing up a few social media posts

▶ is prioritized only when sales are especially low and there's a need for prospecting

▶ is given little thought about the effectiveness of a message to guide a potential customer into a sale.

The problem with this is it creates an inconsistent experience for customers. The key to successful content is to find out what your audience is already looking for and create consistent content around those themes to position your company as a solution to their problem. Here are a few best practices for developing your content strategy while staying sane as an entrepreneur.

- ▶ Offer helpful guidance and be part of a conversation.

- ▶ Plan ahead! Gaps in consistency happen when entrepreneurs get busy. Plan content before it needs to be posted to ensure a consistent presence.

- ▶ Perform keyword research so your word choice matches your ideal client's verbiage.

- ▶ Before you create, think about how you'll repurpose a piece of content. Start with one piece of long-form content, like a blog or video, and consider how it can be used across several different platforms for different reasons. I love starting with a blog post (around 1500 words) and repurposing it for emails, social media post captions, and as an outline for recording video content.

- ▶ Tell stories (the human brain is wired for stories) and focus on meaning-making.

Reflect on topics your audience is looking to learn more about:

....

....

....

....

WEBSITE

Your website will see many iterations. Right now, creating a starting point matters most. If you have chosen to build your site yourself rather than outsource to a web designer, build the site and move on. This is one part of starting a business that turns into a black hole by sucking new entrepreneurs' precious time. When you know better, you do better, and you can always come back later after you gain deeper insight into how your business will fit in the world to refine your message. For now, create your approach and execute, keeping the following best practices in mind:

Remove distractions. Keep the goals you have for your website top of mind. Any content that detracts from visitors reaching those goals should be removed. For example, let's say Faye is an online boutique owner with the goal for website visitors to complete a successful checkout. Faye knows she needs to provide extensive detail about each product for customers to feel comfortable buying a product they've never touched or tried on. Rather than linking to an FAQ page within the product page to answer customers' questions (which seems helpful but is a distraction), Faye should also add the FAQ copy to the product page so customers can more smoothly continue moving forward in the transaction process once they've gathered sufficient information.

Create clear calls to action. Customers need you to tell them what to do next. Make it obvious what their next move should be. Include clear calls to action leading visitors through the Buying Cycle and helping customers navigate to their desired goal. Examples include "Call now," "Learn about our company," "Click to watch," and "Add to cart."

Make it simple when you're asking the customer to think. The average Josephine has so much going on in her life, she won't spend much mental energy figuring out how to buy from you if it's not obvious. Put yourself in the shoes of someone who has never heard of your product or service before. How can you remove the fluff to help busy Josephine understand how to get the result she desires? Oftentimes as business owners, we want to "cast a wide net," so we give too many options, afraid our offering won't satisfy the customer's needs. In fact, the customer just wants to know what the offering is, if it's possible for her to achieve the desired results, and how to buy it. Focus on answering those questions and remove the rest. A practical application for this suggestion is to simplify the information you collect in your forms. Ask only for the information you need in order to help the customer get to the next step. The bigger the commitment feels to the customer, the less likely they are to convert. Keep it simple.

Aim to provide complete but concise information. Help the customer develop a complete understanding of what it would be like to experience your offering and the results it promises. For example, provide product photos from multiple angles, include a video of the product in use, give descriptions to answer who the offering is for, provide bullet points to tell what the coaching process looks like, and clearly and concisely state what the purpose is, why it's important, and how the customer gets results with it.

Include policies, such as terms of use and your return policy. Parting with their money means customers must take a risk. Policies clearly answer what will happen if something goes wrong and help put customers' minds at ease, so the transaction feels less risky. Even if you don't offer returns, for example, a defined understanding of what the customer is agreeing to is better than leaving a big fat question mark in their mind.

Add social proof. As humans, we often feel like our risk of trying something new is lessened if we hear how others have experienced the same situation. Social proof, or accounts of what others' experiences with an offering have been like, are one way to reassure potential customers they're making a great buying decision. Use testimonials, reviews, customer before-and-afters (with permission), "as seen on" logo displays, and client stories to help prospective customers feel comfortable buying from you.

Create content for skimming. The strategic use of short paragraphs (no more than three sentences), easily legible section titles, colored hyperlink text, and bolded keywords help customers find the information they're looking for quickly. Even more, strategically placing optimized keywords (the keywords you already know your customers are using to search for and find your solution) help the language you use in your content to resonate with the way your customers seek information.

Continue leading the visitor through the Buying Cycle. Many websites we audit in my data and analytics business, Simply Integrated (https://simplyinte-gratedllc.com/), are initially built like a billboard. By that, I mean they function as a one-way conversation broadcasting information at the visitor rather than strategically leading them through an experience. Your website should be structured to lead visitors through the experience of buying from you the same way your marketing messages do. Calls to action and opportunities to engage are vital. Each page on your site should meet the psychological need your customer is experiencing at varying stages of the Buying Cycle.

For instance, a first timer likely wants to know who you are, how you provide value, and if they can trust you, so offer a snippet on your home page to develop rapport and call them to visit your About page if they want more information. Site visits to your FAQ page, for example, signal someone is considering buying from you, so you might strategically place a call-to-action button at the bottom of the page leading visitors to explore your services.

Remember, if you don't tell customers where to go next, their likelihood of leaving your site altogether increases. Put yourself in the shoes of the website visitor to explore what the experience would be like at varying stages in the Buying Cycle so you can instinctively lead visitors where they should go next to reach a sale. Even better, ask someone who doesn't know much about your business to browse your website. Then stand close and watch what they do.

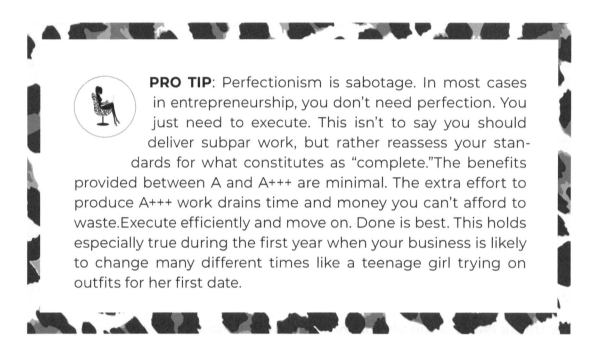

PRO TIP: Perfectionism is sabotage. In most cases in entrepreneurship, you don't need perfection. You just need to execute. This isn't to say you should deliver subpar work, but rather reassess your standards for what constitutes as "complete."The benefits provided between A and A+++ are minimal. The extra effort to produce A+++ work drains time and money you can't afford to waste.Execute efficiently and move on. Done is best. This holds especially true during the first year when your business is likely to change many different times like a teenage girl trying on outfits for her first date.

Basic steps to build a website

1. Choose the platform and pay for the subscription (see our vetted list of options in the Founding Females™ Resource Suite at www. HerBusinessGuide.com).

2. Purchase and connect the domain from a domain registrar. This step can feel technical and intimidating, but it's doable (and you'll be proud of yourself once it's complete!). Since most site platforms and registrars differ, use a search engine to research specific instructions for connecting your domain with your website platform or get a hold of the registrar's customer service for guidance.

3. Plan your site before you dive in by creating the site framework. Included in the next section is a list of best practices for keeping your site optimized

(i.e. searchable via search engines)—information you can incorporate from the beginning. Keep it simple and straightforward. You can always go back and add more later as you gain clarity about your business. For each page:

    a. Brainstorm the content, desired outcomes, and purpose.

    b. Decide how it will link to other pages on the site with buttons and hyperlinked text to purposefully lead visitors through the value you offer and to a sale.

    c. Decide how you'll capture the audience's information for other marketing activities.

4. Build the website according to your plans above.

5. Publish.

6. Promote with your **Phase Four: Launch** strategy coming up.

Use this space to jot notes about your website vision: how customers feel when they browse it, the value they gain, how they contact you, what pages it will contain, and what the overall experience is like:

....

....

....

....

Basic SEO Planning Best Practices

Outline your pages in advance by planning:

   ▶ Which keywords you'll use

   ▶ The title of each page and each section

   ▶ Written copy for each page and each section within each page

- ▶ What photos will be used and where—size them appropriately for web (not too large or you might break the internet!) and organize them in a folder labeled with optimized keywords

- ▶ What videos you'll use and where

- ▶ Which messages you'll craft and on which pages based on the Buying Cycle

- ▶ 3-4 blog posts available for first-time browsers with links leading into other pages on your site

- ▶ Where you'll place email opt-in forms

- ▶ How you'll lead them back to your website after they leave (announcing upcoming content, inviting them to a webinar, or hooking them on a multi-part content series, email marketing, and targeted ads are a handful of ideas)

- ▶ Skimmable copy with short paragraphs (3-4 sentences) and easy-to-read section titles.

- ▶ Hyperlinks within your written copy to other related pages on your site

- ▶ A distraction-free site to keep visitors on your site as long as possible

- ▶ Build a site everyone can enjoy by ensuring your site is ADA compliant. For instructions, visit www.ADA.gov.

SOCIAL CHANNELS

Before you build a presence on any social media platform, first verify your target audience uses the platform. Then, stick to a manageable number of social platforms to ensure you can manage the content well. Social media platforms vary and change frequently from what kind of content is prioritized in the feed to features available for building community.

For a comparison of platforms best suited for different types of audiences, best practices for each social media channel, and basic return on investment, consider setting a keyword alert in Google. When you do, Google will email you with a list of sites that have mentioned the keywords you indicated. It's an efficient way to access a concentrated list of sources discussing changing trends.

Basic social media best practices for small businesses include the following strategies:

- ▶ Be consistent. Create in batches by planning content topics and scheduling content in a publishing tool (see a vetted list in the Founding Females™ Resource Suite) so you don't have to commit time and brain power to it daily. Some social platforms reward posting organically inside the app, but in my experience it's a nearly impossible feat to remain consistent with. I prefer to know the content is accounted for so I can focus precious attention elsewhere in my business.

- ▶ Leverage social platforms for repeat touch points and to build rapport, knowing that most platforms are designed to keep people in the app.

- ▶ Each social media platform has its own best practices. Choose a fewer number of platforms and manage them well rather than trying to maintain a presence across too many platforms. When you do, management of the platforms can become overwhelming, inconsistent, and impersonal.

Use this space to jot notes about your business's social strategy:

EMAIL STRATEGY

It's totally natural if you aren't quite sure what to say in your emails at this point. As your business evolves through the first year, you'll become keenly aware of your audience's needs, personality, and behavior patterns through interacting organically. A robust email strategy can be helpful once your business is a well-oiled machine. At this point, getting started is most important and a basic automated welcome email will do just fine.

Mark your calendar for three months after launch to revisit your welcome series. Then, you can add to the welcome series and make updates to your strategy for funneling customers into a sale.

Lots of fun email marketing platforms are available at low or no cost. See our vetted list of email marketing platforms in the Founding Females™ Resource Suite at www.HerBusinessGuide.com.

Here are a few tips to keep in mind:

- ▸ Create a simple automated welcome email. This will be the email anyone receives when they first subscribe or purchase a product. "Automated" means that no matter when or who subscribes to your list (likely through your website), they will receive an email in their inbox without you having to do a darn thing. Ahh, can you feel the simplicity?

- ▸ After you create your simple welcome email, hash out your plan for a consistent, value-centric email (some call this an email "newsletter"), perhaps weekly or monthly. Cue the happy dance for repeat touch points. The reality is that not everyone will open your email, but most will at least see it in their inbox, even if it's while they delete it from their inbox without opening. (Depressing, I know, but still counts as a touch point.)

- ▸ Never add someone to your list without their permission. Rather, think about making it easy for someone to opt in – on your website, in a call to action with a link in the footer of your personal emails, or as a link in your Instagram bio. In addition, regulations like the General Data Protection Regulation (GDPR)—a privacy and security law governed currently by the European Union—determine how you can collect emails. Be sure to abide by the regulations.

- ▸ Think about meeting someone for the first time whose response was, "Hey, wanna buy my stuff?" You'd probably run. Don't do that. Instead, use your email list to first develop a trusting relationship. You worked hard to earn their presence on your email list. Now nurture the rela- tionship with intentional value. This could be:

  - ▸ Your most recent blog post

  - ▸ Your favorite actionable tip for accomplishing a goal your audi- ence cares about

> ▸ Encouragement helping them see you empathize with what they're going through. (Make them think, "Ooh, this girl gets me."

▸ Craft strong subject lines to help get more of your emails opened. Spend ample time crafting them for the best possible results.

▸ Don't ask readers to do too much. Create concise copy and craft one call to action. Consider what **one** action you want them to take. Visit your blog? Purchase a product? Hit reply and respond?

Your online presence is like a storefront for customers to peek inside and learn about your business. It should be well-branded and authentic to your business. Every account you create will require maintenance, so the simpler and well-automated, the better.

STEP 7

FIGURE OUT YOUR PHYSICAL SPACE

"DISCONNECT FROM EVERYTHING LONG ENOUGH TO SEE IF IT FEEDS YOUR SOUL OR IF IT'S A DISTRACTION. WHAT'S DEEPLY CONNECTED WILL ALWAYS REMAIN." – MARYAM HASNAA

Look around. Why did you choose the space you're in right now? You know yourself well enough to choose your working environment carefully. If you've reached a place in life where you're thinking about starting a business, you don't need me to tell you a carefully crafted environment conducive to doing your best work shouldn't be overlooked. The goal is not to convince you it's important, but to remind you to be intentional about standardizing someplace that uplifts and supports your efforts to do great work.

Distractions steal your productivity in small, hidden chunks: messy papers on your home office desk, a chatty neighbor at the coffee shop, or choppy internet in your basement hideout—the one your kids haven't discovered yet. Challenge yourself to intentionally honor your psychological needs for a physical space that supports your high caliber business dream.

WORKSPACE

The physical space where you'll work will impact your productivity. Maybe a coworking space sounds enticing at first, but you later find the social aspect provides too much of a distraction. Or perhaps you foresee working from home, but then find the background noise of a coffee shop a better fit away from home distractions of laundry, TV, and kids.

Think about what makes you, you. Then plan for optimal productivity for the most efficient use of your time. Workspaces aren't one-size-fits-all. Let's explore.

List the pros and cons of each of the workspaces below:

Home Office

Home offices offer lots of distractions, but you can't beat saving on the overhead of cost of rent or the time savings of only having to walk down the hall. Plus, maybe you prefer the superwoman powers you get from tossing in a load of laundry between client calls. If you choose to work from home, think through safety measures and whether securing a P.O. Box or a virtual mailbox would be a smart alternative to sharing your home address with strangers.

Pros	Cons

Coworking Space

A coworking space often involves a paid membership and is a shared space individuals can use to work solo or collaboratively. Think through the advantages and disadvantages: What's included in the cost of rent? Do interruptions throw you off your a-game or do you thrive being around others? Will you lose productivity by driving to the coworking space every day when you could get started working right away at home? Do the space's hours align with your best working hours?

Pros	Cons

Brick and Mortar

A brick and mortar location is a physical space you buy or lease to operate your business from. Think through these questions: Would it be easy for customers to find? Is it located in a well-populated area where potential customers already travel for other reasons? Will the window front attract potential customers? Can you afford to pay the rent or mortgage?

Pros	Cons

Coffee Shop

Lots of people do their best work in a coffee shop. Something about the aroma of coffee beans mixed with the good-hearted nature of coffee lovers creates an ecosystem for good vibes. Does this environment work well for you? Let's consider: Will you have access to all you need, like a printer (probably not, but this doesn't matter if you won't be printing often), comfortable seating, and quiet space to hold meetings? What will you end up spending by paying for food at the coffee shop rather than making meals from home? Do other well-connected individuals meet at the coffee shop? If so, it might be an opportunity to expand your network or pick up a new client.

Pros	Cons

Alternative option: ....

Have an alternative option in mind to use as your workspace? List it here and outline the pros and cons.

Pros	Cons
....	....
....	....
....	....

Make plans for what your workspace will look, feel, and function like. For example, if you'll be working from home, how will you keep important papers organized? Or, if distractions are your nemesis, create boundaries around how you'll separate work time from social interactions or home responsibilities.

....

....

....

....

....

....

....

....

....

It may not be a corner office overlooking beautiful Manhattan, but your workspace is YOURS. You get to create an environment you love showing up to. Whether it's a quiet spare bedroom turned office at home or a local coffee shop down the road (cue all the amazing smells!), where you choose to work determines how you feel each day and how productive you'll be while you crank through to-do items. Choose wisely!

STEP

BREATHE LIFE INTO YOUR BUSINESS PLAN

Six years later, I pulled out the original business plan for Simply Integrated, LLC—my marketing business—as I organized my thoughts for this book. That precious little baby business was my ticket to freedom and all it took was the self-discipline to put dreams into words. Full disclosure—I skipped the financial section of the business plan altogether because 25-year-old me needed this book like a fish needs water.

It's no surprise the business I dreamt up in that 8-page business plan is nothing like what I'm running today. Of course, your business will change four or forty times. That's the point. Putting your thoughts into words = an action plan.

Action. Plan. Emphasis on *action*.

The purpose of a business plan is to have a starting point to mold, shape, and tweak your business as you go. Your business plan is a target for how you want your business to operate and evolve. It's a project you get to refine as you move closer and closer to your dream. It's your vision, your ticket to freedom, and your vehicle to grow and evolve.

Creating the vision starts with intention. It exposes gaps in your strategy that lead to clarity. Intention helps you ask questions you didn't know you needed to answer. Once your business plan is set, then you get to work backward crafting intentional results into smaller actionable to-dos. Your business plan can be one page (seriously!) or 100. It needs only to serve your intended purpose(s): secure capital, clarify your thoughts, or help convey your ideas to others.

Note the difference between where you were when you started this book and where you are now! Look at you, girl! You've thoroughly considered all aspects of your business. It's time to create your business plan.

Does this step feel intimidating? Don't let that imposter syndrome creep in. A business plan is a detailed outline of how your business will operate, what it stands for, what value it provides, and to whom. Its purpose is to empower you to develop a detailed focus for where your business is headed. Does this sound familiar? It should. The information in your business plan is in the sections you've already detailed in this book! Use it as a reference to add as much or as little detail as you need to be successful. Use the Business Plan Template provided in the back of the book and also available to download in the Founding Females™ Resource Suite to summarize all you've created.

Keep in mind if you'll be requesting loans or investments, a detailed business plan will be critical for showing others your well-rounded plan for becoming profitable.

The sections of your business plan will include:

1. **Executive Summary**. Provide a concise description of your business, your product or service offering, and the value your business provides.

2. **Company Description**. Detail what you do and who you do it for. Describe which strengths, assets, and competitive advantages make your business great.

3. **Market Analysis**. Describe your industry, what the competition looks like, and who your ideal client is.

4. **Organization and Management**. Explain how your company will operate, including its legal structure and an organizational chart of who answers to whom if you have employees.

5. **Marketing and Sales**. Describe your marketing strategy, how you'll gain and retain customers, what the buyer journey looks like from lead

to paying customer to repeat customer, and what your sales process looks like.

6. **Financial Projections**. Include your sales forecast and all financial documents that paint the picture for becoming profitable in your business.

7. **Appendix**. Include graphics, charts, and additional resources to illustrate the viability of your business.

Below is a very simple 1-page business plan template. It may be all you need to record your plans or simply a foundational start to build a more robust business plan later. The simplicity of it allows you to take your many beautiful thoughts and condense them into only the most important ones. Take a moment to flip down the corner of this page. You'll reference it often as you grow your business.

BUSINESS PLAN

1. EXECUTIVE SUMMARY

4. ORGANIZATION AND MANAGEMENT

LEGAL STRUCTURE _____

ORGANIZATIONAL CHART

2. COMPANY DESCRIPTION

3. MARKET ANALYSIS

5. MARKETING AND SALES SYNOPSIS

INDUSTRY DESCRIPTION

COMPETITION SUMMARY

6. FINANCIAL SYNOPSIS

IDEAL CLIENT PERSONA SUMMARY

7. APPENDIX (ATTACHED)

'PHASE THREE: BUILD' CONCLUSION

Girl, schedule that much needed massage or text your best gal pals to book a girls' night out! You deserve a celebration after all you have accomplished. **Phase Three: Build** isn't easy by any stretch and you managed it beautifully! Your brain might feel like mush, but you.took.action! You have a beautiful business plan serving as the blueprint for the future you've been dreaming of. Go celebrate!

How do you feel about your dream business becoming a reality? Can you see the smiles on your customers' faces? Can you feel the freedom that comes with entrepreneurship?

Next up is the launch phase where you'll introduce the world to your amazing business! Hang onto your handbag! This, my friend, will be incredible!

NOTES

NOTES

"GROWTH AND COMFORT DO NOT COEXIST."

Ginni Rometty, CEO IBM

PHASE FOUR
LAUNCH

Congrats! You created a legit business (get it, girl!!), *and* since you're technically ready to trade value for money, you may be tempted to step straight into operation mode. After all, there's a chance you already have a few clients or find yourself bringing in sales from your site. Mark my words: skipping the launch phase would be a huge disservice to the hard work you've invested!

Here's why...

You cannot assume people will suddenly know you're in business. You have to tell them by creating buzz with a launch. Planning and executing an official launch will grace you with an abundance of benefits like:

- ▸ forward momentum long after the launch concludes,

- ▸ drilling down your marketing message to perfection, and

- ▸ a rich opportunity for developing repeat touch points with your excited new audience.

I can look back at my clients' data and clearly tell whether or not they curated a well-planned launch. That's because when something new happens, Sally next door becomes nosy and wants all the deets on what the hype is about. (That's a good thing!) Sally goes to Bible study, her kids' little league games, and workout classes at the gym. Since Sally loves being the epicenter of new buzz, she wants to be the one to share the news with her circle of influence—that's right, who then also become potential customers. Sally's gal pals are just like her and also highly likely to become paying customers because of social proof. If Sally's excited about your offering, they will become excited, too.

And guess what? There are lots of Sallys whose ears perk up at the sound of something "hot and fresh out the kitchen." These consumers are called "innovators" and "early adopters." They're gold to your business because they're the ones who love to be first to try something new. They crave to experience something new before everyone else. Then, like a badge of honor, they tell others about it. Your launch is prime real estate for igniting invaluable word of mouth—the greatest marketing you could ever conjure! The reality: If you fail to execute a launch, you will miss capitalizing on all the sweet benefits that come with it. It's a use it or lose it opportunity, and you've worked too hard to pass this up.

Truly, the opening stage of starting a business is an opportunity to create a great deal of buzz and word of mouth that will trickle through and help you maintain forward momentum. It's a chance for your friends and family to gain a true understanding of this pivot you've initiated in yourself into the role of business owner. It's *your* moment to introduce your new endeavor to the world!

Let's talk about **Phase Four: Launch.** There's no way around it except to *put in the work* to send your business soaring. Form the connections. Execute the content. Focus on the target created by your goals. And finally, release your business into the world. This section will provide guidance for how to make the most impact with your business launch. Keep in mind, from planning to execution, a launch takes weeks, not days. Repeat touch points are crucial for developing rapport with your audience so they trust you, and we'll talk about how to deliver those.

In **Phase Four: Launch**, we'll identify what you want to accomplish with defined goals and objectives and design your message based on what's most likely to resonate with your ideal client and what it will sound like to walk them through the Buying Cycle. You'll pinpoint your promotion plan and which marketing channels you'll leverage.

Then, it's go time! Don't worry—I will shine a bright light on what your 5-week launch sequence will look like and what each week's content will entail. We'll also talk about how to keep those new customers coming back, keeping you in business, and letting you continue to wake up to a business you're totally in love with.

In **Phase Four: Launch**, you will be guided through how to do the following:

- ▶ **Step 1:** Design Your Launch Message
- ▶ **Step 2:** Prep Your Launch
- ▶ **Step 3:** Execute Your Launch
- ▶ **Step 4:** Carry Out Post Launch Promotions

Let's get started launching your business. **You've got this!**

STEP

DESIGN YOUR LAUNCH MESSAGE

I sneaked quietly into business ownership. In my heart, I had just failed at my dream career in the spa industry. My spirit was crushed. I needed a season to lick my wounds as vulnerability seeped from every one of my pores. The last thing I wanted was to shout from the rooftops to the friends and family I needed so desperately in that season of life that I actually thought I had what it took to make something of myself in my own business. I often think about what would have happened if I rode the wave of new business excitement and felt confident telling others about my new endeavor.

Fast forward three years. A new client of mine nearly shook as she shared her business idea with me. The expression on her face told me she was ready, but her voice cracked as she nervously shared her plans. Eventually, she managed to get it out, and the idea was hella good.

Fast forward another two years. Word of mouth was spreading about the results I helped entrepreneurs create. I had become a go-to business consultant for guiding women into their own businesses. In one instance, I was coaching a client through creating her digital presence and the beginning stages of managing her new business. She, too, wanted to quietly slide into business ownership without all the "look at me" she thought came with a launch. By that point, I knew better, and I wasn't about to allow imposter syndrome to spoil the momentum that comes with an incredible business launch.

Why do we try so hard to make ourselves small? The world needs what we have to offer. The dream sewn into our hearts is ours to bring to life and share with others. Do you know how many things we, as women, are capable of?! We accomplish brag-worthy feats before 8am. We rally entire communities. We go to battle for our little ones. We're the glue in our own households. In the words of Beyoncé, we're "strong enough to bear the children, then get back to bid-ness." What she means is that we squeeze watermelons out of our nether regions and return to work six weeks later. We are the literal bomb.com!

We crush it at life and yet, we allow the fear of what others think slow our momentum when it comes to sharing our new business venture with the world. You can't build a successful business without telling people about it, so let's all agree *not* to do that.

Let's all agree to be gosh darn ecstatic when a fellow female launches a business and trust we'll receive that mutual support in return.

Since we're all agreeing we will *not* skip out on creating incredible business launches because of how valuable they are, let's talk about how to design a launch that's freaking amazing!

CREATE REALISTIC LAUNCH GOALS AND OBJECTIVES

To create realistic goals, think honestly about what results your time and resources can produce. Anticipate a learning curve as you complete some tasks for the first time. Scale your expectations up over time. As you play forward what your successes will look like, take into account that your efforts will compound, and successes will build upon each other. In turn, you'll produce increasingly successful results. For instance, it may not be realistic to expect a full book of business by the end of your launch, but if you could sign your first client, consider it a huge win!

Then, build from there. Put into action with your first client what you've learned in this book—nurture them, ask for a review, market the review, and implement a referral program, for instance. As you consistently execute these strategies, your efforts will compound to drive more clients, more sales, and more success.

Quantify your launch goals, such as "gaining your first fifty email subscribers in the first five weeks" or "meeting and following up with three new business contacts at a networking event each week focused on spreading the word about your new business." Each one of these goals adds up, keeps you accountable, and compounds to create your success.

Reflect: What would you like the results of your launch to be? Identify your target and then work backward to identify the mini objectives you'll need to meet on a daily and weekly basis to hit those launch goals.

Here is an example of how we set a goal and work backward: Say you set a goal for 100 transactions in your first month of business. Assuming a 3% conversion rate, you know you'll need to drive 3,333 visitors to your website. To do that, you decide to create "seven days of giveaways." You'll promote the upcoming giveaway for two weeks, run the giveaway week, and follow up with a week of customer reviews for social proof.

Your launch goal is *what* you want to accomplish, and mini objectives are *how* you'll do it.

Launch Goal: 100 transactions, or an average of 3.3 transactions per day.

Mini Objectives:

1. Use email marketing, YouTube, networking, and social media to drive an average of 100 website visitors per day.

2. Use an announcement banner on your website promoting your business launch, social proof through customer reviews (it's fine if they were beta users), and a "related products" section at the bottom of every product page to entice sales.

3. Customize your abandoned cart email with customer reviews, FAQs, and a free shipping code to capture otherwise lost sales.

Now outline your launch goals and corresponding mini objectives.

Launch Goal #1   **Mini Objectives**

Launch Goal #2   **Mini Objectives**

....

          ....

          ....

Launch Goal #3   **Mini Objectives**

....

          ....

          ....

DEVELOP YOUR BUYING JOURNEY MESSAGING

When it comes to creating sales, familiarity wins. The concept of "repeat touchpoints" in marketing refers to potential customers' tendency to need to hear a message multiple times first in order to consider buying. Consistently showing up for your audience is crucial to help them:

1. understand what you do and who you do it for

2. know, like, and trust you

3. consider buying from you.

Without developing this level of rapport with your audience, you risk your message sounding like: **"BUY MY STUFF! BUY MY STUFF! BUY MY STUFF!"**

To start, refer back to the customer's problem you identified in **Phase One: Clarify**. Consider how your customer describes it. What words do they use? How does it make them feel? What are they trying to achieve? What are they currently doing to solve it?

Next, consider what customers might be asking in their minds about your business and offering from these four vantage points of the Buying Cycle:

1. **Awareness - Someone learning about your business for the first time:** What information do they need in order to consider buying from you?

2. **Consideration - Someone considering whether your offering or your competitor's offering is a better fit:** What should you highlight about your value proposition that positions your offering as the winner?

3. **Purchase - Someone who has researched and is ready to buy:** This is where calls to action to buy and expiring bonuses can be effective. What information will help them make the decision? At this point, "Buy my stuff!" should sound more like, "I can help you!"

4. **After-Sale - Someone who has already bought from you:** What do they need to hear and experience in order to become a repeat customer?

These four perspectives describe the buyer's journey through the Buying Cycle as they come to make a buying decision. Lead your audience where you want them to go with calls to action to learn the information they need (outlined above) to travel to the next phase. Consider the following two examples of leading your customer through an experience purposefully:

Scenario #1: A boutique owner leads her social media followers to her website where visitors can read her blog, download her value-packed guide about gift-giving (in exchange for their email, of course), and join her email list. From there, the business owner develops rapport with the audience through a weekly newsletter and delivers value-packed information helping them come to know, like, and trust her as the authority on gift-giving. When leads are ready to make a buying decision, they'll think of her gift baskets. Paying customers then receive a different set of emails helping them better understand how to write thoughtful cards and get the most value from their purchase. Occasionally, the business owner sends an "upsell" email.

Scenario #2: A business owner creates a makeup tutorial YouTube channel and delivers value-packed videos. She includes a link in the video descriptions leading viewers to a free mini course in exchange for their email. Abiding by GDPR, she makes sure to get permission to send recurring messages. Within the course, the business owner delivers information on how to address a common makeup-related problem and offers three consulting packages which have been carefully crafted to meet the need customers struggle with. At the end of the consultation series, she invites them into a paid community where members find peers discussing tips and tricks as they hone their new makeup skills.

The bottom line is to be intentional about the messages you send with an end goal in mind so you can deliver offers to help based on their problem.

Remember, the goal of the Buying Cycle is to first build rapport and trust, then highlight your business as a solution to their need, present a call to action to buy, nurture the existing customer, and finally invite a repeat sale. Start with the marketing channels and messaging you determined in **Phase Three: Build, Step 5: Draw Up Your Marketing Plan**. Then, use this space to develop your launch message from the four phases of the Buying Cycle and to reflect on how you'll carefully lead your audience into each next stage of the buying process.

Here's an example of what each phase of the Buying Cycle looks like with the lead entering the Buying Cycle through the marketing channel, Pinterest.

	AWARENESS	CONSIDERATION	PURCHASE	AFTER-SALE
ENTRY POINT: PINTEREST	The lead learns about your business	The lead considers buying your offering	The lead decides to buy and becomes a paying customer	The customer becomes a loyal fan and repurchases
	What it looks like: Browsing Pinterest, the lead clicks through to a blog post about mindset tips. She likes the post and decides to opt into the mindset coach's email list. She receives the welcome email and the nurture series that follows.	**What it looks like:** The lead finds herself looking forward to each email. The series helps her feel out the coach's personality. The lead feels like she could use mindset coaching and she clicks a link in an email to check on pricing. There, she sees a call to action to sign up for a free 15-minute consultation and thinks, "Why not?."	**What it looks like:** On the free consult call, the mindset coach executes a great sales call, asking the lead about her mindset struggles, providing a roadmap for transformation, and discussing pricing options. The lead decides to purchase five coaching sessions.	**What it looks like:** The client loved her five coaching calls. She now uses her new mindset skills often. The client receives weekly newsletters. Then Black Friday rolls around and she takes advantage of a great deal on the coach's new mini course. All the while, the client raves to everyone she knows about her mindset coach.

Now it's your turn. For each of your selected marketing channels, outline the customer's Buying Cycle journey from lead to paying customer, to repeat customer. If you need more space, use the notes page at the end of the chapter or download the template at the Founding Females™ Resource Suite at www.HerBusinessGuide.com.

ENTRY POINT: _____

AWARENESS	CONSIDERATION	PURCHASE	AFTER-SALE
The lead learns about your business	The lead considers buying your offering	The lead decides to buy and becomes a paying customer	The customer becomes a loyal fan and repurchases
What it looks like:	What it looks like:	What it looks like:	What it looks like:

ENTRY POINT: _____

AWARENESS	CONSIDERATION	PURCHASE	AFTER-SALE
The lead learns about your business	The lead considers buying your offering	The lead decides to buy and becomes a paying customer	The customer becomes a loyal fan and repurchases
What it looks like:	What it looks like:	What it looks like:	What it looks like:

ENTRY POINT: _____

AWARENESS	CONSIDERATION	PURCHASE	AFTER-SALE
The lead learns about your business	The lead considers buying your offering	The lead decides to buy and becomes a paying customer	The customer becomes a loyal fan and repurchases
What it looks like:	What it looks like:	What it looks like:	What it looks like:

ENTRY POINT: _____

AWARENESS	CONSIDERATION	PURCHASE	AFTER-SALE
The lead learns about your business	The lead considers buying your offering	The lead decides to buy and becomes a paying customer	The customer becomes a loyal fan and repurchases
What it looks like:	What it looks like:	What it looks like:	What it looks like:

Girl, you're set. You've mapped out how to strategically welcome newcomers into your ecosystem and then lead them intentionally into a sale. Now let's talk through one more foundational piece of your launch: becoming the hype girl.

PREPARE TO BECOME THE HYPE GIRL

With a savvy strategy for funneling leads into paying customers, you're ready to step into building your audience for the exciting business launch to come. Spoiler Alert! It's likely your audience is small at this point. Ain't no shame. Honestly, girl, that's no surprise. Don't let that hold you back from shouting from the rooftops about something exciting coming. There's something extra special and valuable about the people who jump on board from the beginning. These are your O.G.s. With hard work, your audience will grow, and you'll look back at the small sprinkle of loyal followers who cheered you on from the very beginning.

I've never heard of anyone who turned down a good secret, so you should plan to create build-up leading up to the event. We're humans and humans love learning about new and exciting announcements, and we definitely love being the first to know about anything new with sneak peeks, countdown reminders, interviews, polls, and giveaways. Can you feel the excitement?! Let's cover some basic tips to keep in mind.

LAUNCH PREP TIPS

When it comes to launching, you only get one shot. Plan ahead and consider how you'll create a consistent message to inform and delight.

1. Tell your audience what to expect in advance. Repeat it early and often. A good marketing strategy takes weeks, not days.

2. Have a "one-sheeter" ready and available to send through different channels like email, text, or social media direct message for audience members who ask for more information. Remember—be prepared to

make it easy for the audience to understand what you do and how to buy from you.

3. Reach out to your immediate network to share the exciting news. Your circle of family, community, and friends are in your corner and can help you build positive momentum.

4. Repeat the message several times in several different ways. You may feel like a broken record, but that's what it takes to convey a clear message in a noisy space. Not everyone will hear your message every time. Repeat touch points are your secret to success.

5. Create anticipation by previewing upcoming excitement.

6. Set your launch date and build in a few buffer days in case any last-minute kinks come up so you can be as stress-free as possible.

7. Timing is everything. Select a launch week by looking ahead to avoid big holidays, events, or distraction that will clutter the online space. Then work backward setting your messages and events.

8. Whether your launch is all online or contains an in-person component, automate anything you can to be present for your launch instead of attending to details you could have planned days or weeks in advance, including social media posts, blog posts, and emails. You'll be more confident and collected.

9. Word of mouth is the strongest form of marketing. Keep in mind the key ingredient behind word of mouth is the time it takes for those engagements to trickle through a community—start early and talk about your message often!

10. Launches are exhausting so build rest into your schedule after your launch week by cutting back your working hours for the week (don't go completely dark). Plan and schedule content in advance to capitalize on the momentum you worked so hard to create. Building your business is a marathon. Keep at it, sis!

11. Dress the part. You're creating first impressions, and it's especially important to represent your brand and professionalism in the way you look. This doesn't mean a massage therapist should wear a suit. Rather,

a massage therapist should look like a well-polished massage therapist with clean, well-fitting scrubs and her hair tied back if it's what she looks like while she's performing the service. You are an extension of your brand, so if you show up looking unprofessional before you've earned credibility, don't expect to earn the audience's trust. What will your wardrobe need to include? What will your schedule need to look like to ensure you have adequate time to look presentable each time you are in front of potential customers over the coming 4-8 weeks?

Scan the landscape ahead. Plan your next move, then your next, and your next all the way up to reaching your target. A runner doesn't decide the day before to sign up for a marathon. She creates the desired end results, carefully carves out time to train, plans around rainy days, and tweaks and pivots her training schedule against its original blueprint months in advance.

The mark of an incredible chess player is how many moves she can see ahead. The best chess players learn how to mentally map out the outcomes of multiple moves, often looking ahead eight moves.

Map out your launch. Plan your next eight moves. Decide what results you'll pursue. Then work backward planning each action intentionally according to how to best support your goals.

STEP

PREP YOUR LACK

Brand-new-entrepreneur-me wishes she knew that executing an official launch would have given me an unparalleled leg up. Now, thinking of the missed clarity, inertia, and confidence a detailed launch would have provided makes me smack my hands against both cheeks in agony super dramatic-like. Certainly, this is one hard lesson gained from starting my business without a roadmap. Introducing you to the launch process and knowing how you'll benefit from my marketing misfortune makes it all worth it.

Don't believe there's only one perfect mix of promotional strategies. How you promote your launch must feel (semi-)natural to you. I include the caveat of (semi-)natural because of course you're stepping into uncharted territory, and you must also commit to getting comfy outside your comfort zone. Just do it in a way that feels most authentically like you.

Now, ready for a good pep talk? Let's discuss how you might create buzz to help the word spread about your business.

Here are some promotional ideas:

Family and friends

Reach out to friends, family, your community, and acquaintances individually to share your exciting news. They'll feel excited to be one of the first to know your good news. Let them know what you've built and that you're working hard to prepare for your launch. Be sure to let them know that you'll keep them updated along the way and their support means the world. Give them a call to action, such as "Keep your eyes open for upcoming messages and please open each one for further details." Then, when you follow up, don't forget to reiterate what you're working toward and who you're hoping to help since we can never be certain every one of them will open each email. Plus, a recap is always helpful for driving the information home because, "Hello, busy life."

Record your list of contacts:

....

....

....

....

....

Develop a launch team

Organize a close group of people who will share your message at pre-planned times with their network. Start by creating a list of the people you know who would be willing to help spread your message. Ask them for support and let them know you'll be eager for the opportunity to support them in their upcoming endeavors, too.

Develop the goals for your launch team:

- ☐ Share curated social media graphics, emails, and other communications.

- ☐ Engage with your posted content with likes and comments.

- ☐ Create their own posts about your business launch.

- ☐ Create the schedule and plan for communicating with your launch team.

- ☐ Keep your team in the know. Share wins, successes, and celebrations so they can feel your energy as you go through the launch process.

Develop a spreadsheet to keep track of those who have accepted, and don't forget to thank them for helping promote your business.

Record who you'll ask to be on your launch team:

....

....

....

....

....

Grand Opening

Decide whether you'd like to host an in-person or virtual Grand Opening. If you do, begin developing the details, such as:

☐ Location: _____

☐ Date and time: _____

☐ Invitation list:

....

....

....

....

☐ What the physical invitations will look like or if you'll create a digital invite:

....

....

....

....

☐ Schedule of events:

☐ Entertainment (giveaways, music, food, welcome message & presentation); describe:

☐ What your primary calls to action will be:

☐ What follow-up will look like:

Press Kit

Build a simple press kit reflective of your business and containing all the essential information someone should know about it. Consider who you'd like to develop key collaborations and partnerships with and send your press kit out to:

- ☐ Bloggers
- ☐ Social media influencers
- ☐ Community leaders
- ☐ Podcasters
- ☐ Local media
- ☐ Speaking opportunity organizers

Here's what to include in your press kit:

- ☐ Company description
- ☐ Your bio
- ☐ Description of your product or service offering
- ☐ Description of your target audience
- ☐ Visuals highlighting your work, such as a graphic of the cover of your eBook
- ☐ Sample topics which fall under your expertise
- ☐ Ways you can help bring awareness to the audience you're pitching to
- ☐ Frequently asked questions
- ☐ Contact information
- ☐ A professional headshot
- ☐ Photo(s) of your product (if applicable)
- ☐ Other: _____

Content Strategy

Plan, create, and schedule your content leading up to, during, and after your launch, including social media posts, blog posts, email marketing, and videos. Use pre-recorded videos on social media and duplicate these for use on your website. Live videos can be one-on-one interviews or events.

Calendar of Events

Create a calendar of events and share it with your audience. Events could include:

- ☐ Website reveal
- ☐ Blog debut
- ☐ Live appearances
- ☐ Giveaways
- ☐ Collaborative interviews on podcasts, webinars, and social lives
- ☐ Grand Opening event
- ☐ Ribbon cutting ceremony with the local Chamber of Commerce
- ☐ Organized event with a nonprofit organization whose cause is related to your business. The goal is to spread the message of your new business and align the news with a positive cause.

Lead Magnet

Create a branded lead magnet, which is a valuable checklist or resource related to your business, that the audience can receive and connect your brand with the value you offer customers. The lead magnet should support your goals, not detract from them. For example, a florist would not want to create a checklist teaching people how to DIY their floral arrangements from grocery store bouquets because that doesn't involve buying from her. Instead, she could provide a lead magnet that guides the audience through selecting the right flowers for certain occasions to empower them with that knowledge when buying her product.

240   DREAM, BUILD, GROW

PRO TIP: Fall in love with the process. In the beginning, it's not always easy to see the fruits of your labor, which can feel discouraging at times. I've coached countless women through the "before it worked" stage of their business which is characterized by "planting seeds." Often, they become fearful because their investment of effort isn't creating instant tangible results. Inevitably, they think they're doing something wrong. I remind them there's a lot that happens under the surface after the seed is planted and before it grows into a beautiful flower. Creating your first business will be unlike anything you've ever done. Embrace the challenge, find something you love about each phase, and resolve to keep moving forward. If you feel yourself becoming discouraged, revisit your Why statement and ask yourself, "What steps can I take today to move closer to my goals?" Focus on the next step in front of you, not the whole staircase.

What other ways can you promote your business during your launch?

....

....

....

Your business launch will require lots of moving pieces. Prepping how you'll execute each detail will allow you to carry out your timeline with precision. You now know how to create repeat touch points, develop rapport, craft a strong brand, and repeat your talk track to gain familiarity to help customers move from lead to paying customer. Having an organized plan for what message should be pushed out on which platform will allow you to confidently focus on connecting your message to your goals and serving your audience well.

STEP

EXECUTE YOUR LAUNCH

Girl, let's do the darn thing. You know you're doing it correctly if you feel wisps of butterfly wings in your stomach.

Or maybe launching your business feels as comfortable as a long overdue coffee date with your best girlfriend.

Either way, I'm proud of you! Like you, I want the world to know about your grit, perseverance, and amazing business!

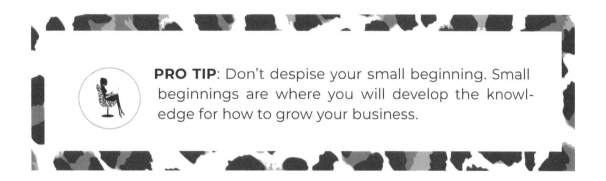

PRO TIP: Don't despise your small beginning. Small beginnings are where you will develop the knowledge for how to grow your business.

The beginning stages are where I see new entrepreneurs feel the most imposter syndrome. Don't let your small beginning deter you from stepping out in front of the audience you have. If one person is showing up, love hard on that one person because one person will turn into two, then into four, then into four hundred. Maybe fewer people than you'd like will hear your message now, but as your audience grows, they'll be able to consume your content and think, "Look how far she's come"—a true marker of progress and development.

You can't wait until you have the audience to step out and start talking. Stepping out now helps drive the audience to you. Small beginnings allow the flexibility to pivot as you see fit (while fewer people are watching!) so it's good practice to build confidence. Take pride in creating something new. Take pride in your insatiable curiosity to learn. This attitude helps open conversations with veteran Founding Females™ who have been where you want to go and can shed insight to sharpen your journey. Small beginnings are a good thing for so many reasons! Embrace yours.

Now that you have the vision for what you want your launch to look like, it's time to DO the darn thing! Remember that 5-week prep sequence I promised to walk you through to take you from business plan to open-for-business? Well, here it is!

WEEK 1: PREP WEEK

Use Week 1 to create content, prepare your thoughts, and organize your marketing channels. During this week, you might consider the following:

Outline Your Messaging Strategy

Put pen to paper or type out line-by-line what your message sounds like. Imagine you're sitting across from the reader who's hearing your messages at various places along the Buying Cycle. If you need a refresher, turn back to **Phase Four: Launch, Step 1: Design Your Launch Message** and what your launch messages will sound like according to each phase. As you craft your message, you'll want to first give a broad overview of what you do and who you do it for. Form a connection by helping the listener feel your experience with the pain your offering meets. Pinpoint what people typically do to try to solve this pain and why it doesn't work. Give a brief but detailed synopsis of your offering, and then make an offer to help.

In this step, form the words for how you'll convey this information. That way, you can refine your message so it sounds clear, confident, and non-salesy.

A content calendar can also be helpful for scheduling which messages go out on which channels and when, including social media posts, blog content, in-person events, social media event details, podcast interviews, video recordings, emails, etc. Find a sample content calendar in the appendix and in the Founding Females™ Resource Suite.Leverage your content in as many ways as possible, but be sure to tailor the message for each channel.

Online community. Become active in online community conversations several times per week on social media, in networking events, and in forums. Make sure you're not just joining groups of peers. For example, if you're a health coach, you'll want to make sure the group members include ideal clients, not other health coaches. Your contribution to the conversation should be just that—conversational. Poorly positioned sales pitches create the 'wince effect' among readers. Instead, contribute to the conversation the same way you would sitting around the table with girlfriends. When there's an opportune moment to offer insight based on your zone of genius, give value and always ask permission to message someone with more info if you think you can help meet their pain. Remember, "Here's how I can help!" *not* "Buy my stuff!" Developing rapport among an audience is crucial for your time investment to pay off.

Personal contacts. Reach out to friends and family (text, email, social media message, phone call, drop by—whatever feels natural to you) to let them know about your new business launch and invite them to begin following your social accounts for support. These people already love you and want you to succeed. However, in my experience, an invitation to become part of the success story always yields better results than assuming they'll support you. As much as you appreciate clearly understanding how you can be most helpful in a given situation, so will they. Provide a few examples of what kind of support could be most beneficial (especially if they aren't an entrepreneur), like sharing posts, tagging friends in the comments, or telling others through word-of-mouth about the accounts.

Content planning. Plan and schedule content in advance. You can batch content creation responsibilities for efficiency, then add them to a content scheduler to "go live" appropriately at your selected time and date instead of having to execute each post in real time. In fact, I urge you to develop a process where you plan for when content will be released, load it into a scheduler, and let the process do the rest. Relying on yourself personally to execute the posts when they're supposed to go out is a grave mistake. Inevitably life takes over, you don't get around to posting, and suddenly your marketing content becomes inconsistent. Make sure all schedulable content is ready to go with a date and time selected. For instance, you can create blog posts on your site, then set them to remain a draft until a certain date and time you determine. At that selected date and time, your post will go live without you having to do anything at all. See our Founding Females™ list of favorite, vetted social media schedulers at www.HerBusinessGuide.com.

Launch your online presence. Finalize your website or create a landing page to capture leads' email addresses. If you're able to finish your website before your official launch, great! If you aren't, a simple landing page could serve a similar purpose as a place to send the audience and capture their contact information to begin generating a list of interested subscribers.

A landing page is a simple, one-page website. Some email marketing platforms provide the option to create a single, customizable page that can serve the same purpose. The landing page should be branded to your business. On your landing page, simply and succinctly provide information about what you do, who you do it for, how to buy from you, and how to get in contact with you. Be sure to capture each potential customer's name and email address so you can deliver repeat value and sales messages after the launch is over.

Email marketing. Test your welcome series to make sure it works. As we discussed in **Phase Three: Build, Step 6: Dream Up Your Digital Space,** a welcome series is a sequence of emails a subscriber receives automatically upon subscribing. Creating a welcome series involves thinking intentionally about how your new lead will travel along the Buying Cycle. For instance, your first email won't sound like, "Buy my stuff!" Rather, you'll welcome and nurture the lead, develop rapport, and eventually make an offer to help over the course of several emails. Your email should have one call to action leading the reader to take some kind of intentional action (visiting your website, responding to the email, signing up for a free webinar, joining your online community, or purchasing a product, for example).

Launch team. Communicate with your launch team and review the plan for the coming weeks. "Communicate" is the key word here. You're intimately familiar with how you want the launch to look, but it's likely they are not. We're all humans and in the core of our being, I believe we all want to sprinkle goodness around like confetti and do well by others.

However, it's no secret most of us live busy lives, so put yourself in members of your launch team's high heels. Communicate clearly what you'd like them to do, when, and why. Provide access to all the resources they'll need via desktop and mobile. Make their job insanely simple and easy to complete for the best results. Then, when they do knock it out of the park, hype them up by giving out double high fives generously. It goes without saying that if some members of your launch team don't meet the mark, have grace. At the end of the day, we're all just trying to make it and life is b-u-s-y! It's likely you won't have a 100% participation rate, so aim to invite more members onto your launch team than you think are necessary to achieve your desired results.

Push your own limits. Go live on social media to create anticipation for the exciting week ahead. Girl, you read that right! I said, "Go live." You've got this. So, what if nobody shows up? You've got to start and when you make it a habit, it gets easier.

Countdown to launch. Post countdowns and encourage your audience with exciting reasons to tune into the conversation, like upcoming giveaways, planned interviews, and expiring bonuses. Creating anticipation is a great way to earn positive attention. Embedded in countdowns are repeat touch-points. You're creating excitement about what's ahead. Plus, countdowns give you a reason to tell them *why* they don't want to miss out on the big announcement. It helps them lock in their own plan to be present.

Check and double check. Double check all details for your Grand Opening event. Play the event forward from 24-hours prior to the event all the way to 24-hours after the event, step by step, day-by-day. (Cue the *Full House* theme song here, or don't if I'm dating myself). Think about who else has a role in the event and reach out to make sure they understand all responsibilities. Put yourself in your attendees' Chuck Taylors—consider what experience you want tied to your brand, how you want them to talk about the event after-ward, how you'll inspire them, what emotions you'll evoke with your stories, and your desired end results. Then, plan to fail. WHAT?!

Plan B, C, and D. Yes, plan to fail. By that, I mean plan out two or three worst-case scenarios and how you'll smoothly pivot if things don't go as planned. Your worst fear holds no power over you if you know how you'll deal with it. Coach yourself to smile through it all with ease and joy. Even though the chance of worst-case-scenarios happening is unlikely, by thinking through alternative outcomes, you'll allow your brain to think more quickly if there are small hiccups along the way.

Get the bonuses in place. Plan out expiring bonuses for launch week. Expiring bonuses are perks your audience can take advantage of ONLY during launch week. They help those customers who are on the fence decide to buy by offering a little something extra—a reward, if you will—that will help your early adopters feel special VIP status. Appropriate expiring bonuses depend on your business model and offering, but here are some examples to get your mind turning: a free one-on-one coaching session with you, a buy-one-gift-one-to-a-friend arrangement, access to an exclusive training, free gift with purchase, or a detailed how-to workbook.

Prepare print material. Develop print material like flyers or postcards and plan out how you'll deliver them. One of my all-time favorite business resources is Canva (www.Canva.com), an online design and publishing tool. Canva is an incredible option for printing marketing materials. Be sure to plan this well in advance since you'll need time to create the graphics, have them mailed to you, address them, add postage, drop them in the mailbox in time to be delivered early enough for recipients to plan to attend your launch. By the way, some Chambers of Commerce offer a bulk mail rate as one of their membership benefits, which can be a significant savings on postage. If you're planning to become a Chamber member anyway, don't miss out on this benefit. You might even be incorporating a ribbon cutting with the local Chamber of Commerce as your grand opening event, so brainstorm with your Chamber contact person to make sure you're capitalizing on all its opportunities. I pinky promise I'm not a Chamber affiliate; I just know good connection opportunities when I see 'em.

🖋 **EXPERT LAUNCH TIP: You're laying the foundation work for a great outcome with rich 20/20 hindsight experience. The work you do this week will support your efforts in the weeks to come.**

WEEK 2: PRIME THE AUDIENCE WITH CONVERSATION

If you suddenly open your business's doors and expect customers to buy from you immediately, you're going to feel disappointed because that's highly unlikely to happen. It's not you, friend. It's just how business, marketing, and psychology work. For your message to stick, you must tell people about the excitement that's about to happen, then tell them while the excitement is happening, and finally, tell people about the opportunities they missed. (Yes! Let them know they missed out so they don't make the same mistake next time.).

Repeat this process continually. Err on the side of over-communicating because eventually you'll see repeating your message (even when you feel like a broken record) is what the audience needs in order to take action. Why? Because we live in a world with so. much. noise. In order for your message to cut through the noise, you must show up consistently to the conversation with your potential customers. Offer value. Follow up with reminders. Repeat.

In the life of your business, it's possible you'll catch a few people who need your offering the moment you tell them about it for the first time. More often, you'll "plant seeds" for the future. That means the majority of your audience won't need your offering at the moment, but your message will position your offering as the solution to a future need they'll encounter. When they do encounter that need, they'll already be primed to buy. That's why good marketing takes time, and that's why you shouldn't become discouraged if you're not up to your eyeballs in sales in the first month.

Here's one example. There's a well-known network marketing company that sells these magical hair care products. Suave has suited me just fine for most of my life, so even though I'm connected with several women who sell this magical shampoo and receive their marketing messages weekly, I've never been enticed to become a long-standing customer. The message was strong, but my need wasn't. That is, until I noticed losing more hair than usual in the shower. Maybe this is a joyous gift from hitting mid-30s. Maybe it's from a change in diet, workout routine, or stress. Whatever the root cause (punny, eh?), I suddenly need magical hair care products, and I know who to throw my money at.

This week in your launch prep it's time to begin priming your audience to buy, just like I was primed to buy magical shampoo, but it doesn't stop after this week. You'll continue the conversation throughout the life of your business, at every opportunity. Prime the audience to buy by showing up to the conversation consistently and authentically. Tell people about the value you provide. Make offers to help them. Show up even when it feels like it's not working (this is the magic key in entrepreneurship everyone's looking for). This committed approach starts now during your business launch and should continue through the life of your business.

Let's recap what this process should sound and feel like. Use what you researched in Phase Two: Research **and leverage the community around you.**

1. Participate in conversations already happening online. What you contribute to those conversations should reflect your views, interests, and life outside of business. Be present and engage in meaningful conversations so your audience hears your voice and begins to build familiarity and trust. There's a time and a place for selling, and even then, selling should sound like offers to help.

2. Purposefully invite the audience into a one-to-one conversation through a meeting conference platform (Zoom coffee date, for example), voice messages, in-person meetings (make sure you trust the other person!), and phone calls. A genuine interest in connection and learning about the other person's life should shine brightest. You can't fake that. Commit to connection for the sake of connection. Commit to care.

3. Attend in-person events. There's something magical and relationship-fusing about eye contact and experiencing someone's body language, tone of voice, and facial expressions *in person*. That's why I always prioritize in-person networking events over virtual opportunities. Both are good, but in-person is better for forming genuine relationships. When I'm in a position to gain clients, I commit to one networking event per week until my book of business is full. If my book of business is full, I scale back slightly, but still commit to attending.

4. Consider creating a support group or monthly/weekly meeting for your audience and facilitate meaningful conversation in a trusted space. Again, connection and trust win.

5. Pay special attention to how your audience speaks and describes their world. Mirror their language and body language. This will help the connection feel like you understand and are like them.

6. Invite the audience to the online and in-person events you create. We all want a crowd who understands us. Plus, you'll be positioned as a leader who knows what she's doing.

✎ **EXPERT LAUNCH TIP: Be consistent and show up through the marketing channels you selected in** Phase Three: Build **with a focus on contributing to the conversation.**

WEEK 3: TALK ABOUT THE PROBLEM YOUR IDEAL CLIENT FACES

Friend, our human brains perpetually seek solutions. Innately, we look for ways to do life better. Dialoguing through the problem you know your ideal client faces situates you on the same team.

In Week 3, it's time to help your audience understand that you have a deep sense of understanding about the problem they face. You, too, have been personally victimized by the absurdity of the problem's existence.

It's time to tell stories about your life experiences and describe the problem in detail so the audience knows you also understand the tiredness of parenthood, the agony of an unclear dress code, the deep devastation of caring for a child in pain, or the confusion behind waking up to 24 brand new hours, yet still getting nothing done every.single.day.

Here are this week's to-dos:

1. Reach out once more to your one-on-one connections sharing all that has transpired over the last two weeks. Aim to stay on their radar. Express your appreciation for their support. Ask if they know anyone who might be interested in the topic. If you're hosting a Grand Opening event, invite them to save the date.

2. Create and deliver necessary content and information for your key collaborations and partnerships. For instance, if you're collaborating for a giveaway, share the details, graphics, and written copy with your co-host. Or if you plan to interview a leader in your industry, send the questions in advance with all the details they need to know to make it an excellent experience.

3. Nurture the new relationships you developed in Weeks 1 and 2. Reach out to say hi. See what's going on in their lives. Support their posts on social media.

4. Keep your launch team up to date and give them specific tasks and calls to action.

5. Talk about your audience's problem in your marketing channels so the audience knows you understand what they're going through. Convey that you understand the problem, too.

6. Offer to guide the audience from where they are now to where they want to be (but don't spill the beans on what that solution is just yet).

7. Talk about common solutions people try that don't work and why.

✏️ **EXPERT LAUNCH TIP: Now that you have a warm audience, bring their attention to solving their problem.**

SELL THE *problem* YOU SOLVE, NOT YOUR PRODUCT OR SERVICE

WEEK 4: MAKE OFFERS TO HELP

Last week, your audience thought to themselves, "Dang, this girl gets me." Now, paint the picture that you are the solutionist they need to overcome their problem. It's time to present the solution they've been looking for.

Here are this week's to-dos:

1. Cut out the fluff and keep your message simple.

2. Talk about the problem your audience faces and make offers to help guide them through to their desired results with your solution.

3. Position your offering as the solution they need.

4. Bring attention to the value and benefits of your offering.

5. Create sales calls to action: Invite the audience to browse your new website, share their stories about dealing with the problem and how they solved it through direct message, sign up for a 15-minute consultation call, sign up for your newsletter, view your new blog post, and check back with you often for updates.

6. Make it easy for them to buy! For example, post URLs directly to the product when you talk about it or invite the audience to book a call and pay right inside a calendar scheduling app.

7. Highlight social proof, such as testimonials.

8. Help them clearly picture what their life would be like with the problem solved.

✏ **EXPERT LAUNCH TIP: You are the guide who can take your ideal client from where they are to where they want to be. Now offer to help.**

WEEK 5: CONVERT YOUR WARM AUDIENCE

Girl, it's launch week. You have poured your heart and soul into your business and now it's time to officially open your doors. Let's talk through how to do that.

Recall that calls to action are clear instructions for the audience for what immediate step to take next. Your message should inspire the audience to take some kind of action toward your intended goal and theirs, too. This is where conversion happens.

As you wrap up your business launch plan, consider what the audience will know about your business up to this point in the process. You've introduced the lead to your business, nurtured them well, and now you're ready to make offers to help change their life with your product or service. Picture a close friend or family member dealing with this issue. Consider what you would tell yourself if you were coaching yourself through this challenge. What emotions would you convey? What word choice would you select? What picture would you paint for what it will be like to *finally* overcome the problem?

Now let's work through what your calls to action might sound like as you encourage your audience to buy your offering. Remember, your audience is already warm. They already know what you do and who you do it for. They've developed a sense of your brand characteristics. They've heard you say how you want to change the world. They know you feel their pain and have a solution to help them. Now it's time for them to make forward momentum and become part of the success story. It's time for them to participate, to invest, to take action.

Here are this week's to-dos:

- ▶ Create a sense of urgency with your expiring bonuses, exciting challenges or giveaways, and event-only opportunities to buy.

- ▶ Follow up with all one-to-one connections you made over the last few weeks and let them know it's time to take action!

- ▶ Check in with your launch team and provide clear direction for how they can help refer their network to your online presence.

- ▶ Execute your Grand Opening event.

- Go live each day sharing information about:

  - The concept of your business.

  - Specific ways your product or service meets your audience's needs.

  - Stories of others who are becoming customers of yours.

  - How to make a purchase from you.

  - Other topics your audience would find helpful and engaging.

- Be present on social media and in your inbox to answer questions and engage with your audience.

- Choose winners for giveaways.

- Wrap up any loose ends and thank your audience for sticking with you. Recap the week, remind them where they can go to purchase with you, and pat yourself on the back. You did it!!

✎ **EXPERT TIP: Consider ways you can keep this momentum going! The last thing you want to do is "go dark" when an audience has become accustomed to hearing your message.**

CONGRATS, YOU'RE OPEN FOR BUSINESS!

You did it!! Sis, picture me wrapping my arms around you, jumping for joy, probably spilling the bubbly we're celebrating with, smiling from ear to ear, and clapping wildly at the success you just created. You just launched your business and joined an esteemed league of entrepreneurial females chasing the dream in their hearts!!

Take a moment to celebrate. Rehash the entire process. Don't be so quick to speed to the next to do. What you have accomplished is rare. It took grit, determination, tenacity, resilience, boldly stepping outside your comfort zone, and a whole lotta heart. It's time to sit back and revel for a moment. I knew you had what it takes!

Send me an update with your good news at YesSheCan@FoundingFemalesCo.com so we can celebrate with a literal happy dance **together**!

STEP 4

POST LAUNCH PROMOTIONS

Now that you've created incredible momentum for your business launch, consider how you can keep the momentum going with consistent processes. Put into practice the tips and tricks you collected in this guide. Mark to-dos on your calendar.

PRO TIP: Embrace the pivot. The best way to run your business tomorrow might vary from the best way to run it today. This book has helped you create a beginning point. After you launch, develop the habit of thinking critically about changing lanes, taking a detour, and altering the course when you need to.

While we're at it, let's talk about some specific ways you can keep the momentum going. You worked too darn hard to create this momentum; now capitalize on it! Here are some ideas:

▶ Reach out to organizations who would be interested in a "lunch and learn," and offer to deliver a presentation that will teach their audience something actionable related to your area of expertise. They buy lunch for their employees. You teach them something valuable.

▶ Keep showing up online and in person where you know your audience is spending time.

▶ Create a regular content schedule and make it a priority to plan ahead and execute.

▶ Mark your calendar to reach out to your one-on-one connections with updates and relationship-building conversation at least quarterly. Staying on the radar of those who already know, like, and trust you is valuable.

▶ Continue podcast, blog, and interview collaborations. If you put the research in upfront, these give you incredible exposure to a concentration of ideal customers and position you as the authority in your area of expertise.

CONTINGENCY PLAN

Every successful business owner has a "before it worked" story. My contingency plan was getting a part-time job for 18 months. In my experience coaching women through the beginning stages of their businesses, I often find most underestimate how long it takes for the business to become "successful," with a consistent incoming flow of customers and revenue. This was my story, too. I was officially open for business June 1st, and by December 31st, I had only made around $8,000. Riding the learning curve takes time, but when you stick with it, your approach improves.

Don't feel discouraged if it takes longer than you originally projected for your business to become successful. You learned how to coach yourself through doing whatever it takes as long as it aligns with your moral compass in **Phase One: Clarify**. Ask yourself, "What will I do if it takes longer than expected for my business to become viable and how will I know when it's time to activate the 'contingency plan'?"

A contingency plan is an alternative route you'll take when things don't go as planned. For instance, my part-time job was at the local hospital in my second and third year of business to support my family's goals while my business gained momentum. Your contingency plan might involve staying employed at your 9-5 longer than expected or picking up extra work on the weekends. There's no shame in allowing a job to fund your business. It's challenges like these that show you what you're made of.

You'll know when it's time to activate the contingency plan based on the numbers. First, keep your financial statements up to date and don't fudge the numbers even when they tell a story you don't want to hear. Real numbers are your best asset when it comes to a realistic picture of how your business is performing financially.

Consider whether you've stepped out of your comfort zone to do everything in your power to make your business successful. If you default only to responsibilities you feel comfortable with, you may find leverage in freshening your approach. Remember, old keys don't unlock new doors.

Lastly, if you see signs your offering is successful but isn't driving as many sales as you'd like, go back and study your customers' data and behaviors. Then, research pockets of customers like them. It may be you incorrectly predicted who your ideal customer was and need to promote your offering to a different crowd.

Consider creating another source of revenue while you build your business. Sure, you may have to become the new favorite barista at the local coffee shop, but without the stress of where your mortgage payment will come from each month, bandwidth and freedom would allow you to build your business on your terms. There is no shame in getting scrappy to make the dream become reality.

'PHASE FOUR: LAUNCH' CONCLUSION

Now you know what it takes to ride the exhilarating journey of launching a business. The world finally knows about your business idea. You carefully planned and developed your launch to make the most of your audience's attention. What an accomplishment to finally be in business!

You've defined your initial business goals and shared your business with friends, family, and customers who may already be benefitting from your offering. Girl, you know exactly what to do now to continue consistent marketing efforts that will keep leads flowing through your pipeline, keep you in business, and help you maintain waking up to a business you're head over heels for.

You're ready to nurture the momentum and positive buzz about your business to carry you well into the future. Now that your business is launched, you'll begin to settle into a routine of running your business and keep the many plates spinning that help it thrive.

Be cautious, however. It's easy to become so caught up in the day-to-day that you forget to work "on" your business. Your business needs a savvy, proactive leader like you who will continue keeping an eye on the target and an ear to the ground for opportunities. Two pivotal seasons of business lie ahead of you: learning how to profit and to scale your amazing business.

In **Phase Five: Profit**, we'll address what you need to know to not just operate a business, but to turn it into a cash- and value-generating powerhouse. Let's turn our attention to what it means to profit.

NOTES

NOTES

"I FEEL LIKE MONEY MAKES YOU MORE OF WHO YOU ALREADY ARE."

Sara Blakely, CEO of Spanx

PHASE FIVE

PROFIT

I find the topic of money fascinating. I gush over stories about kids using their dirt-poor childhood as motivation to totally crush it in their career. I often find myself wishing people would wear signs above their heads reflecting their net worth (never said I wasn't weird), knowing the people who look poor often aren't, and the people who look wealthy often aren't. How would that change things?

An incredible book on this topic is *Millionaire Next Door* by Thomas J. Stanley and William D. Danko. As researchers hired to study the lifestyles of first-generation millionaires, they wanted to make sure the millionaires felt comfortable during their interviews, so they provided the finest, most expensive food and drink. What they found was that the average millionaire walking through their doors typically wore casual clothing, preferred to drink American beer over expensive liquor, and drove Ford F150 trucks. The book also reveals that only a small percentage of wealthy people actually drive luxury cars. Things aren't always as they seem.

Everywhere we turn, messages about money clutter our attention. Even the Bible warns that the love of money is the root of all evil. No wonder the subject of money is such an obscure topic.

What if the thought of having money felt deeply ethical and profit wasn't a dirty word? Imagine with me for a moment, brilliant sister. What if we created a world where it was wired in our brains that profit meant "opportunity" rather than "indulgence"? Our society often paints the picture of people who have money as scandalous and ill-willed. Financial conversations, or lack thereof, can feel as if everyone is striving to get more money and then when they do, suddenly, they've crossed into the dark side.

Often, there's a hidden assumption that if a person has money, he or she must have compromised their morals to get it. Even more, many women I know feel icky about money because they buy into the misconception that money is a zero-sum game, meaning that for you to acquire it, someone else has to lose it. And of course, you'd be fearful of admitting you'd like to make money if that was your perception of what it means to have it.

Rarely does anyone say, "Money is bad," yet the way we talk about it often insinuates that reality. Growing up, we create meaning by hearing what others say—song lyrics, adult conversations, movies, news broadcasts. We create understanding with countless moments of covert meaning—sayings that become so common, they feel like a lesson etched in our minds. Ever heard these?

"Money doesn't grow on trees."

"It's better to be poor and happy than rich and sad."

"Rich people got lucky."

"We're aren't made of money."

"Mo' money, mo' problems." Thank you, Notorious B.I.G.

Hearing a female business owner say, "It's not about the money for me," often indicates to me that she hasn't done her deep inner work, like figuring out her Why statement, creating a vision board to pinpoint all the ways she wants to impact the world, dealing with her baggage and beliefs around having money, or developing an idea of the legacy she wants to leave behind. Maybe it's "not about the money" *for her own indulgence.* To most, that assumption would feel icky. But if we wish to make any kind of mark on this world—my guess is you do!—the money your business produces has to be a top consideration. Money is one of the most obvious and accessible conduits of change.

Imagine with me for a moment. Think of all the good you could do if you performed the inner work to restructure your belief about money and profit. What if you used money and profit as a means to create positive change? Having a desire to make money does not make anyone a bad person. Money is a vehicle to do great things in business, in your own community, and in the world. Money allows you to deliver an ever-better experience and more profound results to your customers. It allows you the leverage to provide jobs to others. It's an instrument which can usher you from who you are now to the expert you strive to become. You could take a paid course or program, earn a degree, or take a sabbatical to write a book, for example. Each of these things allows you to further contribute to your industry at large and to those who need to hear the message in your heart.

Money is a tool that allows each of us to vote about what we believe matters most in the world. Every dollar equals a vote. More money equals more hungry bellies fed by getting behind organizations striving to end hunger. More money equals fewer lives lost to cancer with money donated to research. More money equals more advocating for equality in the midst of outrageous social injustice. More money means changing your family tree from generational poverty to generational wealth for generations to come. More money equals more teaching people about Jesus, more mission trips, or more donations to disaster relief for helping people who don't have the means to help themselves. Prayers are powerful and intentions are important, but in tandem with those two crucial components, money can be one of the greatest tools at your discretion to create good.

Why wouldn't we want to acquire it to then use it as a tool for social good?

I believe it's our responsibility, our right, our obligation to be good stewards of what we've been blessed with. What does it mean to be a good steward of our blessings? It means refraining from spending frivolously (in our personal lives but especially in our businesses). Being good stewards over money means refraining from obsessing over it, or for storing it up only for ourselves. It means intentionally managing our money and maximizing it with the resources we have—for instance, choosing to donate to nonprofits whose financial reports show a proven track record for making the most of every donation dollar.

One of my favorite bloggers and podcasters, Allie Cassaza, said it best: "Change your mindset about money, because this world needs good people to become wealthy so they can make the impact God intends. The world needs people like you with good hearts and charitable hearts who have passion and a mission and a message that will change the world and who will do good things with money. There are corrupt people out there with a lot of power and a lot of money, and us good guys need to get up there and match where they're at so we can counteract that and do good things for the Kingdom of God and the betterment of humanity."[1]

Even typing this, goosebumps line my arms. When I heard Allie say that for the first time, my world turned upside down in the most beautiful way. My entire perception, approach, and understanding of what it means to profit changed. As I reflected on this powerful perspective, I realized I am responsible for rewriting my beliefs about money. Becoming someone with money doesn't teleport you to Beverly Hills or pin you against the Joneses without your consent. You, and only you, get to choose what having money means to you and about you.

My goal for building wealth is to change the world. My husband and I have a "giving fund" set aside separately from what we commit to the church with a mutual understanding that our giving fund allows us to seek opportunities to be Jesus' hands and feet on Earth—to meet another's unmet need, to pay it forward, to initiate good change when we see an opportunity. Uses of the fund have varied from paying a woman's bill at a restaurant whose credit card didn't work to making a donation to a good cause larger than we normally would with our monthly budget and even to helping outfit a new college grad with a professional wardrobe. Without the giving fund, we wouldn't have an intentional means to contribute as wholeheartedly as we can with the fund. Because we set the intention and steward the budgeted fund, we create the ability to make deliberate decisions about doing good for others. Money means opportunity. So, if you're someone who finds yourself saying, "I don't care about the money," perhaps it's time for a gut check or to clarify what it is you really mean.

The Bible mentions money over 800 times. Want the Spark Notes version of what the Bible says about managing money? *Forbes* gives us that in an article entitled, "Is the Bible the Ultimate Financial Guide?"[2] It offers these principles:

- ▸ "Do put money aside for investing."

- ▸ "Debt's not prohibited, but it should be avoided."

- ▸ "The more you make, the more you should give."

- ▸ "Don't focus on acquiring possessions."

If money equals opportunity, what does that mean about managing it within your business? Knowing that money creates opportunity develops the impetus to use money to produce the most impact you can, not just at large by giving it away, but also within the confines of your business's operations. It means reviewing ways to take what you have and create leverage to make even more. If your business is not profitable, it means learning how to make it become profitable. If your business is already profitable, no matter the margin, it means knowing you can always become more profitable and then taking steps to figure out how to do that. Within this section, we'll explore actionable steps for both scenarios for building profitability.

Phase Five: Profit will explore how to make the maximum profit for the work you're already doing. First, we'll define what it means to profit. Hint: Becoming maximally profitable isn't just about driving more revenue. From that mutual understanding, I'll guide you through looking at your business to figure out what revenue is coming in and what costs are going out. We'll talk about how to calculate your profit margin so you can understand how efficient your business is with costs. Then I'll help you comb through over twenty detailed strategies you can apply to reach maximum profitability. Once you learn how to become profitable, we'll work through integrating these strategies into your best practices and equip you with information about data-driven decision-making, an incredible skill set you can embrace in driving your business forward strategically and confidently.

In **Phase Five: Profit**, you will be guided through how to rock your profit with these steps:

- ▸ **Step 1:** Track Your Transactions

- ▸ **Step 2:** Compute Your Profit Margin

- ▸ **Step 3:** Step Up Your Profitability Game

- ▸ **Step 4:** Anchor Your Intuition

STEP

TRACK YOUR TRANSACTIONS

P rofit is an indicator of how efficiently we can use our resources to create a result. I have a friend who grew up without much. Because of this, she developed keen ways to maximize her money. Still to this day, she can walk into a grocery store with $20 and walk out with what seems like an entire week's worth of food. I'm baffled every time I shop with her. She learned early in life to maximize what she had, and now it's inherent in her day-to-day decision-making. She makes do with what she has and uses her budgeted grocery money for maximum results. She is a clear example of someone who uses her resources efficiently. We should aim to do the same with our business budget by leveraging our resources wisely to get the maximum compounded results and make the most profit.

"Becoming profitable" doesn't inherently mean "making more money." The definition of profiting is when revenue exceeds costs, so becoming more profitable means widening the gap between total revenue and total costs required to produce your offering. Increasing revenue *is* one way to become more profitable, but profitability can also mean keeping revenue the same while reducing costs. The greater the positive difference between revenue and costs, the more profitable a business is.

Phase Two: Research, Step 4: Finance Your Future and Phase Three: Build, Step 2: Find Your Financial Finesse guided you through how to keep the financial side of your business dealings orderly. If you haven't established clear accounting processes, take a moment to head back to those sections first before moving forward. Without recording what's coming in and what's going out, you can't measure how profitable your business is, a pivotal first step in taking ownership of the financial success of your business. If you feel you have the time, knowledge, and discipline to manage your own books each month, go for it! If not, you may choose to learn or to outsource the task to your accountant. (See **Phase Three: Build, Step 1: Assemble Your A-Team** for how to build your expert team of support and choose an accountant.)

Your systems are in place for you to make sense of your financial position. It's not enough to work from a gut feeling. Creating your accounting processes in **Phase Two: Research, Step 4: Finance Your Future** and **Phase Three: Build, Step 2: Find Your Financial Finesse** created the foundation to focus on profitability. Commit to show up as the financial manager of your business by reviewing your financial position in your business monthly, or at least quarterly, during the first year. When you do, you'll learn financial patterns that will help you look ahead to make the wisest decisions for the wellbeing of your business.

Numbers don't lie. They tell the story and invite the question, "Now what?" so your business can evolve and improve over time. Having an accurate record of every transaction related to your business establishes the foundation for seeing the whole financial picture clearly and gaining a true sense that either your processes are working as intended, working better than intended, or not working as well as they could be.

If you're reading **Phase Five: Profit** after running your business for some time, but haven't yet tackled accounting responsibilities, start by calculating your business expenses and revenues. We'll use revenue and expenses in **Phase Five: Profit, Step 2: Compute Your Profit Margin** as we cover three different ways to calculate your profit margin.

Take a moment now to check in with your business. Use the space below to record the revenue your business has produced so far this year and its expenses.

Revenue: $ ....

Expenses: $ ....

You can't manage what you don't measure, so if you're unsure what's coming in and going out of your business, it will be impossible to gauge the efficiency of your businesses processes. Tracking your transactions gives you the information to be able to use financial tools and standards. Without these metrics, running a business can feel obscure and uncertain. But with this data, girl, you've got all the information you need to gauge how viable your business is, how well it uses resources, and what areas of opportunity your business has.

STEP 2

COMPUTE YOUR PROFIT MARGIN

Suppose you get a job at the trendiest boutique in town. You love what the shop sells so much that you spend everything you make before you clock out. Your profit margin just vanished, and you have little to show for your hard work. In fact, it's costing you to work at that darling boutique, rather than empowering you to pursue your goals. I get that some people exercise just so they can eat what they want—or work at a boutique just so they can buy cute stuff—but that's not a great strategy in business. Maximizing your profit margin means using as few resources possible to create the greatest amount of profit over and above what it costs to produce your offering.

Your profit margin is the amount that your business's revenue exceeds its costs. Profit margin is a basic and common financial term that helps people understand to what extent a business is profitable, and how efficient your business is with resources. From a bank's perspective, your profit margin lends insight into how likely you are to default on a loan, and it's highlighted on your profit and loss financial statement. For a rundown of what a profit and loss statement is and how it can help you, refer back to **Phase Three: Build, Step 2: Find Your Financial Finesse**.

Aiming for a healthy profit margin helps you as a business owner make important decisions, like whether or not to hire more employees, how and when to order supplies, and how to develop systems that lead to greater efficiency with resources. There are three ways to look at profit margin: Gross Profit Margin, Operating Profit Margin, and Net Profit Margin. Let's define each.

Gross Profit Margin is revenue minus the cost of goods sold, which are expenses directly tied to the production or manufacture of the product, including materials and labor, divided by net sales and multiplied by 100. Service-based companies, such as a bookkeeping company, can use the cost of revenue (total cost to produce a sale) rather than the cost of goods sold (COGS). Net sales are the total amount of gross sales minus returns, allowances, and discounts. Use gross profit margin to help you analyze how profitable your business is compared to what direct labor and materials resources are required to produce the goods/services. To calculate gross profit margin, use the following:

Gross Profit Margin = ((Revenue - Costs of Goods Sold) / Net Sales) x 100

Operating Profit Margin is all income minus the cost of goods sold, overhead, operating costs, administrative expenses, and sales expenses required to run the business. This metric is a reflection of how efficient a business is after also taking into account costs not directly tied to producing the offering to keep the business running. Operating profit margin helps you analyze how profitable your business is compared to a broader view of costs directly (such as the material used to make the t-shirt that customers buy) and indirectly (such as rent) related to producing the goods.

Operating Profit Margin = ((Revenue - Cost of Goods Sold - Indirect Costs) / Revenue) x 100

Net Profit Margin is the total amount of income left over after all additional revenue streams and expenses are considered, multiplied by 100. Net profit margin tends to be the truest reflection of how efficient a business is with its operations because it not only considers the costs to produce the goods and the costs to keep the business running, but it also takes into account payments on debt, taxes, and one-time payments (such as purchasing equipment) and any income generated from investments or secondary operations. In other words, net profit margin takes into consideration a comprehensive view of all factors that play a role in how much money a business makes and owes. Net profit margin helps you understand profitability of the business as a whole.

Net Profit Margin = ((Revenue - COGS - Indirect Costs - Other Expenses - Interest - Taxes) / Revenue) x 100

DO THE MATH

It's a good idea to know all three types of profit margins in your business so you can glean a complete picture of how efficient your business's use of resources is.

Calculate your Gross Profit Margin:

Gross Profit Margin = ((Revenue - Costs of Goods Sold) / Net Sales) x 100

Your Gross Profit Margin: ....

Calculate your operating profit margin:

Operating Profit Margin = (Revenue - Cost of Goods Sold - Indirect Costs) / Revenue) x 100

Your Operating Profit Margin: ....

Calculate your Net Profit Margin:

Net Profit Margin = ((Revenue - COGS - Indirect Costs - Other Expenses - Interest - Taxes) / Revenue) x 100

Your Net Profit Margin: ....

WHAT'S A GOOD PROFIT MARGIN?

A "good" profit margin varies by a business's circumstance, including how long it's been in business, its business model, level of competition, and its industry. A business with low overhead cannot compare its profit margin to a business with lots of overhead and assume it's better run. Some industries require much more to operate than others. For instance, a consulting business with low overhead could have high profit margins (for instance, 75%) and not be run efficiently while a restaurant with high overhead and low profit margins (for instance, 4%) could be running incredibly efficiently.

To find the average profit margin in your industry, perform an online search or seek out a reputable source, like Ibis World or Biz Miner. A subscription to either of these resources is likely out-of-budget for the average entrepreneur; however, there's a chance your local Small Business Development Center (SBDC) or a local library may have access to them for you to use.

Now that you know what your profit margin is, you can see how efficient your business is. With every dollar of revenue, how much does it cost you to stay afloat? Hopefully less than $1. Knowing your numbers is a wise woman move you won't regret. It allows you to become the strong financial decision-maker your business needs. Use that knowledge to empower yourself to manage your resources as the good steward you are.

STEP  3

STEP UP YOUR PROFITABILITY GAME

Like anything else, numbers in themselves don't motivate us much. Suppose you have a fair profit margin for your industry. So what? It's not about striving for great numbers. It's the reality those numbers reflect about your business that really matters. It's about the picture and the vision of your successful company, reflected through the numbers of the impactful business entity you've created.

High profit margins give you leverage, freedom, and opportunity. It's breathing room when things don't go as planned. It's being able to create a charitable component of your organization. It's having the flexibility to create a business you're proud of.

Reaching maximum profitability is about asking yourself what you can do today, this week, or this month, to maximize overall sales rather than solely focusing on one big goal of making six figures, for example. Once you know what your profit margin looks like, it's time to create a plan to improve your profitability. As you've probably gathered from my style of problem-solving, I'm a fan of pinpointing the target result and then working backward, outlining tangible step-by-step to-dos to get there. This section will guide you through several approaches you can take to increase profitability.

DRIVE A GREATER NUMBER OF NEW LEADS AT YOUR CURRENT CONVERSION RATE

This strategy leans heavily on improving the effectiveness of your marketing efforts. You'll need to drive more leads by increasing the number of people who know about your business. In the example of converting leads on a website, if 100 people visited your website each day and 3% (three visitors) converted to customers, your goal using this strategy would be to drive more total visitors to your site and convert customers at the same percentage—3%. The goal is to increase awareness of your business so more potential customers enter the pipeline. Here are four ideas for doing exactly that:

Never stop networking. The 3-Month Rule in business suggests it takes about three months after you start networking consistently for referrals to come into your business consistently. The opposite is also true. It takes about three months after you stop networking consistently for those referrals to drop off. That means, you want to continue networking even when you're busy so leads don't stop flowing through your pipeline.

Create a referral program. Referral programs are a concept we covered in **Phase Three: Build, Step 5: Draw Up Your Marketing Plan.** As a recap, referral programs incentivize customers to refer their friends and family to your business. Strong referral programs can be a great way to generate new consistent leads because the already-delighted customer referring others to your business earns some kind of compensation for passing more customers your way.

Develop a sales team. Outline what an in-house sales team would look like for your business. Bring in someone whose sole responsibility is to drive sales to free you up to focus on your area of expertise or develop your business in other areas. The benefits of having a dedicated person or team include delegating tasks to a uniquely motivated individual to build relationships and help grow the business. Hire someone who is self-motivated, curious, competitive, coachable, not discouraged by a challenge, confident in their own ability, high-energy, and who likes people. Clearly communicate the vision for what your sales team is working toward to set clear expectations about sales goals and incentives.

Collaborate with other businesses that have a complementary audience to yours. Maximize marketing efforts by teaming up with other businesses who target the same audience and cross-promote each other. Be sure their brand image aligns with yours and that you can trust associating with their brand will make a positive impact on yours. Doing this will help your marketing efforts gain momentum because you're able to leverage each other's time, effort, and marketing dollars to create meaning in the minds of an audience you both want to reach. An example is a mobile boutique and a coffee truck aligning their stops at the same local businesses so customers can hit up both. In promotions, both the mobile boutique and the coffee truck mention one another in marketing efforts.

List the strategies you'll use for driving a higher number of leads at your current conversion rate:

....

....

....

....

....

Hash out a step-by-step plan for implementing these strategies into your current operations:

....

....

....

....

....

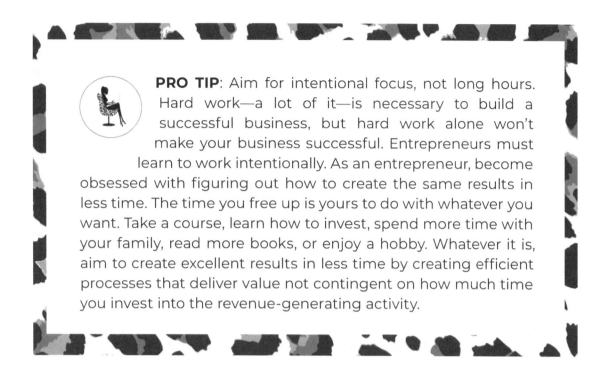

PRO TIP: Aim for intentional focus, not long hours. Hard work—a lot of it—is necessary to build a successful business, but hard work alone won't make your business successful. Entrepreneurs must learn to work intentionally. As an entrepreneur, become obsessed with figuring out how to create the same results in less time. The time you free up is yours to do with whatever you want. Take a course, learn how to invest, spend more time with your family, read more books, or enjoy a hobby. Whatever it is, aim to create excellent results in less time by creating efficient processes that deliver value not contingent on how much time you invest into the revenue-generating activity.

CONVERT EXISTING LEADS AT A HIGHER CONVERSION RATE

Rather than casting a "wider net" and hoping to convert the same percentage of leads, this strategy focuses on converting more of the existing leads already within your net. For this to happen, you'll need to improve effectiveness of your sales efforts. For example, you could sharpen your consultation call skills or find a way to improve your paid ads process to yield a higher percentage of paying customers out of your total leads.

This could also mean increasing your conversion rate on your ecommerce store to capitalize on the traffic already coming to your site. For example, if 100 customers visit your website each day, converting more existing leads would mean increasing the number of people who decide to buy from three paying customers (3% conversion rate) to five paying customers (5% conversion rate) each day. To convert more existing leads, consider the following strategies:

Improve the effectiveness of your consultation calls. A consultation call is where someone sets up a call or meeting to talk with you about your services, and your job is to convert them into a paying customer. Stacey Boehman is an incredible life coach who teaches her audience of life coaches how to improve their sales skills. Even though I'm not a life coach, I've gained a great deal from listening to her podcast titled *Make Money as a Life Coach* because she shares invaluable information about her sales process. One valuable piece of insight, for example, was when she shared the difference between a consult call and a coaching call in Episode 108: "Five Things You're Doing on Consults (And Why Coaching Isn't One of Them)."[3] She explained that we shouldn't coach on a consult nor expect to convert a lead on a coaching call, because the human brain uses different areas to make decisions to buy (selling) or to change behavior (coaching). Utilizing lessons like these and approaching sales opportunities with a defined approach can make a profitable difference between winning or losing a potential client.

Follow up! It seems obvious and logical to follow up with existing leads, but the truth is, both business owners and customers get busy. Sometimes just an extra little push is enough to remind someone to complete the transaction. After all, there's far less competition when you're willing to go the extra mile. This goes for service- and product-based business models, though the approach for each may differ. With service-based business models, reaching out by phone or email or stopping into a lead's office lets those potential customers know you care about their results.

Become a seed planter. I remind my female mastermind members frequently how powerful "seed planting" is. Recall throughout **Phase Four: Launch** when we discussed how important it is to create situations of opportunity and lean into delayed gratification knowing a sale often hinges on the familiarity created by several touch points. As I shared previously, a lot happens under the surface after the seed is planted and before it grows into a beautiful flower. Examples of seed planting include meaningful suggestions for collaboration, offering future support, or using foresight to sell a future need a potential client has. As the popular Chinese proverb goes, "The best time to plant a tree was 20 years ago. The second-best time is now." The time to cultivate valuable relations to acquire new clients is before you need them.

List the strategies you'll use for converting a higher number of leads with your current audience:

....

....

....

....

....

....

Hash out a step-by-step plan for implementing these strategies into your current operations:

....

....

....

....

....

....

INCREASE AVERAGE ORDER VALUE

Average order value (AOV) is the average dollar amount spent by customers. To calculate the AOV, divide total revenue by the total number of transactions. Increasing average order value means driving more revenue from the same number of transactions. Here, your total number of customers and conversion rate could stay the same, but because customers spend more, your business makes more. To do this, the key to success is fulfilling more of your customers' needs or fulfilling their needs with higher priced items. For example, a florist could coach her sales team to lead customers to their top tier and middle tier arrangements rather than the lowest tier. A gift shop could place a rack of specialty cards next to checkout so customers pick up a card at the same time they're buying a gift. A marketing agency could offer to manage a customer's email marketing while they're on a consult call for social media marketing. Increasing the average order value means selling more to the same number of people. Here are a few strategies.

Raise prices. The most obvious way to increase the average order value is to raise prices. Be careful, though. You could end up decreasing demand for your offering, especially if your prices are already set above competitors' prices and customers don't see enough of a valuable differentiator between your offering and your competitor's offering. For example, a gas station likely couldn't raise prices much higher than a competing gas station down the street because it's nearly impossible for customers to differentiate between the two offerings. That is, unless one gas station decided to offer a unique value proposition, such as a free pumping service where drivers didn't even need to leave their car. Many companies take the approach of becoming a specialist at one thing in order to raise prices. Businesses can typically charge a higher price for an offering that meets a specific need rather than a general need, such as in the case of a web designer who designs on drag-and-drop sites versus a web designer who knows how to code customized sites.

Cross sell. Cross selling invites customers to purchase complementary or related products to what they've already decided to purchase. The example above where the gift shop places the card rack next to check out is an example of cross selling. Take a look at how you're already serving customers' needs and consider what other secondary or tertiary needs you could also meet to help them reach their desired results.

Upsell. Upselling is different from cross selling because in upselling, a customer is led to a higher priced alternative to meet the same need. If you head into a car dealership to buy a durable family van and leave with a Ferrari, the saleswoman sold the heck out of you. Good for her!

Bundle. Bundling is where you offer a group of related products at a discounted price. In order to take advantage of the discount, the customer must buy all items in the bundle. Here, customers are enticed by getting a better deal and are willing to spend more to get it. An example of bundling is when an insurance company offers a discount for carrying your home and auto insurance together.

Promote products or services with the lowest cost to you. Another way to increase profit is to sell more offerings with the highest profit margin. Here, reducing costs makes you more money for all the reasons listed in the previous section, **Phase Five: Profit, Step 3: Compute Your Profit Margin**.

Use a dollar threshold for free shipping or a free gift with purchase. Entice customers to buy more by offering free shipping or a free gift with purchase when they meet a certain amount. I fall victim to this strategy nearly every time I lay eyes on the internet because I pride myself on being a savvy spender, as most people do. I'll throw a roll of toilet paper into my cart knowing that I'll need it at some point and that my entire total will go toward products I can use rather than toward shipping costs which add no value to my life.

Offer a higher priced payment plan option. A payment plan allows customers to spread out the money they owe to make it more financially feasible. If you give customers the option for flexible payments, make it worth your risk by slightly increasing the total amount owed. When customers don't have to spend their money all at once, many are willing to spend more because it feels less risky to them and because it gives them time to figure out how to pay the balance.

List the strategies you'll use for increasing average order value:

....

....

....

....

....

....

....

Hash out a step-by-step plan for implementing these strategies into your current operations:

....

....

....

....

....

....

....

....

DECREASE COSTS

As mentioned earlier, profiting doesn't always mean driving more revenue. Sometimes becoming more profitable means leaning up processes, becoming more efficient, and getting rid of unnecessary costs. Here are three cost areas you may be able to decrease:

Cost of customer acquisition. Focus on lower-cost marketing methods to acquire customers. Spend less to drive the same number of customers. Compare the average cost of customer acquisition (marketing spend divided by total number of customers acquired) to their customer lifetime value (how much they'll spend over their lifetime) to gauge how efficient your marketing efforts are. Driving down the cost to acquire customers means more of their revenue can be attributed to your overall profitability. We'll take an even deeper dive into this in more detail in a moment with additional strategies for retaining customers.

Costs of production. How much it costs to produce your offering is a major consideration in how profitable your company can be. Consider each and every component of producing an offering, including the time you spend shopping for or fixing equipment, how much time is required to deliver customers the "extras" like going above and beyond, and the extent of the training required to produce an excellent result. All considerations up until the customer receives the offering are fair game for scrutiny when it comes to driving down costs of production.

Costs of overhead. Overhead costs are what you're responsible for paying for, unrelated to what's required for the direct production of a product. Office space, extra plush toilet paper, and the newest smartphone are examples. Sometimes, investing in overhead can increase efficiency or productivity, but not always. One of my favorite podcasters, Nick Huber, who hosts *The Sweaty Startup* (https://sweatystartup.com/podcast/), talks often about purchasing used but durable, non-fancy moving vans when he and his partners started their college moving business. They could have opted for fancy new vans, but the benefits would have been negligible. Look for less expensive options in your business for overhead expenses that will still create a similar or identical result.

List the strategies you'll use for driving down costs in your business:

....

....

....

....

....

Hash out a step-by-step plan for implementing these strategies into your current operations:

....

....

....

....

....

RETAIN CUSTOMERS

Retaining customers is a crucial way of decreasing the cost of customer acquisition because there is always a cost attached to bringing new leads into your business. You can decrease the cost of acquiring new customers when you retain the customers you already have. Existing customers are the easiest and least expensive to sell to, so be sure you're capitalizing on the customers you've worked so hard to acquire in the first place.

They previously made the decision to buy, and the cost to acquire them as repeat customers is much lower than the cost of driving brand new leads. Plus, nurturing the relationships you've already established can be far more beneficial than starting a relationship with new customers. For example, not only do existing customers already trust you, but they also don't have to be convinced that your product works, so their average order value is likely to go up with subsequent purchases.

Additionally, customers who already know about you are more likely to spread the word about your business to others, and word of mouth is a powerful form of marketing. Taking special care to nurture your current customer base by showing appreciation and attention is an especially strategic way to become more profitable. Here are some ways to approach retaining customers:

Lower your churn rate. "Customer churn rate measures the percentage of customers who end their relationship with a company in a particular period," according to Harvard Business Review[4]. When churn rate is high, repeat customer rate is low. To avoid this, create a process in your business for following up with customers who haven't purchased in a while. For instance, if a bottle of a beekeeper's local honey typically lasts one month, a great time to follow up with her customers is before a customer's bottle of honey runs out. Like the savvy beekeeper boss lady she is, she also makes it easy for them to refill their stock by offering a subscription model. In another example, an SEO strategist might recommend to customers a quarterly audit service where she keeps an eye out for new emerging opportunities to drive organic traffic for customers and automatically sends new annual contracts at the first of the year.

Offer a customer loyalty program. Customer loyalty programs motivate customers' loyalty and entice more frequent purchases because they offer an incentive to do so. For example, Hotels.com offers free stays in hotels after a certain number of nights purchased. Coffee shops offer a free cup of joe after a certain number of purchases. Our favorite daddy-daughter date night spot is a sno-cone shack along Broadripple Avenue near Indianapolis that offers punch cards. I'm not sure we've ever completely filled a punch card (though we have about 10 different cards laying around), yet the lure of earning a free sno-cone keeps us coming back. The unfilled punch cards have become a memento for us and a reminder about all the reasons to get excited when the Midwest summer turns warm in the springtime.

Implement a customer survey. Customer surveys are powerful for more than gathering information about what a customer's experience is like. They can also serve as a safety net for customers who unfortunately had a bad experience. See, most people simply want to be heard and to know their feelings matter. If given the opportunity, a customer might vent about their poor experience in the form of a survey knowing it's a direct line to someone who can repair the damage rather than telling their 100 closest friends and family and damaging your business's reputation.

Another way to use this strategy is to implement information-gathering in the off-boarding process with a 1:1 interview or survey. This strategy works best for customers who have a comprehensive customer experience, such as a home remodel, extensive coaching services, or a wholesaler who sells large amounts of products to a customer. A survey at the off-boarding process helps you understand the benefits and challenges customers experience in working with your company so you can then implement recommendations to improve your current processes. Don't be afraid of hearing the hard truth; it's one of the few and most valuable insights that allow your business to become not just good, but great. The more you become curious and caring about who buys from you, the more you can tailor an experience to delight the customer and help them develop loyalty to your offering and brand.

Continually strengthen your value proposition. By definition, your value proposition is the reason your customer chooses you over your competitors. You defined your value proposition in **Phase Three: Build, Step 5: Draw Up Your Marketing Plan**. Your unique value proposition earns repeat business from loyal customers because no other business has your secret sauce. Every so often, a company decides to create a new, fresher iteration of its brand. When that time comes for you, be sure to evaluate your value proposition to be sure it aligns with the evolution of your business.

COLLECT MONEY QUICKER AND TAKE THE FULL TERM TO PAY

Shortening your terms, meaning the amount of time customers have to pay you, allows you to collect money quicker for products or services rendered. For example, you may decide invoices are due upon receipt rather than giving your customers 30 days to pay. Offering terms of 10, 30, or 90 days is essentially loaning out money to your customers. You're doing them a favor for buying from you. Perhaps this is one strategy businesses use to acquire and retain customers, but it shouldn't be offered by default or obligation. After all, your customer gets to enjoy your offering for free until money is due. If you've offered products or services to customers, you are owed money and have no obligation to provide a grace period for them to pay. Even though this strategy doesn't directly increase the total amount of cash you're driving into your business, it is a way for you to leverage the use of cash at your disposal as you wish.

Alternatively, taking the full term to pay your vendors allows you to keep cash flow in your bank account for a longer period of time and accrue even the tiniest amount of interest your bank might offer. I must mention here some companies take advantage of this strategy by taking longer than the stated terms to pay, or by not paying at all for products or services they've already received. This strategy doesn't sit well with my conscience, because I believe in adequately compensating people and businesses for the value they've delivered. Play fair and do the right thing.

How might you collect money more quickly in your business?

....

....

....

....

....

Small changes can create profound results in your business. Implementing even one or two of the strategies listed within this section could be enough to meet your new revenue goals each year. Profiting strategies often come in handy the most once you've developed your business beyond the proof-of-concept phase, having established a strong foundation to build upon. With past experience to pull from, you can more clearly see how to improve your business's processes to become better, faster, or more efficient, always continuing to build the dream that was sewn into your heart.

STEP

ANCHOR YOUR INTUITION

I remember staring at my Google Analytics dashboard completely bewildered. The graphs on my screen felt like a foreign language. In fact, I was bragging to myself that I even figured out how to link Google Analytics to my website in the first place. I trusted the power of the behemoth, Google, but had no clue how to leverage the tools at my fingertips.

When I was in school, the online space was still on the verge of making data widely accessible to the average Jane. But in those early stages of running my business, I read time and again how entrepreneurs were creating incredible results by learning how to read the story the data told about their online presence, so I leaned in.

Four years later, that's how I eat. Data is now what I do and reading the story of the data is how I provide value to customers of Simply Integrated, LLC. My entrepreneurial passion is to empower women-owned businesses, so I do that with their data. My team and I apply search engine optimization (SEO) strategy to drive organic traffic to a client's website. Then we help them design the site's infrastructure and content to lead visitors through the Buying Cycle and into a sale. It's my job to comb through pages of data to help businesses determine how to improve, and I never would have made it to this point without allowing my brain to grow into someone who used data-driven decision-making.

You, my friend, can leverage the same power in your business to read the story the data tells and make informed decisions about your business. It's beautiful, isn't it? We can become better, more intellectual versions of ourselves by leaning into a challenge!

Learning to manage by numbers is a critical skill for women growing businesses. Driving profits and scaling your business, like we'll cover in **Phase 6: Scale** of *Dream, Build, Grow*, requires you to become an even more fine-tuned decision-maker. It's time to embrace using data to become proficient at the analytics side of your business.

Data analytics refers to datasets that help you draw conclusions. One of the greatest benefits to the entrepreneurial ecosystem today is the vast amount of data insights we have available at our fingertips—often for free! Don't worry, you're ready for this! Revisit **Phase Three: Build, Step 5: Draw Up Your Marketing Plan** for a refresher on what key performance indicators (KPIs) are.

Email marketing software, social media platforms, and your website all have tools to help you learn which of your content is performing well, lending insight into how to create more effective content in the future. For example, reviewing website analytics data could help you understand which blog posts drive the highest number of visitors and even the greatest number of sales. At that point, you can review the post to figure out why it performed well and then implement the insight into your best practices when writing posts in the future to increase website traffic and sales with every subsequent post.

Step into the driver's seat behind the analytics tools so you can create powerful meaning out of the insights. Note Google has the large majority of search market share when it comes to search engines and offers robust tools for you to easily understand the nuances of visitor behavior on your site. Consider taking a Udemy (https://www.udemy.com/) beginner's course about Google Analytics.

If you haven't leaned into understanding analytics for decision-making for your online presence, now is the perfect time. The goal is not to compare your stats to your competitors' or to your girlfriends' businesses. The goal is to create a benchmark to compare your own business's progress against your own goals for it over time.

Each decision we make (cause) creates some kind of result (effect). Every system is perfectly designed to create the results it does based on the input it's given. Results are not random; we just need to figure out how to leverage the data to understand why things are happening.

For example, Monroe's website produces the conversion rate, website traffic, and abandoned cart rate it does because of how it was designed. If she makes tweaks to the website, those numbers will fluctuate to produce different results. Let's say she hires an SEO expert to optimize her site to drive more organic search traffic. The SEO expert runs a site audit and produces a list of 25 things to accomplish for Monroe's site to earn better organic traffic from the search engines. Monroe and her team implement the changes to the website and content. The changes result in improvement via more organic traffic, visitors spending a longer amount of time on the site, increased conversion, and a lower abandoned cart rate. Monroe initiated an improvement to her website to produce one designed to yield more successful results.

The following section provides information for you to record your current stats so you can flip to this section later and compare your growth. If you're looking at me like I'm crazy for asking you to do this, fabulous! Consider this a sign you need it the most. You don't have to become a pro. You just have to become familiar with where to find information so you can leverage it periodically in your business to make decisions.

Your website's platform analytics

How to find your data: Depending on what platform you built your site on, your site analytics could be obvious upon login to your site dashboard or slightly less obvious, as in the case of needing a WordPress plugin or connection to Google Analytics to view data. If you are unsure, perform a quick Google search to find out where on the backend of your site your analytics are housed and record the following data for a specific timeframe.

Note: Whether you choose a weekly, monthly, or annual timeframe for your data snapshot depends on how long you've been in business. If you have the data, I recommend looking over a longer period of time to get a feel for the ebb and flow of trends and then zoom into shorter lengths of time for a closer look at why a variation from the norm happened.

Use the following space to record your stats:

Site visits (website's analytics/Google Analytics): ....

Unique visitors (website's analytics/Google Analytics): ....

Total sales (website's analytics): ....

Average order value (website's analytics/calculate on your own: ....

Dispersion of traffic (website's analytics/Google Analytics)**:**

>   Direct traffic: ....

>   Search traffic: ....

>   Social traffic: ....

>   Email traffic: ....

Bounce rate: ....

Average session duration: ....

Social Media Analytics

Each social media platform is different in how to find your data. Note you'll likely need business-designated profiles/accounts to have access to data insights rather than the personal accounts you may be more familiar with.

Take your top 2-3 social media platforms and record the following baseline for each:

> **Platform:** ....

>> Number of followers: ....

>> Interactions: ....

>> Ratio of followers to non-followers who view your content: ....

>> Commonalities among best performing posts: ....

>> Profile visits: ....

Button taps: ....

Content Interactions: ....

Platform: ....

Number of followers: ....

Interactions: ....

Ratio of followers to non-followers who view your content: ....

Commonalities among best performing posts: ....

Profile visits: ....

Button taps: ....

Content Interactions: ....

Platform: ....

Number of followers: ....

Interactions: ....

Ratio of followers to non-followers who view your content: ....

Commonalities among best performing posts: ....

Profile visits: ....

Button taps: ....

Content Interactions: ....

Email Marketing Analytics

Email stats will be available inside your email marketing platform, such as MailChimp, Active Campaign, and Constant Contact, either by individual email campaigns sent or under a separately housed "Reports" area in your dashboard that shows trends and averages. Become familiar with the following:

Total subscribers: ....

Average open rate: ....

Average click rate: ....

Average unsubscribe rate: ....

Make it a goal to revisit data sources monthly. Mark a standing data date with yourself in the first week of each month to review last month's performance. Learning to read the story the data tells is a skill you'll develop over time and will pay dividends. For now, commit to showing up, and your decision-making ability will evolve.

APPLY DATA-DRIVEN MARKETING STRATEGY TO YOUR WEBSITE

Data-driven decision-making is using facts, metrics, and data to guide strategic business decisions. Now that you have your baseline metrics, let's shine light on strategies to enhance the effectiveness of your website. Here, you'll learn what factors most impact the success of your site when it comes to turning leads into paying customers. The following guidance will help you view your website content from an intentional perspective rather than what "looks right." Whether you built your website yourself or hired help, the conversion rate optimization insights you'll find below are ones that few people know to implement.

A/B test. A/B testing, or "split testing," is comparing two variations of a page or elements of it, measuring the results, and then implementing the result with the better metric. Don't be afraid to switch things up, but go slowly and keep changes small and incremental. If you change everything at once, you may have a harder time pinpointing specifically what worked better (or didn't). Let the data direct your decisions by pinpointing the base metric and how the result changes when you make a slight change. Pinpoint a baseline and make it a game to see how much you can improve over time by getting creative with how you tweak content.

Keep visitors on the site longer. Your goal is to keep visitors on your site as long as possible. The longer they stay, the more familiarity they build and the more likely they are to buy. Blog posts, videos, professional-looking photography, frequently asked questions, and informative pages that teach visitors about your area of expertise are helpful resources to aid the visitor in developing rapport with your business. Be sure to add links via hyperlinked text and clickable buttons leading to other pages and sections on your site to increase number of pages per session and dwell time.

Create a strong abandoned cart strategy. The reality is that the large majority of people who come to a website aren't ready to buy. Some sources cite up to 90% aren't yet ready to make a purchase. Even those who fill their cart often abandon it, but that doesn't mean they won't change their minds later. An abandoned cart strategy is an effort to recoup otherwise lost sales when customers fill their cart, but leave before checking out. Sending follow up emails or leveraging a pop-up when visitors go to exit the site can be helpful for winning a portion of those sales.

Look to see where traffic is dropping off. Use Google Analytics to understand where visitors are most likely to leave your site. Then focus on improving the content on those pages and leveraging calls to action to lead visitors to where you want them to go next. The Top Exit Pages report can be found in Google Analytics (Login > Behavior Tab > Site Content > Exit Pages) if you have it linked with your site.

Add convenient payment options. As mobile use increases, it's vital customers can check out easily using their phones. Convenient payment options like Apple Pay and PayPal allow customers to complete a transaction with ease. The easier and more convenient the checkout process, the higher your conversion will be. Even the smallest distraction or inconvenience can deter the most eager customers from completing a transaction, so scrutinize the transaction process and continually ask how you can make it simpler.

Create great copy. Everyone suggests this, but what does it mean? Great copy isn't just content that sounds great. It's copy that speaks the language of your audience's brains. This also means fancy copy—no matter how cute—isn't effective if it doesn't give your customer a reason to buy in terms that matter to them. I hate to break it to you, but your audience cares about your company only to the extent it benefits them. Your written copy—website copy, email copy, social copy, and anywhere your customers read your marketing messages— must bridge the gap between your products and their priorities. One great resource for learning how to write copy that moves customers to action is *Building a Story Brand* by Donald Miller where he explains why and how to position your customer as the hero of their own story.

Keep your site speed in check. Customers typically won't wait longer than five seconds for a website to load. If your site is slow, it's working against your goals. Running multiple third-party platforms, large photos (in terms of kilobytes), and files that aren't compressed are a few reasons sites run slow. Check your site speed with Google's Site Speed tool (https://developers. google.com/speed/pagespeed/insights/). If this topic or making improvements to site speed feels out of your league, contact a web developer or search engine optimization strategist for help.

Data-driven decision-making has the answers you might be seeking about what is and isn't working to drive sales. Empower yourself by keeping an open mind and learning about making decisions with data. The more you learn, the more you can improve your business and the customer's experience.

'PHASE FIVE: PROFIT' CONCLUSION

Can you believe it?! You have become the savvy female business owner I knew you'd one day be when you picked up this book. You built your business. You launched it. And now you have a thorough understanding of how to make the most profit for the work you're already doing. I hope you feel empowered. I hope you feel confident. I hope you never again underestimate your ability to accomplish amazing things.

In **Phase Five: Profit**, we dove deep into working smarter, not harder, by applying intentional strategies to drive more revenue, lower costs, and create the largest profit margin available to you. In this phase of building a successful business, it's no longer about doing the right things but rather analyzing the right things, and you just got a crash course in what all those "right things" are.

Highly scalable businesses (what we'll talk about next in **Phase Six: Scale**) tend to have a higher profit margin. Less scalable businesses tend to have a lower profit margin. Pinpointing your current profit margin gave you a starting point to discuss the strategies companies use to maximize profitability and identify which ones to implement in your business. By this point in the process, you know it's not enough to *know* what to do. You must take action and make appropriate changes to daily processes so your business can realize the power of those changes.

The data-driven decision-making we talked about in this phase—one of my favorite business topics of all time because of the immense leverage it provides—means YOU know how to get and analyze the information you need to make sound decisions in your business. That's right, sis. You don't have to guess when you know how to read the data.

Look at how far you've come, girlfriend. You've now moved through five of the six phases of creating a successful business. There's one phase left: **Phase Six: Scale**. There's no stopping now. See you there!

NOTES

"DON'T YOU DARE UNDERESTIMATE THE POWER OF YOUR OWN INSTINCT."

Barbara Corcoran, Business Mogul

PHASE SIX
SCALE

Madam C.J. Walker, whose parents were both slaves, was born into poverty and learned its hardships throughout her youth. When her first husband died before her 21st birthday, Madam C.J. Walker struggled to feed her young children with her meager salary. Her business idea, hair care remedies, was born out of a solution to a challenge she faced in her own life: a scalp disorder. The hair care concoction she developed turned into a line of hair care products under the Madam C.J. Walker brand. Word spread quickly of her new offering in 1905, and Madam C.J. Walker became the first American female millionaire.

Let's take another example. In some parts of the world, connection isn't so easy. Even with an excellent business idea and workable processes, businesses in some countries face the challenge of connecting their idea with an appropriate market. That's why Nigerian entrepreneur Hasfah Jumare created an app called CoAmana with the purpose of closing societal gaps through "market-enabling" technologies. Her goal is to connect small businesses with a larger global market.

Another example: In 1998, at 27-years-old, Sara Blakely started her company, Spanx, with $5,000 in savings while selling fax machines door-to-door. Up until she sold her business in 2021 for $1.2 billion (yup, that's a "b"), Sara Blakely owned 100% of the company, which means she didn't give up ownership in exchange for investments. She got her start through bootstrapping the business and continued to self-fund. In the beginning, she leveraged purchase orders and revenue soared through sales in big box stores like Neiman Marcus.

These stories of women inventing solutions to common problems give me chills, a sense of pride, and the empowering sense I can do anything! These women had an idea and scaled their businesses to break barriers and impact the world. There's no stopping you or me from doing the same. A business's scalability describes its ability to meet increased market demand. In the product space, this means ramping up production and leveraging economies of scale. With more recent introduction of technology, this can also now mean delivering an offering to an unlimited number of people such as in the case of app accessibility or online courses.

Scaling a business can feel like an impossible feat. Let's change that. This final **Phase Six: Scale** focuses on what it means to scale, why it's important, and how to do it. First, we'll define scalable business models and the types of offerings that scale well. We'll also cover why scaling your business is important if you want to become financially independent with more access to spend your time the way you want.

Next, we'll talk through the challenges of scaling, especially the mindset shift in approaching the problem-solving required to scale. We'll also discuss how to know whether or not you're ready to scale and what to do about it if you're not there yet. We'll look at main issues in your business and walk through a training exercise for how to identify the root cause of issues.

Then, I'll cover the seven different revenue streams and various methods for offering value to customers you may not have considered yet. This is where you'll pinpoint how you'll scale your business based on which revenue streams are right for your business, offering, and business model.

Once you learn how to become the decision-maker your scaled business needs and pinpoint which revenue streams you'll incorporate, you'll then create a detailed vision of your target goals so you know where you're headed, and you can lead your team to get there. You'll also learn how to set your business up for success by reflecting on your new self-concept shift, exploring options for raising capital, refreshing core documents which define your business, and imagining qualities and characteristics of team members you'll likely need to surround yourself with.

By this point in running your business, you've operated long enough to work out the kinks and create efficient processes. The next step in this phase will focus on identifying which processes to detail, how to create your processes and repeatable systems, and how to integrate them into your business so all employees, team members, and stakeholders are on board. Finally, we'll discuss what an exit strategy is and why you need one.

In **Phase Six: Scale**, you will be guided through how to do the following:

- ▸ **Step 1:** Gauge Your Readiness to Scale

- ▸ **Step 2:** Reinforce Your Revenue Streams

- ▸ **Step 3:** Refine Your Vision

- ▸ **Step 4:** Grow into the CEO

- ▸ **Step 5:** Protect Your Processes

- ▸ **Step 6:** Develop an Exit Strategy

WHAT IT MEANS TO SCALE

Scaling a business is making an offering widely available without a directly proportional incremental increase in costs. Scaling is a shift in a business approach from incremental growth to compounded growth. The ability to scale is the deciding factor between building an asset and earning a paycheck. By necessity, a scalable business is one where you can make its products or services widely available to the public.

A scalable business is able to grow out of proportion with the costs and resources required to create it, meaning an additional sale does not require an equal amount of additional costs. Freelance, for example, is unlikely scalable because you trade one hour of your time for a set number of dollars. A freelance graphic designer, however, could scale her business by selling printable files of her work with unlimited potential for sales. Since service-based businesses are limited in the number of hours available, they're also limited in the amount of money they can make providing services in exchange for incremental income. Scaling, on the other hand, is offering additional value without directly proportional additional costs.

Examples of scalable business models include software (apps, CRM, retail chains, ecommerce), monetized content (blogs, podcasts, YouTube), digital downloads (stock photos, podcast intro music, graphic designs, music, books, movies), courses, membership communities, and subscriptions (meal delivery, Amazon Prime, "wine of the month" clubs).

A business is ready to scale only after it has become predictably profitable, gained a strong footing in the market, and has enough experience and lessons learned to broaden its reach while making efficient use of resources. Profiting and scaling are mutually exclusive, although they have many overlapping qualities and indicators by definition. For example, it's important for a company to be profitable before scaling, but both profiting and scaling involve the efficient use of resources to maximize results.

The journey to become profitable primes a business to scale because during that season of business, product or service bugs are worked out, marketing messages are refined, and processes tend to become more efficient over time. Setting up to scale your business is unlike anything you've accomplished to this point.

WHY SCALING EQUALS FREEDOM

If you want to determine your own earning potential, it's critical to consider how your business can scale. For example, Amiah owns a single mobile boutique which is not scalable because she's limited by her resource of time and geographic location. She can only sell out of her mobile boutique to as many pop-ups as she can drive her mobile boutique to. Even if she maps out the most efficient route, chooses the biggest and best pop-ups, and cuts back on sleep, she still has a threshold she cannot surpass because of time limitations. However, suppose Amiah opens an online store where customers can order from anywhere in the world and shop the same products she offers in her mobile boutique. This additional revenue stream adds a scalable aspect to her business model because anyone anywhere can order from her store, making her selling ability unlimited.

Also take Vivian for example. Vivian creates a course about parenting. Selling the course to 100 customers uses nearly the same number of resources as selling the course to 1000 customers. Zoe put the effort in upfront to create the content, but afterward, selling to an additional customer does not require much, if any, additional time. That's why her course business is scalable. While it's true she might have to handle an occasional customer service issue and spend time marketing, those requirements of time and capital are not in direct proportion to each additional sale.

Scaling is about systemizing, because at some point, your business will grow to a point where you can no longer pull every lever. You will hit your capacity limit to manage every aspect and move every piece, and when demand exceeds capacity, you'll face missed opportunities. From a lifestyle perspective, a scalable business allows you to make more money working less time, freeing up your precious resource of time to spend your days on your terms—starting another business, vacationing, spending time with your kids or grandkids, volunteering, enjoying hobbies. If starting a business is your ticket to live life on your own terms, a scalable business is your ticket to freedom of time.

PRO TIP: Allow your challenges to spur improvements. Ever noticed how some of your most difficult life circumstances helped shape you into the incredible person you are today? Like a diamond under pressure, beautiful things can come from challenging circumstances. The same goes with business challenges. It's the struggles that force us to face the flaws and refine our processes to create better results and outcomes. Constraints contribute to innovations. Constraints increase creativity. That's why I encourage you to embrace challenges. Welcome the criticism. Leverage the insights that hard times present. When something isn't working, ask yourself what the ideal outcome would be and then work backward to create a process that produces that outcome. In the beginning, it may seem like another challenge hides around every corner. Nevertheless, persist, my friend! You were made to rise above hard challenges. Just like happiness, improving processes is a journey, not a destination.

Let's move into the action steps to help you foresee opportunity and take action to scale your business.

STEP

GAUGE YOUR READINESS TO SCALE

Your business craves a problem solver, someone who actively participates and continually asks, "How can we make this better?" As you transition into a scalable business model, recognize your problem-solving must evolve as your business does. As the saying goes, "New levels, new devils." Look the challenge in the eyes and commit.

Up to this point, it's likely your leadership leaned heavily on what seemed most logical. If successful businesses were run on logic, most anyone could knock it out of the park. It's time to put your business knowledge and experience to work to look beneath the surface to run your business. Just like the cause and effect of economics, problems are rarely what they seem. My friend and processes expert, Dean Heffta, once said: "More often, what we think is a problem is actually a symptom of a problem."[1] This is an interesting concept to grasp, and it applies directly to the problem-solving skills you'll need to develop into the owner your business needs, so let's talk through two examples:

Example #1: Let's say a manager of one of your retail locations sends you an email saying, "We need to recruit another employee before the busy season ramps up next month. Our first shift crew is not making the cut." At face value, you might think, "Gosh, she's right. We ought to hire a better fit quickly before the busy season ramps up." Then, like the wise woman you are, you stop and think about the situation. You realize rehiring is expensive, and it may not solve the root issue. You consider a different angle. Maybe it's not the employee's performance that should be scrutinized, but rather the training process or communication of expectations that should be refined instead to help the first shift crew better understand expected results. The employee's performance is not the problem, but rather a symptom of a problem. When you look beneath the surface, you realize the real problem is a faulty training program and the absence of employee-wide communication about performance expectations.

Example #2: You're a nervous wreck biweekly as your responsibility of running payroll draws near. Your cash reserves seem to be dwindling without revenues matching projections and you're beginning to wonder if you'll run out of cash to pay employees. For the millionth time, you try to come up with some brilliant idea to market better, sell more effectively, or get one-time customers through your doors again in order to generate more cash flow. Then it dawns on you. Too much of your cash is tied up in monthly subscription costs you don't use and over-ordering, causing the holding of excess inventory. In essence, your employees' paychecks are sitting on the shelves of the warehouse in unused and unnecessary inventory. Once these problems are resolved, your cash flow returns to a much healthier state. The shortage of cash is a symptom of the problem, which is tying up too much cash flow. Once you pinpoint how to better leverage your cash, you realize your cash flow problems resolve and profit margin improves.

These examples illustrate basic constraints. If they were approached differently, it would allow the business to ebb, flow, and evolve as a scalable entity. Next, let's visit symptoms which may indicate more serious problems in your business which should be addressed before attempting to scale.

You are not ready to scale your business if:

- ► Your business has an inconsistent/unpredictable cash flow.

- ► You lack proof of concept.

- ► You don't have cash or access to capital to invest in the necessary resources to scale.

- You struggle to delegate and insist on managing every aspect of the business.

- Customer satisfaction is lacking.

Each of these symptoms connects back to a bigger problem—a crack in the foundation—and should be addressed in order to prepare your business to scale. Inconsistent cash flow might indicate you haven't nailed your marketing messaging or created adequate marketing channels to drive consistent sales. It could also signal poor management of cash and the need to outsource the accounting responsibilities. Lacking proof of concept might mean your offering needs some tweaks or you misjudged who your ideal customer is. Your resistance to delegation might indicate your leadership team is lacking the necessary skill set for future growth.

As you face problems in your business, pull back the curtain to see what factors cause the symptoms. W. Edwards Deming once said, "Every system is perfectly designed to get the results it does." In other words, the results you're seeing were initiated by some kind of input. It's the input which needs to be addressed, and your job is to find out what that input is.

Reflect on your three most daunting challenges. In the space below, list each challenge and reverse engineer (meaning, "work backward, step by step") the circumstance until you arrive at the root issue. Use the problem-solving perspective detailed above to work backward. An example is provided.

Example:

Problem: First shift employees are under-performing.

Why is this a problem? They're not meeting sales numbers, which is contributing to the retail location missing sales goals. In addition, customer satisfaction scores are the lowest from customers who shopped during the same time of day those employees were working.

Investigate: Upon talking to the first shift employees, you learn they're unaware of company-wide sales goals. They feel confused about the branded selling method, so they're afraid to engage with customers. When you ask what their training and on-boarding was like, you find out these employees were hired during a transition of management and didn't receive the employee handbook or proper training, which outline the company-branded selling method and employee expectations.

308   DREAM, BUILD, GROW

Takeaway: If employees were aware of their sales goals and how to guide customers in making a purchasing decision, perhaps they would feel more comfortable to engage with the customers and make sales.

Solution: You address the issue in the following ways:

▸ Discuss your findings with the store manager and come up with a plan.

▸ Schedule a two-day training for first shift employees, which includes a review of the company handbook, group role playing to improve sales skills, and revisiting the brand standards so employees feel confident in the business's mission and vision and understand how their contributions play an important role.

▸ Have the location manager schedule a sit-down with each employee to review sales expectations regularly and ask for input on how they can feel supported through meeting their goals.

▸ Establish easy access for employees to check on their sales goals and progress during each shift so they know how close they are to their goals.

▸ Use this situation as an opportunity to roll process improvements out to all locations.

Reflect: **How will this problem-solving method contribute to your goal to scale?** Rolling out process improvements positively impacts employees at all levels of the organization because many problems root in a lack of understanding about expectations. Clarifying expectations can synergize each team member's efforts so all employees row in the same direction. At the end of the day, employees want to know what's expected of them and what they can expect from others.

Your turn. Use the problem-solving process to consider the major challenges you face in your business currently.

Problem #1:

Why is this a problem?

Investigate:

Takeaway:

Solution: You address the issue in the following ways:

....

....

Reflect: How will this problem-solving method contribute to your goal to scale?

....

....

....

....

....

Problem #2: ....

Why is this a problem?

....

....

....

....

Investigate:

....

....

....

....

Takeaway:

Solution: You address the issue in the following ways:

Reflect: How will this problem-solving method contribute to your goal to scale?

Problem #3:

Why is this a problem?

....

....

Investigate:

....

....

....

....

....

Takeaway:

....

....

....

....

Solution: You address the issue in the following ways:

....

....

....

Reflect: How will this problem-solving method contribute to your goal to scale?

....

....

On the flip side, you may be ready to scale if you feel confident in your problem-solving skills, which likely means many or most of the following apply to you.

Signs you're ready to scale:

▸ You feel confident in the foundation of your business, and financial numbers warrant your optimism with adequate cash flow and a profit margin that indicates operational efficiency.

▸ High customer retention rates mean you have a loyal core customer base that can help carry your business through the process of scaling.

▸ You're confident in your team, and you have identified positions which will need to be filled based on defined markers, such as adding one new salesperson for each additional $100,000 in revenue.

▸ Your business has been profitable for a while, which likely means you've worked out major kinks in your processes to get to this point.

▸ Demand exceeds capacity and you have a plan for meeting such capacity.

▸ You have planned for how you'll maintain the strength of your brand through the transition.

Few people pause to consider whether their business is primed to scale, so kudos! Your forethought in first pinpointing solvable challenges before scaling up your operations will allow you to dive headfirst into the new initiative without all the mind drama. You have taken an unbiased look at your business's operations, hashed out a plan for solving impeding challenges, and included the necessary process improvements that will help your business scale uninhibited. Now let's talk about the importance of establishing multiple revenue streams.

STEP

REINFORCE YOUR REVENUE STREAMS

According to the book *The Millionaire Next Door* by Thomas J. Stanley & William D. Danko, the average millionaire has seven revenue streams. This is not to say all millionaires are business owners, though many are. Rather, millionaires have created a combination of revenue opportunities, such as a full-time job, commercial or residential real estate investments, a stock portfolio, licensing fees from intellectual property, revenue from paid speaking engagements, etc.

You, too, can take a similar approach as you build multiple revenue streams in your business, knowing that more revenue streams typically hedge your risk. Building revenue streams helps diversify your income, making it less risky if something were to happen and obliterate your sole revenue source. One example is a landscaping service who also offers snow removal in the wintertime.

The key is to create a value ladder with a combination of active and/or passive revenue streams. In this space, we'll explore the different revenue streams, and then you'll define which revenue streams are right for your business. Finally, you'll have space to journal about what role each plays in your business, the timeline for when it will be introduced to your business, and how it best serves the customer.

First, let's explore the types of revenue streams you might use in your business. The following revenue streams come from The Business Model Canvas[2], another incredible resource for starting your business.

Selling assets. This means you sell something, someone buys it, and it's theirs to do with it what they please. You purchased this book. Mary bought Maggie's business. Chantell crushed her quarterly goals and bought herself a latte to celebrate. In each of these examples, the customer takes ownership of the purchased offering and the business they bought it from no longer has discretion over it.

Usage fees. With this revenue stream, you make money based on how often someone uses your service. You offer a monthly social media management package, and the customer pays you each month for the service. A hotel sells rooms and customers pay per night. Your electricity bill comes each month, and you pay based on how much electricity you used.

Subscriptions. The subscription revenue stream means someone purchases the right to access an offering on an ongoing basis. Examples include accessing Netflix, receiving monthly meal delivery, and becoming a member of a paid mastermind group.

Renting, leasing, and lending. Here, a customer temporarily uses an asset for a specified period of time. With this revenue stream, the owner of the asset is able to justify the cost of the item and then earn recurring revenue above what it cost to purchase. Examples include renting real estate or leasing a car.

Licensing to third parties. With this revenue stream, the owner keeps a copyright, but allows others to use it for a fee. Suppose you'd like soothing instrumentals to play during the intro to your podcast. You don't make music, so you purchase the rights to use music someone else made.

Brokerage fees. Brokerage fees are defined as the income someone makes who pairs people or businesses together. An insurance broker, for example, helps customers find the best insurance company and deal rather than working for any one insurance company. A real estate agent is another example of a broker because she pairs homeowners selling their homes with interested parties looking to buy a home.

Advertising Fees. With advertising fees, you agree to allow someone to advertise their offering in a space you own in exchange for a fee. Examples include fees from triathlon sponsorship spots, like my friend Leann offers to businesses for her kids' triathlon, Tri2BeatMS.

Which revenue stream(s) does your business currently fit into?

....

....

....

....

....

Challenge: Find 2-3 additional revenue streams from the list above that you could leverage in your business and/or personal wealth-building strategy. Explore them in detail in the space provided, including how you could execute each revenue stream, the value it would provide to your business, and what would be involved in setting up the revenue stream in your business.

Revenue Stream #1: ....

....

....

....

....

....

....

Revenue Stream #2: ....

....

....

....

Revenue Stream #3:

Reflect on what the transition could look like as you switch from your current business model into one which integrates additional revenue streams. Consider how relationships, roles, and operations will also shift.

What role does or will each revenue stream play in your business? For example, I have intentionally developed offerings (also revenue streams) to serve my three ideal client personas—DIY Dolly, Passionate Pearl, and Full-Scale Fiona. Each revenue stream serves as a valuable resource for helping each ideal client persona reach the next level.

Not all new revenue streams need to be introduced immediately. Consider the timing of rolling out each new revenue stream based on the workload your business can manage now and in the future. For example, say you want to add the revenue stream of group workshops in the next 12 months and a course which encompasses similar content in the next 3-5 years. What does the timing look like for your new revenue streams?

Finally, reflect on how each revenue stream serves your customer. Keep the value your customer experiences from each revenue stream top of mind. Each revenue stream should be purposeful to them and to your business.

STEP

REFINE YOUR VISION

October is goal-setting month in my world. I spend the entire month thinking about what I want the next calendar year to look like. I comb through the seven dimensions of wellness—social, emotional, spiritual, physical, environmental, intellectual, and my favorite, occupational, to be sure I create a holistic approach to intentionally designing my life. I narrow what I hope to accomplish in the next 365 days into a single focus word. One year, my focus word was "transformation." I visualize and map out which accomplishments and results will be realized through my efforts, knowing that most mornings, I'll wake to the same journal prompt, "How will what I do today push me closer to my goals?"

Why October rather than November, December, or January? Girl, I can't remember to put underwear on during the holiday craziness, much less think clear thoughts as crucial to my success as visualizing an entire year's intentional results. Starting in January is too late to give my mind ample time to prepare. I believe a vivid picture of where you're going is exactly *that* important. Otherwise, as long as you're in survival mode, your brain will work only to continue producing the status quo.

Recently in a mastermind meeting, I explained to my girl gang how my brain works. I'm literal, black and white, process-oriented, and realistic, so channeling my right brain genius really stretches me. I shared the same boring excuse and, up to that point, I believed it. I told the group, "I have a hard time visualizing something that hasn't yet happened. It feels like I don't know what

I want sometimes." And no sooner did I say that than another mastermind member and friend, Reagan, drop the accountability I needed.

"Francie, you know what you want," she said. "You have to be willing to dream outside of what feels realistic." Whoa. She knew exactly what I needed to hear. Our thoughts hold incredible power, and when it comes to creating your ideal business through process development, it's no different. You must first have a clear vision of what that highest, ultimate, top-performing business ideally looks like to achieve it, even when it feels ludicrous to your brain at the moment.

Knowing where you desire to take your business is a critical factor to arriving there successfully. You must know your destination in such depth that you can see, hear, smell, taste, and touch what it will be like. As we discussed at length in **Phase One: Clarify**, developing a vision creates a target for your brain to create specific and intentional results. Planning and purpose align all your efforts to row in the same direction cohesively.

Imagine a group of ambitious athletic leaders jumping into a rowboat with the collective goal to "arrive at the destination." The problem is, nobody set parameters for where the destination was or how to get there. No common understanding about what constitutes success was established. No method for measuring whether or not the group was going in the right or wrong direction was communicated. There the group sits in the middle of the lake arguing in favor of their own ideas and goals. Instead of making progress toward the target, their energy is expended laying the groundwork for how the feat should be accomplished.

Don't allow your company to become the equivalent of a haphazard rowing ordeal. Manage your growth, or your growth will manage you. Define your destination and imagine what the journey to get there might look or feel like. Desensitize your brain and heart to the unknown so you can advance forward into your new ecosystem full of changes and opportunity. Determine which factors signal success and which factors signal a need for redirecting the vessel onto a straighter path toward the target.

Hope is not a strategy. Use the following space to visualize your intention to scale your business.

Break your current operations down to identify what parts are scalable and what parts are not scalable:

Scalable

....

....

....

....

....

....

....

Not Scalable

....

....

....

....

....

Dig deeper to analyze the factors in your business which are currently preventing it from scaling. Could it be lack of vision, capital, equipment, space, hired help, connection, or confidence?

....

....

....

....

....

Brainstorm ways to fill each of the gaps you listed above.

For instance, if you're lacking the confidence to take your business to the next level, you could 1) seek out a mentor who has been where you want to go, 2) dedicate a day to researching what the path toward success looks like so it doesn't feel so scary, 3) hire a business coach to lead you through the change, 4) reflect deeply on where your fears of failure are rooted to pinpoint and address your hesitation, 5) take a business course online or at a local college, 6) listen to audiobooks about how to scale your business.

List the gap and how you'll fill it:

Gap: ....

How you'll fill it: ....

....

....

....

....

....

....

Take inventory of what processes and systems you have in place currently supporting your success. Then pinpoint how you can leverage those processes and systems to create a value ladder of products and services. Remember, creating a value ladder is the process of organizing your offerings in ascending order based on value and price to create options for customers based on their needs. The offerings along your value ladder should support your ideal customer's goals and needs and provide options for meeting them. Add offerings intentionally and keep it simple and obvious which option is the best fit based on the customer's needs.

For example, word of mouth has spread about Chloe's corporate developmental training workshops and demand has especially increased over the last six months to the point where she's fully booked out for the remainder of the year. She could raise her rates, which would incrementally improve her financial standing. However, if she does this, she's still capped by her availability of time and the constant traveling is taking its toll on her family life.

The good news is Chloe has some options. She could alternatively offer online webinars, an efficiency improvement because this would allow her to execute the training workshops from her own office. Plus, she could execute more trainings in less time without the need to travel. The disadvantage here is she would still need to be present for each transaction. In other words, her business depends on her time and the execution of each training program. Chloe is still trading time for money.

Another option is to package her training workshops into a course to develop an additional revenue stream and reach a new market of customers who can't afford her full-scale training workshops. Here, she's not limited to the number of courses she can sell, and each additional sale doesn't require additional time. In fact, a combination of all options listed would meet many of Chloe's goals—raising her rates (highest tier), providing a webinar option (mid-level tier), and offering the content in a paid course (lowest tier) defines her value ladder. Additionally, Chloe now has a scalable option (the course), and two higher-priced paid tiers still position her as the expert, but also alleviate her time constraint and serve her customers with options to fit their needs.

How can you deliver your value differently to appeal to a wider audience and scale your business?

What will a scaled business look like for you? How might your lifestyle change? How might your financial standing change? How might your business's position in the market change? Use the space below to journal through changes you can anticipate:

....

....

....

....

....

....

You never grow out of dreaming as an entrepreneur. Reaching new seasons of business requires you to cling to your roots. Dream big audacious dreams and visualize the highest standard you can possibly fathom. Visualize your results, even if you don't know in the present how you'll achieve them. Simply creating the target gives your brain a vision of what it must create. Always remember, if you can dream it, you can do it. So, go on! Create a business that doesn't need you. Create a business that's so fine-tuned it throws heaps of freedom at you on the regular.

STEP

GROW INTO THE CEO

It became obvious "what got you here won't get you there" when I realized I'd need to restructure my service business to scale it. Growth had plateaued, and time was my limitation. I wish I could say as soon as the light bulb flickered on, I knew what my business needed and thereafter promptly executed. Actually, it was more like Bambi testing her legs for the first time. All the nurturing that made my business initially successful was nothing like the strategy that would transform it into the entity it was destined to become.

Recently, I listened to a *Bigger Pockets* podcast episode[3] highlighting the importance of stair-stepping your success. To stairstep your success, the episode explained, you must reach the new level and be willing to ride the learning curve of that phase as you get the hang of it, only to take the next step up and do it all over again. Leave your ego at the door and be willing to suck.

It's likely scaling your business will require different skills and responsibilities from you, your business's leader. Every season of entrepreneurship has a beautiful way of encouraging you to bloom. With its glorious newness peeking around every corner, we frequently face the harsh reality of stepping outside our beloved comfort zones. It's likely scaling your business might stretch you in ways no season before it has.

This is where many business owners get hung up because they can't relinquish the responsibilities of touching each aspect of the business. That must change. As you scale your business, you must learn to delegate, outsource, and leverage resources for the greater good. In order to grow, you'll need to embrace a new role—the role of CEO. For example, there may be a phasing out of you personally performing revenue-generating tasks within your business replaced by a phasing in of embracing more of CEO-related responsibilities.

We hear the term CEO (Chief Executive Officer) often, but what role does a CEO play? The CEO is responsible for painting the broader vision for all divisions and stakeholders within the company. She makes strategic business decisions, manages big picture operations, serves as the main source of communication among company leaders, and is the glue that holds a business together through its evolution. See, as your business transitions, you'll also have to transition into a broader visionary role. You'll need to free up your time to "sail the ship," which often means giving up your seat rowing the boat.

Phase Six: Scale, Step 4: Grow into the CEO focuses on transforming into a visionary who can lead through change. Here, you'll begin to take the pulse of your business's current operations and anticipate what changes and intentional shifts are necessary to ready yourself and your business for growth.

Consider the ways your job description will shift over the coming 6-18 months as you work toward your goals of scaling:

What new skillset(s) might you need to learn to become the leader your future business needs? For example, does your business need you to be able to manage people well? Leverage cash more strategically? Travel extensively? Generate new and innovative product designs for others to execute? Speak publicly?

....

....

....

....

....

....

Your incredible brain is your most important asset, and the beauty is that you can learn to manage your mind for better success. Your thoughts determine your outcomes and your potential. How might your self-talk and self-perception need to shift as you transition into your new role leading your business into future growth?

....

....

....

....

....

....

....

....

....

Scaling your business means many things for its operations. One consideration you should anticipate is using cash differently than you do currently because scaling will likely require an investment of cash in equipment or other resources, labor, or new facilities. A certified accountant can provide guidance for how to best use your resources for tax purposes, like writing off depreciating assets.

Use the space below to brainstorm your future need for cash in your business. Also take this time to call or email your accountant to set up a meeting to discuss your plans for the future of your business.

....

....

....

....

....

....

....

CONSIDER RAISING CAPITAL TO SCALE YOUR BUSINESS

After considering your business's future cash requirements and after talking with your accountant, consider whether you have the cash on hand to execute your plans to scale. If you don't currently have the necessary cash you need, it might be an indication you'll need to either wait to execute your plans until cash flow is available or raise capital. Keep in mind the types of loans available to you are typically based on your legal business structure. Your lawyer or banker can help guide you through financing options fit for your situation and your legal structure.

Common methods for raising capital include:

Bootstrapping - If you have the cash on hand to carry out the investments you need to scale your business as Sara Blakely did in the section's introduction, this might be the best option. While using your own cash seems like the obvious solution, many factors play into whether that's so. For example, if the interest rate is extremely low on a short-term loan, your accountant, banker, or lawyer may recommend keeping your cash and borrowing money from the bank for little interest (cost) to you.

Crowdfunding - Crowdfunding is raising funds through a collective effort from friends, family, customers, and individual investors. Rather than a few people contributing a lot, with crowdfunding, a lot of people typically contribute less individually than larger scale investors to help propel an idea forward.

Angel Investor - An angel investor is an individual with a high net worth who uses their own funds to invest in small businesses and is typically seeking high returns.

Venture Capitalist - A venture capitalist is a person or company that uses money pooled together from several sources to invest in small companies.

Short-term and long-term loans - Short-term loans are generally for less than one year and come with a higher interest rate. Long-term loans are generally for longer than one year and offer lower interest rates. Because the debt is repaid periodically over a longer time period with long-term loans, the interest amount paid tends to be higher in total. See your banker for options. Also consider loans from the Small Business Administration.

Peer-to-peer lending - This financing option pairs individuals who want to invest with individuals who need financing. This option allows more flexibility by crafting repayment under terms you agree upon with the lender. To find such opportunities, research peer-to-peer lending and explore your options to find one best suited for your needs.

Use this space to jot notes about your lending needs and which options might be the best fit for you:

....

....

....

....

....

REVISIT YOUR BUSINESS'S CORE DOCUMENTS

Depending on how long ago you launched your business, it may be time to revisit your business plan, brand standards, and marketing plan to update these core documents steering how your business operates and where you plan to take it in the future. I recommend refreshing your core documents annually on your business's anniversary anyway, but especially before your plans to scale come to fruition.

In my experience growing my own businesses and in consulting other females through starting their businesses, I can confidently say many things tend to change through the first year of business ownership. That doesn't mean you're doing it wrong. It's impossible to forecast perfectly how reality will transpire so when you need to, pivot. Whether what changes is characteristics of your ideal client, how the product is received compared to what you anticipated, brand messaging, or processes, some things you cannot know until you step into business operations and take action. That's why launching your business is a starting point and focusing on the profiting and scaling aspects of your business can be addressed once you have gained experience to apply. With upcoming changes in your business as you scale, now is a great time to get those core documents updated.

You've become more knowledgeable about your business, your offering, your customers, and your best practices since you originally created the documents. The practice of working back through the content will help instill "what got you here" so you can use the same evolution to consider what it will take to take to "get you there."

Once you've revisited each document, make necessary changes and disperse the documents to all necessary stakeholders. Check the appropriate boxes below when each task is complete.

- ☐ Business Plan
- ☐ Marketing Plan
- ☐ Brand Standards

CONSIDER HOW YOUR TEAM WILL GROW

Many business models cannot scale without growing their team. Hiring and managing a team is one of the trickiest aspects of running a business, but it's one you do not want to leave to chance. Just like your ideal client persona is the person best suited to buy from you, you should also consider what ideal characteristics someone should possess for each position within your company.

Recall from **Phase Three: Build, Step 1: Assemble Your A-Team** this season of business might be appropriate to consider engaging a human resources consultant or hiring a human resources manager depending on how large your business has grown. The right time to transition to a full-time, in-house human resources manager can be a balancing act. Bring a full-time, in-house HR manager on before your business needs one and they might spend time and energy perfecting unnecessary aspects of your business. Bring an HR manager on too late and you could find yourself in legal challenges with employees you don't know how to handle. Engaging an HR consultant until you're ready for a full-time HR manager is one way to mitigate this risk.

Take time to think about how you foresee your team growing. If you already have employees, what characteristics make them great? How have they adapted to, contributed to, and helped evolve your company culture?

....

....

....

What characteristics and skill sets do employees of your company ideally possess?

What kind of people are not a good fit for your organization? For instance, someone who wants a desk job may not be a good fit for a position that requires moving around continually. In another example, someone who prefers to work independently or remotely may not be a good fit for your social, collaborative culture.

Think about what qualities and cultural values make your business great. Then, consider personal qualities that don't match up with those priorities. Document your thoughts below.

How can you hire skill sets complementary to yours for positions you'll be working closely with? For example, if you're someone who thinks concretely, it could be advantageous for you to hire a leader who thinks creatively.

What type of thinker(s) and problem solver(s) will you need to grow your business into your scaled vision? For example, an optimistic, diligent, hard-working personality could provide the momentum your business needs to carry out large, daunting marketing campaigns.

How will you know when it's time to hire? In a previous example, I shared perhaps you'd consider hiring an additional salesperson for each additional $100k in revenue. Many experts will say revenue-generating employees should be able to produce at least 2.5x their salary in revenue to justify employment.

What goals, when met, will trigger the need for additional hiring in your business?

....

....

....

....

....

....

CONSIDER YOUR NEW CIRCLE OF INFLUENCE

If you haven't yet secured a mentor, now would be a great time to become diligent and intentional about opening yourself up to opportunities where you could form a connection with someone who can lend mentorship. Here are some ideas for possible sources to find a mentor:

- ▸ Local networking events (National Association of Women Business Owners, Women in Leadership groups, Rotary Club, and Chamber of Commerce events, for example)

- ▸ Industry-specific conferences (introduce yourself to the speakers and conference organizers and ask to grab coffee to create a relationship and potentially ask him/her to mentor you)

- ▸ A seasoned business owner who has achieved the success you desire

If you already have a mentor, take this opportunity to reach out to him/her to schedule a sit-down. There, provide updates and ask for guidance on your path forward to scaling. If your mentor doesn't have specific experience in what you're aiming to accomplish through scaling or if you don't have a mentor yet, use the space below to brainstorm possible mentor relationships or opportunities where you could seek out a mentor to guide this new business challenge.

More than anything, mentally preparing to show up differently in your business is necessary to become the leader your business needs to scale. This season of business will stretch and pull you in new ways. You can no longer workhorse your way to success. Many entrepreneurs before you have tried. Nope. Now, you'll need to think, plan, and approach your business more strategically, with more finesse, and more CEO gumption.

How do you prepare? Consider the financial needs of your future business and return to your roots by revisiting what makes your business special. Think about the new roles your business will require and surround yourself with people several steps ahead of you who can lead you in the right direction.

Scaling your business means engraving it with a fresh purpose—one that makes a bigger impact, stretches beyond old limitations, and serves more customers with intellectual intentionality. You can do this. You were made for this!

STEP  5

PROTECT YOUR PROCESSES

W.Edwards Deming was many things—engineer, statistician, author— but most of all, he was known as the master of processes. He recognized that much of what is broken about any business is the processes it follows to get results. Don't mistake his process orientation for lack of care for people. Processes were what he helped companies utilize to profoundly impact their workforce satisfaction. He knew in the core of their being, employees wanted to understand what was expected of them and what they could expect from their company. Processes do that. He knew that processes were the key to effective management of any kind.

Repeatable day-to-day processes and maximized workflows are critical for scaling a business. Creating repeatable processes forces a business's leader(s) to thoroughly review how business activities are accomplished compared to how they would ideally be accomplished. If methods and processes are relegated to the mind of the person who does them, they aren't repeatable or scalable.

To put it simply, processes are your key to creating a business that doesn't rely on you. If your business relies on you, it's not scalable. The goal of this phase, then, is to help you create a business that works primarily through processes.

Defined processes help anyone involved in your business to understand expectations behind how to produce a result and create consistent experiences for customers. Ask yourself, "How can I accomplish the same results in the simplest way possible?"

Keeping processes woven in your mind won't cut it anymore. If you're the only one who has access to how to accomplish tasks and goals, your business growth's bottleneck will be you. Team members must be able to access documents outlining how and why things are done the way they are. The right way to run your business must come out of your thoughts and into a digital format so others can help carry the load for growing the business in their respective areas of expertise. Scaling is predicated on designing a system where results can be achieved without your involvement. What is the best way to accomplish each task? Handpick team members with a skill set full of potential to evolve as your business does. Provide clear communication about how to accomplish goals through documented processes. Paint a vision for the goals everyone is working toward. Communicate clearly along the way.

Repeatable systems develop momentum in your business, allowing you to focus on revenue-generating activities rather than non-revenue-generating activities. The goal of creating processes is not to eliminate problems, but to increase value in the time spent on tasks. The benefits of processes are many, but most especially helping stakeholders in an organization understand expectations—what's expected of them and what they can expect from others.

Processes create a common dialogue for problem-solving and context for pinpointing where there is a disconnect between what should ideally happen and what is happening. This section will help you consider which processes within your business can be outlined and detailed so you can develop a consistent experience for customers, work out inefficiencies internally, and leverage them to grow your business in the future. Remember, the goal is to create a business that leads to freedom so consider how you can automate, delegate, or eliminate wherever possible with hired help, machinery, or online platforms.

There is a business saying that goes like this: "Create assets, not paychecks." When you create an asset, you create something that can exist (and potentially bring recurring income) after your direct involvement. This is where you involve the strategy of "delegate, automate, or eliminate" so the business can still produce value by someone else or automatically, freeing your time to do other things (focus on growing and scaling the business, build another business, spend more time with family, or sip martinis on an island in Tahiti—a girl can dream, right?!) while you still earn an income. Building your business as an asset also requires you to consider the standard operating procedures—the processes your business follows to create results. SOPs create efficiency, consistency, and the opportunity for someone else—an employee or a potential buyer of the business someday—to understand what input creates your valuable output.

Conversely, when you create a paycheck, you're creating a way to earn a living. The business depends on you to "pull each lever" and do all the heavy lifting to create outcomes. At the end of the day, you created all the results. If you get sick, take a vacation, or otherwise step away from your business, the results come to a halt. Without you, the business doesn't run. In other words, you're not creating inherent value in your business, because if someone wanted to buy your business, they'd have no idea how to run it. All the processes are in your mind and without relaying how the results are created, no one else would know how to create the value you do.

The more your business relies on you to handle each task, the harder it is to scale or eventually sell. If your business depends on you to move each piece forward, you're earning a paycheck, not building an asset you could potentially sell to an interested buyer in the future. The ability to step away from your business while it runs without you is a sign you have created an asset, not just a paycheck.

Your personal mission: make business tasks NOT about you completing each task. Instead, create business tasks that anyone can do well, even if you're the sole person operating it. Standard operating procedures (SOPs) help you do that.

A savvy female business colleague of mine, Chelsie, once said in a mastermind meeting if you find yourself saying the same thing more than once each week, turn it into a process.

Processes you might consider documenting include:

- ▶ Accounting practices
- ▶ Content creation and execution
- ▶ Onboarding and offboarding clients
- ▶ New client consultations

- ▶ Criteria for vetting suppliers, collaborators, or other third-party stakeholders

- ▶ Hiring and firing employees

- ▶ Employee training

- ▶ Updating your website

- ▶ Requirements for staying accredited

- ▶ Criteria for when in-person meetings are necessary and how to run them efficiently

- ▶ Criteria for vetting costs in a business

- ▶ Customer service support

- ▶ Social media management

Use the space below to determine which processes in your business will allow you to create repeatable consistency within your organization.

CUSTOMER-FACING PROCESSES

Transactions

What does the transaction process look like? Online? Point of sale?

How long should the transaction take?

What kind of equipment or subscription does your team need access to in order to complete the transaction, and what should someone know about managing it?

How does a customer experience your brand as they come to make a buying decision, purchase, and decide whether to make a repeat purchase?

How is the transaction process accomplished by your competitors?

Do you see any areas for thinking outside the box to increase efficiency?

Remove all friction. For instance, contactless payment technology, like Apple Pay, is one feature of purchasing online which makes it simple for customers to pay from their phones. Alternatively, some box stores empower employees with point-of-sale equipment throughout the store rather than at a checkout counter so customers can check out anywhere in the store rather than only at the checkout counter.

How can your team make it easy for customers to pay on their terms?

....

....

....

....

....

....

....

....

PRO TIP: "Will it make the boat go faster?" After a long streak of disappointing performances leading up to and including the Rowing World Championships, the Great Britain men's rowing team set out to achieve a profound goal: Win the gold medal at the 2000 Sydney Olympics. For two years, each member of the team fostered an intense focus on improvement in order to reach the collective goal by changing how they approached preparing for the competition. With every decision, the rowing team asked themselves, "Will it make the boat go faster?" Each decision was made under the premise that if a small change in their routine or processes made the boat go faster, they'd keep doing it. If it didn't make the boat go faster, they'd try something else. The team in fact improved significantly over those two years and went on to win the gold medal at the Olympics. Applying the same concept to your business is a focused way to achieve your goals.

Handling a New Customer Inquiry

What aspects of new customer inquiries can your team turn into a process for ultimate efficiency? For instance, perhaps if a customer wants to book a consultation, how can they quickly and simply do it without the back-and-forth emailing required to find a time that works for both of your schedules? An online calendar manager or a canned email asking the potential client to offer three available times to meet are two examples.

....

....

....

....

....

Which customer touch points need a human element (non-automated) so the potential customer isn't met by what feels like a robot?

....

....

....

....

....

....

....

....

What are your goals for each new inquiry?

How can you lead the potential customer to each next phase in the Buying Cycle?

Consultation Call

What information is important to cover during the initial 1-on-1 consultation call?

What criteria do you use to determine if the potential client is a good fit for your business?

How long should the call be?

How do you know if the context of the conversation would be better suited for a paid consulting session rather than a complimentary (if you offer this) consultation?

Design Your Client Onboarding and Offboarding Processes

Create two checklists – one for onboarding and one for offboarding. Consider what should be communicated to the client to create a smooth process of working together. For example, if you run a web design company, your process might look like this: Initial Consultation > Contract > Collect Deposit > Intake Form > Official Timeline and Deadline > Mid-Project Updates > Delivery of First Draft > Allow 1 Week for Customer Feedback > Site Edits > Project Delivery > Final Payment.

Document what onboarding processes look like:

....

....

....

....

....

....

....

....

For offboarding, consider how you can best leave that client and prime them to work with you again in the future. For example, a web designer's offboarding process might look like this: Send Final Invoice > Email Client Synopsis, Including future Service Recommendations > Write and Mail Hand Written Thank You Note > Email Client Outtake Form Collecting Information about Their Experience, Including Asking for a Review > Set CRM to Remind You to Check Back in 90 Days.

Document what offboarding processes look like:

....

....

....

....

....

....

....

....

Customer Service

What FAQs could you turn into a page on your website or one-sheeter to help customers better understand what it's like to work with your business?

....

....

....

....

....

....

....

How do you pinpoint potential opportunities to improve your business based on feedback you receive in customer service conversations?

If someone else is handling the customer service in your business, what skills or information do you need to equip them with to relieve you of the need to be closely involved?

Events

What online and in-person events take place in your business? What should they look and feel like?

....

....

....

....

....

What is the criteria for determining if an event is valuable to your business? For example, if your business is a remote boutique, how do you decide which seasonal pop-up markets to attend?

....

....

....

....

What are the goals and results you're looking for with each event?

....

....

....

....

How do you wish to integrate your brand into events? Signage? Branded fliers? Introductions?

....

....

....

....

....

Create a checklist for events, such as creating a Facebook event, sending out invitations, booking the venue, etc., so you can reference it in the preparation phase for each event and make the process as efficient as possible.

....

....

....

....

....

How does your business close out each event to document and integrate lessons learned and best practices to make the next event even better?

....

....

....

....

....

....

INTERNAL PROCESSES

Team Communication

How should questions be escalated within your organization? Who has the authority to address issues and challenges of various degrees?

....

....

....

....

What is the process for keeping all employees updated on news and events within your organization? A monthly newsletter? A daily team meeting? Weekly manager check-ins?

....

....

....

....

What other expectations about team communication can you develop to help all team members understand how best to communicate with other team members? For instance, when one manager is clocking in, and the other is clocking out, what kind of information should be communicated about the day's activities during the transition so all are in-the-know about important information? Could you create a checklist as accountability for a smooth transition?

How often do team leaders communicate with employees 1-on-1, such as in the case of performance reviews, goal setting, and other important check-ins?

MONTHLY, QUARTERLY, AND ANNUAL GOAL SETTING

How often does your leadership team set goals?

How often does your leadership team check in on the progress of your goals?

....

....

....

....

How does your team remain accountable to its goals?

....

....

....

....

How do you gauge success in your business?

....

....

....

....

How can you develop standards for communication so your entire team understands how individual actions and performance impact company-wide goals?

....

....

....

....

Networking

How do you determine whether a networking event is worth yours or employees' valuable time?

What goals and expected results do you have for attending networking events? Meet three new people? Volunteer time to speak to groups of ideal clients?

What should follow up look like from each networking event? Sending an email? Connecting on LinkedIn? Setting up coffee meetings with important connections? Other?

Time Management

Time is undoubtedly your most precious resource. Use this space to set a precedent in your business to develop good time management habits.

What activities does your team need to perform weekly, monthly, quarterly, and annually to accomplish big picture goals?

Weekly:

Monthly:

Quarterly:

Annually:

How does your team perform revenue-generating activities in your business? For example, if your business is service-oriented, client work is an example of a revenue-generating activity. What are the standards and expectations for all value created in your business?

What are the parameters around performing non-revenue-generating or "support" activities? For example, invoicing for client work is a "support" activity.

Which activities can you automate, delegate, or eliminate?

....

....

....

....

What does your work schedule ideally look like?

....

....

....

....

What boundaries do you need to set with others to ensure your work hours take the appropriate priority of your time?

....

....

....

....

Where in your business can your team batch work, like planning and scheduling your content calendar, developing blog content, or planning a month's worth of weekly newsletters?

....

....

....

....

Accounting

How does your team...

Invoice: ....

....

....

....

....

Budget: ....

....

....

....

....

Manage cash flow: ....

....

....

....

....

File taxes: ....

....

....

....

Pay employees and contractors:

....

....

....

....

Pay bills:

....

....

....

....

Hiring and Firing

PRO TIP: "Be willing to train them." When my business reached capacity, I was lamenting to a group of wise women at a networking event the same agonizing problem many entrepreneurs face – "I just wish I could find another me," I told the women. One of the women replied, "You have to be willing to train them." Cue the epiphany. She was right. If there were another "me" out there, she wouldn't need to work for someone else. She'd likely go start her own business and keep more of the profit. If you can't find someone affordable who has the exact skillset you're looking for, then find someone who has the personal qualities to be coachable and teach them how to create the results you're looking for.

What does your business's hiring process look like?

What criteria do you use to determine if someone is a good fit to work with/ for your company?

How do you know if an employee or contractor is not meeting the standards?

If you find that an employee or contractor is not meeting your standards, what steps does your team need to take to better communicate expectations?

What does the process look like if you need to let an employee or contractor go?

....

....

....

....

Customer Management

Do you need a customer relationship management (CRM) solution? This resource allows businesses to manage relationships and the data and information associated with them. A CRM is one system that can manage email integration, project management, documents, email marketing, sales calls, and relationship progression.

What is your process for managing information pertaining to important business relationships?

....

....

....

....

What is your business's strategy for building its email list? What are the main points of entry? Remember, it's important to have their consent to join.

....

....

....

PROCESS EXECUTION

Don't waste time creating anything that won't be tended to. Where many companies fall short is they devote time to *talking* about what needs to happen, but they don't spend mental brain power to execute habit changes or perform the necessary course correcting to create a new normal that reflects process improvements. In many organizations that try to make change, it never sticks because leaders get hyped about the potential but allow the execution to fall by the wayside[1]. Intentions are a solid start, but intentions don't count on your income statement. Taking time to think through processes and then implementing them in your business operations will ensure your communication and efforts are carefully considered and thoughtfully executed for maximum impact.

So how do you implement processes into your organization? Remember the advice my friend Leann gives me about parenting because it applies here too: "High expectations for behavior, low expectations for how long it takes to get there." If currently your business is only you, you may be able to deploy new processes in a snap. If you have a team rallying around you who each have their own way in which they see the world, it might take a bit longer.

Communicate the "why" behind new processes. Understanding the purpose behind behavior change helps team members get on board, so be sure to share your vision aloud and often. Keep process changes at the forefront of conversation. Remind the team about them during group discussions, like team meetings. Without the proper follow through, employees may resist the change in hopes the expectation will disappear (can't blame them— resisting change is how our brains are wired). The leadership responsibility falls on your shoulders and the shoulders of the other appointed leaders in your business. Continuing to talk about the new expectations and intended results helps employees grasp the transition.

As you implement changes, hold tight to that which you defined in **Phase Five: Profit** regarding your evolved value proposition. Consider putting one single person in charge of making sure nothing rocks the boat in that specific area and strengthening that aspect of your business as you roll out changes. Staying true to your brand values is vital, but it won't be easy unless someone is intentional about locking your brand into new processes, new markets, and new messages with each step up as the business evolves. If your loyal customer base senses that what makes your business special has been sacrificed for growth and profitability, you could have a much bigger challenge on your hands.

STEP  6

DEVELOP AN EXIT STRATEGY

My dad always vowed he'd never retire but rather would take more vacations. For almost 40 years, he worked countless hours, carried the burden of heavy risk, molded the industry for the positive, and developed an unprecedented reputation as a man of impact. It was hard to imagine a separation between him and the businesses he had grown to become so fruitful.

But eventually the time came, and he retired. To celebrate, my brothers and I requested stories, photos, and memories from his colleagues and friends around the world to compile in a printed book for him to keep. After all, he has visited 78 countries with stories to tell from each one, many because his business connected him to people around the world. Emails and letters poured in, many in broken English, from incredible people who had crafted excellent reputations themselves.

In this new season of life, he gets to chase colorful interests, including weekly pickleball, bird watching, decoy carving and collecting, hunting, fishing, bike riding, gardening, golfing, playing make believe with his grandchildren, nightly ping pong tournaments with his bride, and still at a ripe age of 68, traveling the world.

At some point, you will no longer run your business. I know you're probably thinking, *Francie, I'm just revving up, and you wanna talk about the end?* And yes, I do.

When you begin anything with the end in mind, your business included, you're likely to make much more strategic and thoughtful decisions than when you make decisions solely for short-term gain. Girlfriend, do you realize you have the opportunity to create an entity that could exist after your involvement?

Stop and consider what your end goal is. I should note, too, that if creating a business is solely your alternative to working for someone else and you're not interested in creating an entity that could be sold as an asset, there's nothing wrong with that. I'm still sending hugs and high fives to you, girlfriend, for making your own way, carving your own path, and doin' the darn thing.

Realize, though, a little extra effort of intentionally figuring out how to make the business run without you could allow you to transfer the value of a business on to someone else—your children or an interested buyer—and benefit financially long after you use the revenue as your household's monthly paycheck.

What is your end goal? Initially your goal is likely to create a source of income on your terms, but someday there will come an end to your involvement with your business. What might that look like? Will you sell your business? Pass it along to your kids? Dissolve it? Work on it until you take your last breath?

Take a moment to define the details of your exit strategy:

....

....

....

....

....

....

....

....

....

'PHASE SIX: SCALE' CONCLUSION

Breathe in. Breathe out. You did it! You have completed *Dream, Build, Grow: A Female's Step-By-Step Guide for How to Start a Business.* Think back to when you first picked up this book. You had questions in your mind about how to run a business. You held hope in your heart for all the possibilities. You wondered if you had the decision-making ability your business would need. And you did it! Girlfriend...you did it!!

You took action. You overcame obstacles. You built something that once only existed in your heart. Stop for a moment and take it all in.

You worked through the six phases of clarifying your dream, researching how to make it real, building your business's infrastructure, launching your business and telling the world, making your business more profitable, and scaling your business. You have started, refined, and grown your business from idea to a plan for it to run even without you. What an accomplishment! This is *your* vision coming to life, and you've created a beautiful plan for the life you've always wanted.

NOTES

WHAT'S NEXT?

Sis, you already have what it takes to run your business successfully.

Transformation doesn't happen overnight. You'll jump back and forth (mostly forth) between versions of your old self and a marvelous version of the self you're becoming. Enjoy it. This is what it feels like to transform intentionally.

As you look to the future, continue painting your beautiful vision. Continue focusing on changing lives. Continue pursuing your mission. Only you can define what's next, and I can't wait to hear about it inside the Founding Females™ Start-Up Community. (Find it at www.HerBusinessGuide.com).

There's no doubt you'll become stuck at some point. It happens to the best of us. When you do find yourself stuck or at a plateau, remember moments of stuck can become moments of breakthrough. Here are ideas for discovering inspiration to move through challenges:

Present the challenge to your entrepreneur community of support. Ask how others have solved the same problem. As women, we thrive in connection. Whether it's our innate nature to nurture or the way society has shaped us to build community to our advantage, breaking through glass ceilings and overcoming obstacles happens best in the context of a community who understands what you're going through. Consider feedback from someone with a different perspective on how they might handle the situation. What assumptions are you making that may not be helpful? Open your thoughts to what transformation might be taking shape because of this current challenge.

Talk with your mentor. If you haven't found your "official" mentor yet, contact someone who you know has been where you want to go. Challenges are a primary purpose for cultivating relationships with people who have created the kinds of success you desire.

Journal. Committing to daily journaling is the most needle-moving habit I've created as an entrepreneur. Journaling is like having a conversation with the best parts of myself—parts I never knew existed and which yield deeper understanding, more confidence in my decisions, and ideas I didn't know I had. Don't know where to start? Start by telling yourself about what's happening in your business and why it's happening. Journal about the results you'd rather be experiencing in your business and what action you'll need to take for those results to become your reality.

Research. The entrepreneur community is full of people who are self-taught and there's zero shame in being a "figure-outer." In fact, this may become your greatest asset. As a "figure-outer" myself, this is where I derive the belief that I can literally do anything I put my mind to. It's my secret weapon and the quality which I attribute to my success. I truly believe that if someone else has done it or if I can fathom it with my brain, I can make it a reality. If you have a question, others have likely asked that question, too. Make it a fundamental habit when you have a question to go back into research mode and become diligent to figure it out.

Forge new territory. It may be that you're taking a brand-new approach to a challenge in your industry that has never been taken, so take pride and revel in confidence knowing you're a trailblazer. Become comfortable with making decisions when you don't have all the facts, knowing you've developed the muscle that allows you to pivot.

Take a defined cool off period of one week. Mark it in your calendar. Step away from the problem. Focus your thoughts, time, and attention on something besides work. Designate a space to jot down notes for the purpose of getting them out of your brain and recording them on paper for a later date. Don't dwell on them. The point here is to capture good ideas as they come but allow a mental refresh with time away from pouring into your business. Sometimes we become landlocked when we try to force an outcome or decision, so intentional time to refill your cup can release the pressure your brain is feeling to then create better results.

Reflect on your Why statement and your non-negotiables. Allow everything else to become secondary. When you make decisions based on who you are and not what you *should* do, you set the precedent to stay true to yourself. Honor this. It's what develops your gut instinct. It's hard to put into words, but almost always leads you in the right direction.

Consider your progress in multiple forms of success, not just the number of clients you have or the revenue your business generates. Flip back to **Phase One: Clarify** as a reminder of what success means to you. Examples include the impact your business is making on the client, the industry, and the world. Consider the freedom you've found through business ownership to make decisions as you please. Think about the freshening of your soul by doing work you enjoy. Celebrate the unlimited potential you have for the future.

Lean into the savvy of other female entrepreneurs in your circle. Trade business audits with a community member and coach each other through findings. Your eyes will be opened to just how much knowledge you've gained, and you'll continue to see new insights by applying that knowledge to real life circumstances. It's just like education—you can study textbooks and ace the tests, but until you apply the knowledge to a variety of situations, it's really just memorization. Go out and do, take action, and apply.

Re-read Phase One: Clarify of this book. You have now developed a much more comprehensive understanding of starting and launching your business as you've completed **Phase Two: Research**, **Phase Three: Build**, **Phase Four: Launch, Phase Five: Profit, and Phase Six: Scale**. **Phase One: Clarify** intentionally guided you through the development of a baseline starting point for creating an abiding connection to the purpose behind this life change. In my experience, revisiting the basic foundational elements developed in **Phase One: Clarify** can help as you apply and execute business tasks. You now understand what to do and why—a true marker of understanding—rather than memorizing the steps to take. Engrain your values into your every thought, decision, and action. This will transition you from needing guidance from a book into becoming someone who uses her own internal compass to carve the path forward with every step.

CONCLUSION

Celebrate the transformation that has taken shape in your mind and heart. Delight in the possibilities you've created as you worked through each question and to-do within these pages. Your dream has transformed into a company blueprint for the business that was sewn into your heart. What once showcased crisp, blank pages ready to capture your thoughts, ideas, and dreams has become a living version of what once only occupied the depths of your soul.

Has it dawned on you, friend, that with hard work and vivacious tenacity, you created something that never existed before? You are an innovator. A trailblazer. A leader. You're also a wise woman for first obtaining a guide to light your path in committing to the processes within this book. As we visited several times throughout the phases of this guided journal, smart women learn from the experiences and mistakes of others. By consuming the business savvy in *Dream, Build, Grow: A Female's Step-By-Step Guide for How to Start a Business*, you gained an advantage. You rejected the erroneous assumption that you must learn all the hard lessons yourself. You wisely sought counsel. You opened your heart to guidance. By doing this, you committed to leveraging your resources to their maximum advantage, a habit that will pay dividends as you further develop your business.

Each phase of this book led you upward along a crucial pyramid to create a well-laid foundation. You polished your planning expertise to play forward, to define, to imagine, ultimately creating a target on your own unique roadmap. When you began, the vision looked cloudy, confusing, disoriented. Now, you have honed your power by asking the hard questions and by taking time to ruminate carefully. You also honored the advantages of taking action before you have all the answers. You've gained a sense of balance, wisely seeking information and proactively making decisions. Look at how far you've come!

You're now among an elite class of Founding Females™ chock full of ambition who uplift, impact, dare, and believe. No longer do you feel debilitated by confusion or alone on your own island. You've surrounded yourself with inspiring energy, benefiting from the synergy that permeates throughout the female entrepreneurial community around the world. Perhaps without realizing it, you've also laid the groundwork for future generations of female entrepreneurs—maybe your daughter, niece, or neighbor.

In **Phase One: Clarify**, you spent time figuring out who you are and what you want. You intentionally defined the direction where you were headed. In **Phase Two: Research**, you sought answers to questions and informed yourself deliberately to set into position the puzzle pieces of your beautiful vision. In **Phase Three: Build**, you brought your business to life by giving it structure, personality, and strategic plans. Then, in **Phase Four: Launch**, you defined your plan for telling the world about the value of your offering and positioning it in their hearts. **Phase Five: Profit** led you through approaching business management decision-making to work smarter, not harder. Finally, **Phase Six: Scale** showed you how to begin driving compounded revenue rather than incremental revenue.

Your due diligence will serve you well. Your openness to learn and to transform are qualities your business deserves. You have a heart for entrepreneurship and a soul for impacting the world with your ideas.

You have what it takes, but you already knew that, didn't you? You don't need me to tell you that you will change the world. You were well on your way when you purchased this book. You know you have what it takes, and you feel it reverberating in the fibers of your heart.

While this concludes the last chapter of *Dream, Build, Grow: A Female's Step-by-Step Guide for How to Start a Business,* it's only the start to your incredible business journey. The secret to your success is knowing it never has to be perfect.It can always get better with time and experience. You're the boss of your results. You'll test and tweak, test and tweak as you move closer and closer to your targets.

If you didn't believe you could start and run your successful business, you never would have invested the money or, more importantly, committed your precious time. You never would have listened to the calling or believed in this book to be the vehicle to guide you into business ownership. You are now in the driver's seat of the vehicle that will make your dream a reality—a reality of freedom, power, and potential.

Welcome to the good life, sis. Don't forget me when you're ~~famous~~ wildly fulfilled and changing the world.

RIDING ON THE TRASH TRUCK

I would be amiss to exclude the story of my faith journey and how God's incredible grace and guidance have impacted the journey in creating this resource for you. I liken my business routine to that of a trash truck. Before you laugh, hear this... My young daughter, Myla, loves when the trash truck drives around our neighborhood. Every Wednesday morning, we stand together on the back patio and watch as the green behemoth rumbles by.

Inside the front seat, the driver guides the route. The driver's teammate rides on the back of the vehicle, anticipating the next stop. At each stop, the teammate on the back of the truck hops off to do the heavy lifting, then hops back onto the truck again to anticipate the next stop. All the while, the teammate in back is content to trust that the driver will guide the truck to its destination. Season after season, this dynamic duo works together to create positive results.

God is the driver of my business, and I am the teammate on the back following His lead. I'm incredibly thankful He's willing to guide my life forward, and I try hard to let him steer by asking for His continual guidance. My business is actually God's business. He uses me as a vehicle to impact, uplift, guide, and love hard on His precious people. I'm honored to be His hands and feet here on Earth, and I pray daily that He'll continue gripping my heart and using me for His glory. In fact, I repeat this positive affirmation almost daily: "I 10x God's resources for the glory of His kingdom."

As you continue on your trash route, my prayer is that you'll seek His guidance, that you'll ask what He wants the results to look like. He's ready to help; you need only ask. His resources are far better than we could ever source on our own, and His plans are much more fruitful and beautifully impactful. I've prayed countless prayers for you already, sis, as you start your business journey, and I won't stop until I take my last breath. Founding Females™ all over the world are on my heart, and I stand in their corner, cheering them on and praying faithfully for the work they do. God hears our prayers, and He's ready to help. All you have to do is hop aboard ready to fulfill His perfect plan. After all, He is the greatest entrepreneur that ever existed.

APPENDIX

BRAINSTORM YOUR BUSINESS IDEA

D on't have a business idea or don't love the one you have? No biggie! This space is for brainstorming ideas that could be a good fit for you. Your business idea doesn't need to be revolutionary to be successful so don't feel pressure to create a one-of-a-kind idea.

Let's begin by igniting a brainstorming session. Use the space provided to record all business ideas that come to mind:

1.

2.

3.

4.

5.

6.

7.

8.

9.

10.

11.

12.

13. ....

14. ....

15. ....

Next, think about any business idea you've ever tossed around, even in passing. Nothing is off limits or too ridiculous. Now add those ideas to the list above.

Next, explore the following and add additional business ideas that could fit you well.

1. Ask friends, family, and business colleagues what product or service they wish existed. Think through which products or services you wish existed.

2. Evaluate your skill set. What do people compliment you on most often?

3. Call the Chamber of Commerce and ask if they see any gaps in the local area or if they receive inquiries regarding unmet needs.

4. As you use products and services in your own life, ask yourself, "How could I do this better?"

5. Consider your dream job. What about it feels alluring? How can you turn that idea into a business?

6. Assess the responsibilities other people dislike but you don't mind. For instance, I prefer doing laundry any day over scrubbing toilets. Doing laundry allows me to be active as I walk back and forth to the laundry room. Mindlessly folding laundry while I listen to an audio book is my idea of therapy. Offering laundry services could be a great business idea for me because it meets a need others are willing to pay for, and I enjoy the work (crucial!). What is the equivalent for you? How could you meet others' needs and still enjoy your work?

7. Think about what you're most passionate about. Global warming? Fitness? Preventing child abuse? Equality? What unmet needs do you see within community members who share that passion and how can you turn it into a business idea by creating value others are willing to pay for?

ADD YOUR BUSINESS IDEAS TO THE LIST ABOVE

Lastly, review the following list of business ideas. Add the ideas that might be a good fit to the list above. Imagine each idea, even if it doesn't feel like the *perfect* fit. Consider the different roles involved in delivering the final product to the customer. Take meal delivery for example. Perhaps you don't care to interact with customers to deliver the meals, but sourcing the clean products that go into the meals feels like a much better fit. In that case, your customer could be the businesses serving meal delivery businesses rather than the consumer. For the business ideas listed below, there are hundreds of related roles you might consider, so use what's listed as a starting point and explore potential related ideas in the ecosystem.

Home Services. Become an errand runner, laundry doer, paid accountability partner, window washer, trash can sprayer, personal organizer, cabinet painter, or healthy meal planner. Still others include lawn care, personal wardrobe shopper, fish tank care, pool cleaner, or at-home oil changes.

Teach a Skill. Show others how to do something that comes naturally to you: How to choose makeup, clothes, or jewelry based on their features, strategies for stress management, or how to use watercolors. Then, consider the medium through which you would deliver the training—webinar, course, book, guide, or public presentation.

Invest in Real Estate. Learn how to leverage your cash, flip properties, or house hack.

Create an Online Store. Have a product you're passionate about? Source from your favorite vendors and offer them on an optimized ecommerce site like Shopify (www.Shopify.com).

Become a Coach. Become a support person for people trying to accomplish difficult goals. Ideas include general life coaching, weight loss or health coaching, career coaching, parenting coaching, relationship coaching, college prep coaching, and young adult guidance coaching.

Offer Online Services to Small Businesses. It has now become customary even for brick-and-mortar businesses to operate online. That means any small business is a potential customer. Offer to help them run their business online by creating content, managing their website, helping them market, or managing their communications. A Virtual Assistant is someone who offers online assistance from a remote office (this is how I got my start!).

Become a Digital Marketing Manager. Similarly to online services, specializing in marketing allows you to advertise yourself as an expert in the area of marketing for businesses that operate online.

Become a Party Planner. Offer general event services or specialize in something specific. One idea is to become a "Lunch and Learn" planner where you source a presenter, order a meal, and offer a learning experience to corporate teams. Another idea is to offer picnic-style events for special occasions, like engagement parties, baby showers, and girls' nights out.

Pet Care. Offer mobile pet grooming, pet sitting, pet training, or pet walking.

Become a Writer. Offer to create long-form content optimized for organic search like blog posts or website page copy. Become a ghost writer or an author of a book or series of books.

Become an Online Reseller. Resellers are people who source item—sometimes used and sometimes new—and resell them to the general public. For instance, there's a home decor giant that offers free returns. Instead of restocking returned items, the home decor giant will sell returns by the truckload and a designated local reseller will turn around and sell the returned items to the public. Others source items through garage sales or thrift stores and resell them on eBay or other online marketplaces.

Tutor Children. Have basic knowledge of education or a love for teaching? Offer online or in-person tutoring services for school-aged kids.

Start a Food Truck or Mobile Boutique. Enjoy the benefits of a brick-and-mortar and the flexibility of an online store. Arrange a schedule with local businesses and advertise in advance where you'll be parked. Secure event opportunities at local fairs, Farmers' Markets, weddings, or pop-ups. Research well-trafficked events to maximize your route and schedule.

Become a video editor. Video content has become increasingly valuable in the online space. Businesses know they should leverage video content, but few know how to edit the content to make it look good. Take a course to learn how to edit videos and leverage YouTube. Then connect with online businesses to offer your service.

SAMPLE CONTENT CALENDAR

APRIL 20XX

SUNDAY	MONDAY	TUESDAY	WEDNESDAY	THURSDAY	FRIDAY	SATURDAY
			1 Blog: New post Social: Motivational story or quote	2 Social: Event reminder	3 Email: Fri-YAY newsletter	4
5	6 Social: Team member introduction	7 Social: Tip Tuesday	8 Social: Motivational story or quote	9 Social: How-to video	10 Email: Fri-YAY newsletter	11
12	13 Social: Team member introduction	14 Social: Tip Tuesday	15 Blog: New post Social: Motivational story or quote	16 Social: Event reminder	17 Email: Fri-YAY newsletter	18
19	20 Social: Team member introduction	21 Social: Tip Tuesday	22 Social: Motivational story or quote	23 Social: How-to video	24 Email: Fri-YAY newsletter	25
26	27 Social: Team member introduction	28 Social: Tip Tuesday	29 Social: Motivational story or quote	30 Social: Event reminder	31 Email: Fri-YAY newsletter Event: Ladies Happy Hour	1

GLOSSARY

Abandoned Cart Rate - The number of customers who add items to their online shopping cart but abandon it before checking out compared to the total number of shopping carts created.

Analytics - Using data to answer business questions, discover relationships, predict future outcomes.

Assets - In business, an item of value owned by a company, including a vehicle, real estate, equipment, and office furniture.

Average Order Value (AOV) - The average dollar amount spent by customers. To calculate the AOV, divide total revenue by the total number of transactions.

B2B - Stands for business-to-business and is when a business's customers are other businesses.

B2C - Stands for business-to-consumer and is when a business's customers are consumers.

Bootstrapping - A term that describes starting a business only with the cash a business owner has in the bank without taking out a loan or sourcing any additional funding.

Bottom Line - A term used in business that refers to how much money a business makes after expenses are considered. The bottom line can be improved by increasing revenue or decreasing costs.

Break Even Point - The point where the cost to produce one unit of an item equals the revenue the item generates.

Brokerage Fees - The income someone makes who pairs people or businesses together.

Bundle - A sales strategy where a customer is offered a group of related products at a discounted price.

Business Model Canvas - A concept used to describe, visualize, assess, and change business models.

Capital - Money a company has available to pay for day-to-day operations and to fund future growth.

Cash Flow - Measures the ability of a company to pay its bills and is the cash coming into the business minus the cash paid out during a time period.

Cash on Hand - The cash a business has immediate access to.

Churn Rate - Metric that measures the percentage of customers who end their relationship with a company in a particular period.

Consultation Call - The first call between a business and a potential client to discuss working together.

Conversion Rate - The number of people who buy compared to the total number in the audience (visitors on a website, for example).

Conversion Rate Optimization (CRO) - The process of improving the effectiveness of a marketing strategy to increase the number of people who take a desired action.

Cost of Goods Sold (COGS) - The direct costs of producing or acquiring a product to sell.

Cross Sell - A strategy for increasing sales that involves inviting customers to purchase complementary or related products to what they've already decided to purchase.

Crowdfunding - Sourcing a small amount of capital for starting a business from a large number of individuals.

Customer Relationship Management (CRM) - Technology for managing a company's relationships and interactions with customers and potential customers.

Data - Facts and statistics collected together for reference or analysis.

Data-Driven Decision-Making - Using facts, metrics, and data to guide strategic business decisions.

Elasticity - An economic term that describes the extent of a change in supply and demand at varying prices and availability of an offering.

Equity - The value of a business owned by shareholders. If a business has no shareholders, the business owner has 100% equity.

Expense - A cost of operations that a company incurs to generate revenue.

Gross Profit Margin - Revenue minus the cost of goods sold divided by net sales and multiplied by 100.

Gross Revenue - Also referred to as "top line" revenue because it's presented at the top of financial statements and is the total amount of sales a business generates without taking expenses into consideration.

"Imposter Syndrome" - A form of intellectual self-doubt where high achievers often attribute their accomplishments to luck rather than to ability and fear that others will eventually unmask them as a fraud.

Indirect Costs - Costs not directly related to production.

Intellectual Property (IP) - Creations of the mind, like literary works, inventions, designs, or symbols.

Interest - The money owed when borrowing or paid when lending.

Interest Rate - The amount charged by a lender to a borrower for the use of assets and typically expressed as an annual percentage of the loan's outstanding principal balance.

Key Performance Indicators (KPIs) - A measurement term that reflects the critical indicators of progress toward an intended result.

Liabilities - Something the company owes, usually a sum of money, and part of ongoing and long-term operations.

License - An agreement through which a licensee leases the rights to a legally-protected piece of intellectual property from a licensor.

Lifestyle Creep - When a person's lifestyle spending increases as their discretionary income increases.

Market Share - A portion of the market controlled by a company or product and expressed as a percentage as sales divided by an industry's total revenue.

Markup - The difference between what a product or service costs the business to make or acquire and the price it sells the product for.

Net Income - Sales minus cost of goods sold, general and administrative expenses, operating expenses, depreciation, interest, taxes, and other expenses.

Net Profit Margin - The total amount of income left over after all additional revenue streams and expenses are considered, divided by total revenue and multiplied by 100.

Net Sales - The total amount of gross sales minus returns, allowances, and discounts.

Operating Expense - What it costs the business to stay in business during a specified time period, including things like rent, inventory costs, marketing, payroll, and insurance.

Operating Profit Margin - Income minus the cost of goods sold, overhead, operating administrative, and sales expenses required to run the business.

Opportunity Costs - The alternative options given up when another option is chosen.

Overhead - Ongoing expenses not directly tied to creating a product or service but necessary for the running of the business, such as rent, salaries, insurance.

Payment Terms - Specified conditions surrounding the payment for a sale.

Principal - In terms of investing, the original amount invested. In terms of loans, the amount of money the borrower agrees to pay back in addition to interest.

Profit - The amount earned after taking into account the amount spent to produce something.

Profit Margin - A performance measure used to understand the degree to which a business makes money. In simple terms, it's a ratio of how many cents a business generates for each dollar of sales.

Proof of Concept - A test to see if a product or service is viable.

Referral Program - A program instituted by a business for incentivizing customers to refer their friends and family to become customers of the business.

Return on Investment (ROI) - A performance measure in percentage or ratio used to understand the efficiency of an investment by how much income is generated compared to the amount of the investment.

Revenue - The income a business generates from the sale of a product or service.

Revenue Model - The strategy for managing a company's incoming revenue streams and the resources required for each.

Revenue Stream - Various sources that a business makes money from through the sale of products or services.

Scale - Growing a business to make an offering widely available without an incremental increase in costs.

Search Engine Optimization (SEO) - The strategy of improving a website to increase visibility in relevant searches.

"Shiny Object Syndrome" - The tendency to follow trends and results without first determining if they're aligned with big picture goals.

Site Speed - A metric that reports how quickly users are able to see and interact with content on a website.

Subscription Model - Selling a product or service to receive monthly or yearly recurring subscription revenue.

Substitutes - Alternatives for an item that seem almost the same or identical to customers.

Supply and Demand - The relationship between the quantity of an offering that producers are willing to sell and the quantity that customers are willing to buy at varying prices.

Taxes - Mandatory payments levied on people and organizations by the government, based on income.

The Buying Cycle - The process a customer goes through when purchasing a product or service.

Unemployment Rate - The percentage of the labor force without a job and currently seeking work.

Upsell - A sales strategy where a customer is led to purchase a higher priced option to meet the same need.

Usage Fees - A revenue stream based on how often someone uses a service.

Value Ladder - The process of organizing your offerings in ascending order based on value and price to create options for customers based on their needs.

Value Proposition - A specific quality about a business or its offering that is attractive to customers.

REFERENCES

Phase 1: Clarify

1. Sinek, S. (2009). Start with why: How great leaders get everyone on the same page. Portfolio.

2. Economy, P. (2018, February 28). *This is the way you need to write down your goals for faster success.* Inc.com. Retrieved November 24, 2021, from https://www.inc.com/peter-economy/this-is-way-you-need-to-write-down-your-goals-for-faster-success.html.

3. Weir, K. (2013). *Feel like a fraud?* American Psychological Association. Retrieved November 24, 2021, from https://www.apa.org/gradpsych/2013/11/fraud.

4. U.S. Bureau of Labor Statistics. (2016, April 28). *Business establishment age.* U.S. Bureau of Labor Statistics. Retrieved November 25, 2021, from https://www.bls.gov/bdm/entrepreneurship/entrepreneurship.htm.

5. Top reason why businesses fail: https://www.score.org/blog/1-reason-small-businesses-fail-and-how-avoid-it

Phase 2: Research

1. Apply for an employer identification number (EIN) online. Internal Revenue Service. (2021, August 6). Retrieved November 25, 2021, from https://www.irs.gov/businesses/small-businesses-self-employed/apply-for-an-employer-identification-number-ein-online.

2. The ideal team player: how to recognize and cultivate the three essential virtues: a leadership fable, Lencioni - Wiley India - 2018

Phase 3: Build

1. The Independent Community Bankers of America. Retrieved November 25, 2021, from https://www.icba.org/.

2. Top reason why businesses fail: https://www.score.org/blog/1-reason-small-businesses-fail-and-how-avoid-it

Phase 5: Profit

1. Cassaza. (2018, January 17) Re: Episode 006: How my blog got my husband out of his 9 to 5. https://podcasts.apple.com/us/podcast/ep-006-how-my-blog-got-my-husband-out-of-his-9-to-5

2. Nance-Nash, S. (2021, June 30). *Is the Bible the ultimate financial guide?* Forbes. Retrieved November 22, 2021, from https://www.forbes.com/sites/sherylnancenash/2012/05/24/is-the-bible-the-ultimate-financial-guide/?sh=5400cc846493.

3. *Ep #108: Five things you're doing on consults (and why coaching isn't one of them)*. Stacey Boehman. (n.d.). Retrieved November 22, 2021, from https://staceyboehman.com/five-things-on-consults/.

4. *The value of keeping the right customers*. Harvard Business Review. (2014, November 5). Retrieved November 23, 2021, from https://hbr.org/2014/10/the-value-of-keeping-the-right-customers.

Phase 6: Scale

1. Heffta, D. (2021, May 18). Processes in Business [Morton Chamber of Commerce Presentation] Morton, IL, United States.

2. Osterwalder, A., Pigneur, Y., Clark, T., & Smith, A. (2010). Business model generation: A handbook for visionaries, game changers, and Challengers. Wiley.

3. Podcast, T. B. P. (2021, September 12). *Biggerpockets Podcast 504: The millionaire formula: 10 steps to hit 7-figure net worth (part 2)*. The BiggerPockets Blog | Real Estate Investing & Personal Finance Advice. Retrieved November 23, 2021, from https://www.biggerpockets.com/blog/biggerpockets-podcast-504-part-2.

ABOUT THE AUTHOR

Francie Hinrichsen is a business enthusiast who empowers female entrepreneurs to breathe life into the business dreams God called them to. After feeling like a misfit in the corporate world, Francie discovered a life she loved waking up to through business ownership. Francie is the author of *Dream, Build, Grow: A Female's Step-by-Step Guide for How to Start a Business*. She's a passionate entrepreneurship hype girl, female leader, published writer, public speaker, and community enthusiast. A Master's degree in business administration and more than ten years of experience between a corporate career and business ownership have positioned her to teach other women modern strategies for starting and growing successful businesses.

Francie concurrently owns and operates two businesses, Simply Integrated, LLC, a data and analytics marketing company, and Founding Females™ where she leads a team of female entrepreneurs in specially curated communities designed for members to support and uplift one another.

As a community leader, Francie helps other women business owners to thrive with the right guidance and support. Francie created the Founding Females™ Startup Community and Founding Females™ Mastermind, entrepreneurship communities that coach women through improving their business mindset and operations. She believes that anyone with a dream on their heart can pull up a seat to change the world through entrepreneurship.

Made in United States
Troutdale, OR
03/06/2024

18261962R00217